THIS BOOK BELONGS TO

Kathleen A Farstad

RAISING
Resilient
CHILDREN

FOSTERING STRENGTH, HOPE, AND
OPTIMISM IN YOUR CHILD

RAISING
Resilient
CHILDREN

ROBERT BROOKS, PH.D., AND
SAM GOLDSTEIN, PH.D.

CB
CONTEMPORARY BOOKS

Library of Congress Cataloging-in-Publication Data

Brooks, Robert B.
    Raising resilient children : fostering strength, hope, and optimism in your child /
Robert Brooks, Sam Goldstein.
       p.   cm.
    Includes bibliographical references and index.
    ISBN 0-8092-9764-7
    1. Child rearing.   2. Parent and child.   3. Resilience (personality trait) in
children.   I. Goldstein, Sam, 1952–   II. Title.
HQ769 .B6817   2001
649'.1—dc21   00-60316
                                                                          CIP

Interior design by Nick Panos

Published by Contemporary Books
A division of NTC/Contemporary Publishing Group, Inc.
4255 West Touhy Avenue, Lincolnwood (Chicago), Illinois 60712-1975 U.S.A.
Copyright © 2001 by Robert Brooks and Sam Goldstein
All rights reserved. No part of this book may be reproduced, stored in a retrieval system, or
transmitted in any form or by any means, electronic, mechanical, photocopying, recording, or
otherwise, without the prior written permission of NTC/Contemporary Publishing Group, Inc.
Printed in the United States of America
International Standard Book Number: 0-8092-9764-7

01 02 03 04 05 06 MV 20 19 18 17 16 15 14 13 12 11 10 9 8 7 6 5 4 3 2 1

Parental influences on child development are neither as unambiguous as earlier researchers suggested nor as insubstantial as current critics claim.

—W. ANDREW COLLINS

If you want things to be different, perhaps the answer is to become different yourself.

—NORMAN VINCENT PEALE

In memory of my parents, Eva and David, and in appreciation of my wife, Marilyn, and my sons, Richard and Douglas. From all of you, I have learned the true meaning of love and resilience.

R.B.

In memory of my mother, Sarah. For Janet, Allyson, and Ryan and to future generations with our promise of a bright tomorrow.

S.G.

Thanks to Kathleen Gardner for her invaluable assistance in the preparation of this manuscript. Thanks also to James Levine and Matthew Carnicelli for sharing our vision.

S.G.
R.B.

Contents

Preface

In the summer of 1944, after many years in hiding, Anne Frank wrote in her diary:

I have lots of courage, I always feel so strong and as if I can bear a great deal, I feel so free and so young! I was glad when I first realized it, because I don't think I shall easily bow down before the blows that inevitably come to everyone. (Frank 1993, 260)

The words of this resilient young girl written more than fifty years ago define the essence and goals of this book. The qualities of resilience that Anne Frank so eloquently described helped her face and cope with years of great adversity. The qualities of a resilient mindset are no less important for today's youth. For hundreds of millions of children worldwide, daily adversity compromises their current and future well-being.

After fifty years of combined clinical practice, we have come to realize the great importance that these qualities of resilience play in children's lives. A resilient mindset, the ability to cope with and overcome adversity, is not a luxury or a blessing possessed by some children but an essential component for all children. Such a mindset has become increasingly important as the technological complexity of our society grows at such a dramatic pace.

In this book, we have set out to synthesize and present in a practical way a large volume of research about the qualities of resilience and the abilities of some children to face and overcome great adversity. Instilling these qualities in our children, we believe, is perhaps the most important role of parents and educators.

This belief in the significance of resilience came to us at a high price. As we look back on our years of clinical practice, we realize how many children were lost because parents and professionals expended time and energy to fix deficits rather than to build assets in children.

The focus of parents on fixing their child's problems is not difficult to understand. As professionals, we too came by this bias honestly; it is how we were trained. Clinical psychologists are typically taught to identify that which is different in a negative way and prescribe interventions to reduce symptoms or problems. The professional field has come to learn that the "deficit model" is fine for identifying how and why children are different and even for prescribing strategies to improve those differences, but we now believe that our highest goal is to improve the future of all children by identifying and harnessing their strengths. The deficit model has fallen far short in helping us to achieve this goal. Symptom relief has simply not been found to be synonymous with changing long-term outcome. We have come to appreciate that the qualities of resilience, the qualities we describe and teach you to instill in your children in this book, do in fact change the future.

Our profession has enabled us to work with countless children and adolescents experiencing a wide range of medical, developmental, emotional, and behavioral problems. Over the years, we have found ourselves spending more and more time with the parents of the children with whom we work. We have served on the faculties of two major universities, authored fifteen books and dozens of articles and chapters, and sat on the editorial boards of professional journals. Our individual experiences as psychologists led us to a shared vision that represents the heart of this text.

We have written this book in a style that permits you to read and reread our words in different ways. We present a description of the main characteristics of a resilient mindset in children as well as the mindset that we as adults must possess to nurture hope and resilience in our children. We offer many specific ideas and strategies to develop a resilient mindset. Given your particular interests and the dynamics of your family, you may wish to invest time and energy on one strategy more than others. You may also wish to skip ahead to a particular chapter or review a certain chapter several times. At the end of the book, you'll find an Appendix containing a chapter-by-chapter summary of the obstacles as well as the strategies involved in nurturing a resilient mindset. However you choose to use this book, our goal is that you gain an understanding of the importance of resilience as well as practical ideas on how to raise resilient children.

The many families you will meet in this book are representative of the populations with whom we have worked in our clinical practices. Though some stories are compilations of experiences, all of the examples reflect the course of events for real individuals and families. It is our hope that these ideas, principles, and guidelines will make a positive difference in your life and the lives of your children.

RAISING
Resilient
CHILDREN

1

The Dreams and Wishes of Parents

What is it that most parents want for their children? Happiness, success in school, satisfaction with their lives, and solid friendships quickly come to mind. If we examine our parental goals, it would not be an over-simplification to conclude that realization of these goals requires that our children have the inner strength to deal competently and successfully, day after day, with the challenges and demands they encounter. We call this capacity to cope and feel competent *resilience.*

Resilience embraces the ability of a child to deal more effectively with stress and pressure, to cope with everyday challenges, to bounce back from disappointments, adversity, and trauma, to develop clear and realistic goals, to solve problems, to relate comfortably with others, and to treat oneself and others with respect. Numerous scientific studies of children facing great adversity in their lives support the importance of resilience as a powerful force. Resilience explains why some children overcome overwhelming obstacles, sometimes clawing and scraping their way to successful adulthood, while others become victims of their early experiences and environments.

In presenting the concept of resilience in this way, we believe that regardless of ethical, cultural, religious, or scientific beliefs, we can all agree that we must strive to raise resilient youngsters. However, knowing what needs to be done is not the same as knowing how to do it. Although many of us may increasingly view the world as a hostile place in which to raise children, a place in which even Beaver Cleaver would be at risk, the solution of constructing taller walls around our families and double locking the front door in order to keep out a seemingly toxic culture is unrealistic. Blaming the world around us, which we all are in fact a part of and have to some extent been responsible for shaping, as an antifamily, child-poisoning culture does little to relieve our ominous sense that great adversity awaits in our children's future.

As we watch, wonder, and worry about our children and ourselves, most parents agree that our children require a healthy dose of resilience but are uncertain where to begin. According to a recent USA/CNN/Gallup Poll, most parents concur that it is much more difficult today to raise children to be "good people" than it was twenty years ago (Donahue 1998, 1d). Two out of three parents feel they are doing a "worse job." Seventy-five percent report that they are attempting to do things differently but are unsure what to do or if in fact what they are doing will be effective. Many hold out changing the world around them as the place in which the solution lies, yet feel overwhelmed with the daunting task of having an impact on a world moving at Mach speed.

No child is immune in this environment. In this fast-paced, stress-filled world, the number of children facing adversity and the number of adversities they face continue to increase dramatically. Even children who are fortunate enough not to face significant adversity or trauma, or to be burdened by intense stress or anxiety, experience the pressures around them and the expectations placed on them.

Thus, we believe that if we want to raise resilient children, we must not concentrate all of our energy on changing the world around us, but rather we must begin by changing what we do with our children. We must begin by appreciating that we can no longer afford the luxury of assuming that if our children don't face significant stress or adversity they will turn out "just fine."

Our contact with thousands of parents in our clinical practices and workshops confirms our opinion that the concept of resilience should take center stage in this process. Yet, our experiences also suggest that many well-meaning, loving parents either do not understand the parental practices that contribute to raising a resilient child or do not use what they know. Stresses as parents, "excess baggage" from the past, and lack of knowledge about new research pertaining to child development are just a few of the obstacles to engaging in the seemingly obvious practices that would promote resilience. Time and time again, our discussions with parents testify to this point.

Most parents are aware that children will feel more competent and self-assured if they're helped to navigate challenging situations. Yet, when Michael, a twelve-year-old, became frustrated while attempting to build a radio from a kit and walked away, his father, Mr. Burton, responded angrily, "I told you it wouldn't work. You don't have enough patience to read the directions carefully." While Mr. Burton knew that what his son needed at that moment was encouragement and assistance rather than criticism, his own frustration led him astray from a helpful response to one that actually weakened Michael's resolve to persevere with more difficult tasks.

Similarly, nine-year-old Jane came home from school in tears and sobbed to her mother, Mrs. Jones, that some of her friends refused to sit with her at lunch, telling her they did not want her around. Jane was confused and distressed and asked her mother what to do. Mrs. Jones knew that one of the most important skills that children develop, a skill that is a basic component of resilience, is the ability to solve problems on their own. However, rather than engaging her daughter in a dialogue about possible solutions, Mrs. Jones, feeling anxious, immediately replied that Jane should tell the other girls that if they did not want to play with her, she did not want to play with them. While this motherly advice may have been appropriate, quickly telling Jane what to do and not involving her in a consideration of other possible solutions robbed her of an opportunity to strengthen her own problem-solving skills.

While raising resilient children is a goal that should unite all parents, it is a process that is neither taught nor, until very recently, even highlighted for many parents. We believe that the absence of this concept in guiding our parenting skills has escalated the problems that beset so many children, leaving them unprepared to meet future challenges. A lack of knowledge about resilience may lead to parenting efforts that fail or even are counterproductive. Thus, the obvious and prudent course of parenting is often sidetracked by an absence of information as well as a failure to use the information available.

We believe that the concept of resilience defines a process of parenting that is essential if we are to prepare our children for success in all areas of their future lives. Given this belief, a guiding principle in all of our interactions with children should be to strengthen their ability to be resilient and to meet life's challenges with thoughtfulness, confidence, purpose, and empathy.

Although in some scientific circles the word *resilience* has typically been applied to youngsters who have overcome stress and hardship, it should be understood as a vital ingredient in the process of parenting *every* child. Each family develops unique goals and values based on myriad factors, but in the course of achieving these goals and living in concert with one's values, the principles involved in raising resilient youngsters can serve as guideposts. The process of teaching children about friendships, religion, athletics, dealing with mistakes, learning to share with siblings, and meeting responsibilities will be enhanced by an understanding of the components of resiliency.

Each interaction with our children provides an educational opportunity to help them weave a strong and resilient personal fabric. While the *outcome* of a specific issue may be important, even more vital are the *lessons* learned from the process of dealing with each issue or problem. The knowledge gained provides the nutrients from which the seeds of resiliency will develop and flourish.

This book is not intended to prescribe what values or goals to set for yourself and your family. Rather, it reflects our belief that if you set your sights on raising a resilient child, then all aspects of parenting—including teaching values, disciplining your children, helping your children to feel special and appreciated, assisting them to persevere, helping them to make decisions and to feel comfortable with those decisions, and encouraging satisfying interpersonal relations—can be guided by this priority. The chapters that follow articulate and explore the mindset of resilient children as well as the mindset of parents who focus on resilience, examining how this parental mindset leads to specific ways of interacting with our children.

Before proceeding, we would be remiss if we did not note that questions have been raised recently about the importance of parents in influencing their children's lives. Many parents may not appreciate how different each child is at birth and, thus, may assume more responsibility for their children's success and more blame for their children's failure than is warranted. We believe, however, that even given these innate and environmental differences, parents play a major role in their children's development. More than fifty years of research with parents and children, not only of our species but also of others such as monkeys, has consistently demonstrated the powerful role that parents play in nurturing and shaping the behavior and attitudes of their offspring.

In fact, nearly fifty years ago, experimental psychologist Harry Harlow demonstrated that although infants require sustenance, if given the choice, they choose maternal contact and comfort, not only when stressed but even when hungry. Further, a recent review of parenting research concluded that "the expression of heritable traits depends, often strongly, on experience including specific parental behaviors" (Collins, Maccoby, et al. 2000, 228). However, as will be discussed, it is essential that we understand the parameters of our influence so that we can set realistic goals and expectations for ourselves and our children.

To understand the mindset of a parent capable of developing and reinforcing resiliency in children, we must also understand the mindset or perspective of a resilient child. We must ask what are the major characteristics, skills, and abilities that contribute to a child's resilience, to a child's perceiving the future in a hopeful, confident manner. In grasping the mindset of a resilient child, we gain an invaluable source of information to guide our parenting practices as we attempt to reinforce the components of this mindset in our children. This introductory chapter briefly describes the mindset of the resilient child and the parent who fosters resilience. This grounding will help you to understand what can be done in the parenting process to nurture these features. Subsequent chapters specify strategies for reinforcing resilience.

The Mindset of a Resilient Child

Resilient children possess certain qualities and/or ways of viewing themselves and the world that are not apparent in youngsters who have not been successful in meeting challenges and pressures. Resilient youngsters are able to translate this view, or mindset, into effective action. Resilient children are also hopeful and possess high self-worth. What contributes to this sense of hopefulness and self-worth?

Resilient youngsters feel special and appreciated. They have learned to set realistic goals and expectations for themselves. They have developed the ability to solve problems and make decisions and thus are more likely to view mistakes, hardships, and obstacles as challenges to confront rather than as stressors to avoid. They rely on productive coping strategies that are growth-fostering rather than self-defeating. They are aware of their weaknesses and vulnerabilities, but they also recognize their strong points and talents. Their self-concept is filled with images of strength and competence. They have developed effective interpersonal skills with peers and adults alike. They are able to seek out assistance and nurturance in a comfortable, appropriate manner from adults who can provide the support they need. Finally, they are able to define the aspects of their lives over which they have control and to focus their energy and attention on these rather than on factors over which they have little, if any, influence.

Developing a resilient mindset is what we would hope for all children. A resilient child is an emotionally healthy child, equipped to successfully confront challenges and bounce back from setbacks. In a sense, the child just described is a "product"; it is how we would like our children to turn out, how we would like our children to view themselves and others. How do we use every situation, every interaction we have with our children as part of a process to reinforce this product? How do we develop an approach that continually works to strengthen a child's resilience?

The Mindset of the Parent Who Fosters Resilience in Children

Parents who engage in the process of raising resilient youngsters possess an understanding that is sometimes explicit, at other times implicit or intuitive, of what they can do to nurture a resilient mindset and behaviors in their children. Such parents know about and appreciate the components of resilience, so that their interactions with their children are guided by a blueprint of important principles, ideas, and actions. However, grasping the complexities of this blueprint is an ongoing process filled with challenges, frustrations, setbacks, and successes. As one parent commented, "It might be easier if children arrived with an owner's manual or road map."

This is a thought that all parents have entertained at various times. It would be reassuring to believe in the existence of one set of operating guidelines, one direct course to follow, as we prepare our children for what lies ahead. Though some may wish for a true, proved, golden path to the future, that path does not exist. Nonetheless, we can be comforted by the knowledge that we have certain guideposts to help us traverse and appreciate each child's unique road. While each road is shaped by a variety of factors, including the child's inborn temperament, family style and values, educational experiences, and the broader society or culture in which the child is raised, these guideposts provide principles and ideas applicable for all roads and thus can direct us in raising resilient children.

This chapter describes each of the guideposts and how they shape the mindset and action of parents. The principles and actions in each of these guideposts are examined in greater detail in subsequent chapters. Remember that these principles and ideas shape parenting practices and beliefs that are important for *all* children, not just those who have experienced hardship, adversity, or trauma. The fast-paced, changing world of the twenty-first century requires that all children acquire the outlook and skills associated with resilience. Following is a list of ten guideposts that form the foundation for helping to reinforce the mindset of resilient youth. These may seem to be obvious, commonsense practices that most reasonable parents would follow without difficulty. However, as noted earlier, even the principles and practices of effective parenting that appear obvious require continuous thought and reflection so that we don't lose sight of what is truly important in our parenting behaviors. The guideposts embedded in the mindset of parents who foster resilience in their youngsters include:

1. Being empathic
2. Communicating effectively and listening actively
3. Changing "negative scripts"
4. Loving our children in ways that help them to feel special and appreciated
5. Accepting our children for who they are and helping them to set realistic expectations and goals
6. Helping our children experience success by identifying and reinforcing their "islands of competence"
7. Helping children recognize that mistakes are experiences from which to learn
8. Developing responsibility, compassion, and a social conscience by providing children with opportunities to contribute
9. Teaching our children to solve problems and make decisions
10. Disciplining in a way that promotes self-discipline and self-worth

Let's get acquainted with each of these parenting guideposts and the principles and actions they exemplify.

1. Being Empathic

A basic foundation of any relationship—parent-child, husband-wife, teacher-student—is empathy. Simply defined, in the parenting relationship empathy is the capacity of parents to put themselves inside the shoes of their youngsters and to see the world through their eyes. Empathy does not imply that you agree with everything your children do, but rather that you attempt to appreciate and validate their point of view.

While many parents believe that they are empathic, experience shows that it is easier to be empathic when our children do what we ask them to do, are successful in their activities, and are warm and responsive. It is much more difficult to be empathic when we are upset, angry, annoyed, or disappointed with our children. When we feel this way, even well-meaning parents say or do things that actually work against a child in developing resilience.

The following two examples capture the extent to which frustration can compromise a parent's capacity to be empathic.

John's parents, Mr. and Mrs. Kahn, couldn't understand why their seemingly intelligent seventh-grade son experienced so much difficulty completing his homework. John was athletically gifted but had a long history of problems learning to read. His parents, observing John's lack of interest in school activities, believed he could do the work if he "put his mind to it" and frequently exhorted him to "try harder." They chided him as to how awful he would feel as a senior in high school when he was not accepted into the college of his choice.

In an effort to motivate John, his parents told him that he would not be allowed to participate in any after-school sports, an area in which he excelled, if he obtained a grade lower than a B. In telling John to "try harder," while perhaps well intentioned, they failed to consider how these words were experienced by John. Many youngsters who are repeatedly told to "try harder" hear these not as helpful words but rather as judgmental or accusatory, increasing their existing frustration with school rather than their motivation to succeed. Thus, the words the Kahns used worked *against* their goal to motivate John.

Sally, a shy eight-year-old, was often prompted by her parents, Mr. and Mrs. Carter, to say hello when encountering family friends. Yet, from a young age, Sally seemed anxious, fearful, and easily overwhelmed in new situations. She would hide behind her mother in public places or when strangers came to the house. The Carters couldn't comprehend why Sally appeared so nervous around others, especially since they saw themselves as loving parents. They told Sally that if she didn't learn to say hello, other people would not want to be with her. At best, Sally was able to glance down and whisper, "Hi."

Sally's parents, wanting their daughter to be more outgoing, failed to appreciate that Sally's shyness was an inborn temperamental trait and could not be overcome simply by telling her to "say hello" to others. Frequently reminding shy children to say hello can heighten their anxiety and increase their tendency to withdraw as a means of escaping an uncomfortable situation.

Parents who are empathic think about how they would feel if someone said or did the same things to them that they said or did to their children. If we are trying our best, yet struggling with an activity, would we find it helpful to have someone exhort, "Try harder!"? How many shy adults would welcome the advice to "go out and make friends"? If a child is shy, an empathic statement together with words of encouragement is more likely to lead to success, self-worth, and resilience.

For example, one father told his shy daughter that many kids find it difficult to say hello and that he would be of whatever help he could so that it might become easier for her to greet people in the future. Such a statement validates what the child is experiencing in a nonjudgmental way and offers hope for change. It creates a climate in which resilience is able to thrive.

We are often asked if people can increase their ability to be empathic. We believe they can. Parents can be guided by certain questions that help foster empathy, such as: "How would I hope my child describes me?"; "How would my child actually describe me, and how close is that to how I hope my child would describe me?"; "When I talk to or do things with my children, am I behaving in a way that will make them most responsive to listening to me?"; and "Would I want anyone to speak to me the way I am speaking to my child?" Parents who are able to go beyond their frustration or annoyance and ask these kinds of questions of themselves are practicing empathy, a key component of an effective parenting mindset.

2. *Communicating Effectively and Listening Actively*

Empathy colors the ways in which we communicate with our children. Communication has many features. It is not simply how we speak with another person. Effective communication involves actively listening to our children, understanding and validating what they are attempting to say, and responding in ways that avoid power struggles by not interrupting them, by not telling them how they should be feeling, by not putting them down, and by not using absolutes such as *always* and *never* in a demeaning fashion (e.g., "You never help out"; "You always show disrespect").

Resilient children develop a capacity to communicate effectively aided by parents, who are important models in this process. Mr. Burton's response to Michael's difficulty in completing a radio kit, "I told you it wouldn't work. You don't have enough patience to read the directions carefully," is an example of a message that actually works against the development of a resilient mindset since it contains an accusatory tone. The art of communication has important implications for many components of behaviors associated with resilience, including interpersonal skills, empathy, and problem-solving and decision-making abilities.

3. Changing "Negative Scripts"

The most well-meaning parents have been known to apply the same approach with their children for weeks, months, or years when the approach has proved unsuccessful. For instance, we know of one set of parents who nagged their children for years to clean their rooms, but the children never obeyed. From our discussions with families, it is evident that one of the main reasons parents continue to engage in unproductive behaviors is their belief that children should be the ones to change, not them. However, as many parents can attest, children will "outlast" us in that standoff.

A parent with a resilient mindset recognizes that if something we have said or done for a reasonable time does not work, then we must change our "script" if our children are to change theirs. We must have the insight and courage to think about what we can do differently, lest we become embroiled in useless power struggles.

Often a parent's negative scripts are based on "myths" or excess baggage that we bring from our own childhoods. An example is what occurred in seven-year-old Billy's home when he spilled a glass of milk for the third time in a week. The milk dripped over the counter and onto the floor.

His parents, Mr. and Mrs. Murray, although typically patient, became annoyed. His father said tersely, "Why can't you be less clumsy! You just don't seem to think about what you're doing."

Billy was hurt and embarrassed. He had not intentionally spilled the milk; it just happened. He promised his parents that it would not happen again and that he would be more careful. Yet, the next day, Billy spilled some juice.

Mrs. Murray took away the juice and said, "I hope that helps you to remember to hold your glass right!"

If Billy's parents had been aware of the significant temperamental differences among children, they might not have interpreted his continually spilling drinks as a sign of careless, willful, or oppositional behavior and might not have responded with punishment. A change in mindset would allow Mr. and Mrs. Murray to appreciate what hindered Billy from holding his glass and perhaps change their approach, including providing him a glass with a cover.

When parents change their own scripts, it does not imply "giving in to" or "spoiling" children; rather, it serves to teach youngsters that there are alternative ways of solving problems. If anything, it helps children learn to be more responsible and more accountable in handling difficult situations.

4. Loving Our Children in Ways That Help Them to Feel Special and Appreciated

A basic guidepost for building resilience is the presence of at least one adult (hopefully several) who believes in the worth of the child. The late Dr. Julius Segal referred to that person as a "charismatic adult," an adult from whom a child "gathers strength." Never underestimate the power of one person to redirect a child toward a more productive, successful, satisfying life. As parents, we must find ways in which to help children feel special and appreciated without indulging them.

One possible approach is to schedule "special times" alone with each of our children so that we can give them our undivided attention and have opportunities to convey a belief in them. However, this is often more difficult to accomplish than one realizes, as evidenced by what occurred in eight-year-old Stephanie's house.

Stephanie's parents, Mr. and Mrs. Grant, put time aside each evening to either read or play games with her. Stephanie greatly enjoyed this time. Nonetheless, when the phone rang, they would interrupt their activity with Stephanie, explaining that phone calls were important. Stephanie soon chose to watch television rather than be continually disappointed.

In helping our children to feel special and appreciated, we must give our love unconditionally. This does not mean an absence of discipline or accountability; it means that even if they transgress, we still love and accept them.

5. Accepting Our Children for Who They Are and Helping Them to Set Realistic Expectations and Goals

One of the most difficult leaps for parents is to accept their children's unique temperament. When this acceptance is present, parents can successfully set expectations and goals consistent with the child's temperament. Every child is unique from the moment of birth. Some youngsters come into the world with so-called easy temperaments, others with "difficult" temperaments, and still others with shy or cautious temperaments. When parents are unaware of their child's inborn temperament, they may say or do things that impede satisfying relationships, expecting things from their children that the children cannot deliver.

For example, school was an environment in which ten-year-old Carl experienced little success. In the morning he appeared to dawdle, often missing the school bus. His parents, Mr. and Mrs. Thomas, would then find themselves obligated to drive him to school. A neighbor advised them not to drive Carl; if he ended up missing school for the day, it would teach him a valuable lesson. Mr. and Mrs. Thomas took the advice but, to their dismay, discovered that Carl was no better prepared to get ready for school the next day. They were bewildered about what to do next and became increasingly angry at Carl for his seeming irresponsibility. In desperation they decided to restrict many of his pleasurable activities.

Carl's parents were unaware that Carl was late not because he was irresponsible but rather because, similar to a number of other children, he was distractible, often becoming drawn into other activities, and moved at a slow pace. Instead of yelling or punishing, it would be more effective to accept that this is Carl's style and to engage him in a discussion of what he thinks could help and/or to work closely with the school to have a motivating job or responsibility waiting for him at the beginning of the school day. For example, a child with whom we worked was given the job of "tardy monitor" at school, a position that entailed arriving early and keeping track of which students were late. The child loved the responsibility and arrived dutifully on time.

Accepting children for who they are and appreciating their different temperaments does not mean that we excuse inappropriate, unacceptable behavior but rather that we understand this behavior and help to change it in a manner that does not erode a child's self-esteem and sense of dignity.

6. Helping Our Children Experience Success by Identifying and Reinforcing Their "Islands of Competence"

Resilient children do not deny the problems they face, but they recognize and focus on their strengths. Unfortunately, many youngsters who feel poorly about themselves and their abilities experience a diminished sense of hope. This often leads them to minimize or fail to appreciate their strengths. Parents sometimes report that the positive comments they offer their children fall on "deaf ears," resulting in parents' becoming frustrated and reducing positive feedback.

Parents must realize that when children have low self-worth, they are less apt to accept our positive feedback. We should continue to offer this feedback, but, most important, we must recognize that true self-worth, hope, and resilience are based on children's experiencing success in areas of their lives that they and others deem to be important. This requires parents to identify and reinforce a child's "islands of competence." Every child possesses these islands of competence, or areas of strength, and we must promote these rather than overemphasize the child's weaknesses.

Fifteen-year-old Laurie had difficulty getting along with her peers, but young children gravitated toward her. As her parents, Mr. and Mrs. Laramie, put it, she was the "pied piper" of the neighborhood. Given this strength, she began to baby-sit. As she developed confidence, she was more willing to examine and change her approach with her peers, which led to greater acceptance.

We also knew a boy with reading difficulties who discovered that he was "gifted" in artwork, especially drawing cartoons. His parents and teachers displayed his cartoons at home and school, an action that boosted his self-esteem and in a concrete way communicated that he had strengths.

When children discover their strengths, they are more willing to confront even those areas that have proved to be problematic for them.

7. Helping Children Recognize That Mistakes Are Experiences from Which to Learn

There is a significant difference in the way in which resilient children view mistakes compared with nonresilient children. Resilient children tend to view mistakes as opportunities for learning. In contrast, children who are not very hopeful often experience mistakes as an indication that they are failures. In response to this pessimistic view, they are likely to retreat from challenges, feeling inadequate and blaming others for their problems. Thus, if parents are to raise resilient children, they must help them develop a healthy outlook about mistakes from an early age.

Mr. Burton criticizing Michael for not being able to complete the radio kit and Mrs. Murray punishing Billy for spilling milk are communicating (perhaps without even realizing it) that mistakes are terrible and punishable.

Instead, in promoting a more positive attitude toward mistakes, it is helpful for parents to reflect on how their children would answer the following questions: "When your parents make a mistake, what do they do?" and "When you make a mistake, or if something doesn't go right, what do your parents say or do with you?"

In frustration, many parents respond to mistakes in ways that actually lessen a child's confidence. If parents are to reinforce a resilient mindset in their children, their words and actions must communicate a belief that we can learn from mistakes. The fear of making mistakes is one of the most potent obstacles to learning, one that is incompatible with a resilient mindset.

8. Developing Responsibility, Compassion, and a Social Conscience by Providing Children with Opportunities to Contribute

Resilient children possess a sense of responsibility. But how do we reinforce responsibility in our youngsters? Too often, we call the first responsibilities we give children "chores." Most children and adults are not thrilled about doing chores, whereas almost every child from a very early age appears motivated to help others. The presence of this "helping drive" is supported by research in which adults were asked to reflect on their school experiences and to write about one of their most positive moments. One of the most common responses centered on being asked to help others in some manner (tutoring a younger child, painting murals in the school, running the film projector).

Parents with a resilient mindset recognize that resilience and self-worth are enhanced when children are provided with opportunities to shine and taste success, especially by making a positive difference in their world. Parents who involve their children in charitable work, such as walks for hunger or AIDS or food drives, appreciate the importance of such activities in fostering self-esteem and a social conscience.

9. Teaching Our Children to Solve Problems and Make Decisions

Hopeful children with high self-esteem and resilience believe that they are masters of their own fate. They believe that they have control of their lives. Having and maintaining control over one's life is critical for all of us. When parents help their children learn how to make decisions and solve problems independently, they provide a vital ingredient in the process of developing that control. Resilient children are able to define problems, consider different solutions, attempt what they judge to be the most appropriate solution, and learn from the outcome.

If parents are to reinforce this problem-solving attitude in their children, they must be careful not to tell children what to do. Instead they must engage children in thinking about possible solutions. To facilitate this process, it is helpful for parents to set aside a "family meeting time" every week or every other week during which problems can be discussed and solutions articulated.

Recall that Jane, the child whose friends refused to sit with her at school, asked her mother what she should do. Mrs. Jones was well meaning, but by offering Jane a solution before asking *her* to think about what might help, she was depriving her daughter of an opportunity to develop problem-solving skills.

Here's a similar example: Barry and his older brother, Len, constantly bickered and argued. They fought about everything, including who would sit in the front seat of the car and which television program to watch. Len was frequently admonished by his parents to be more tolerant since he was the older of the two. They warned him that his failure to do so would result in his being punished. Len's response was to become distant and reject interactions with Barry. Asking the boys to come up with a solution to their fighting would likely have been more effective.

We have often been pleasantly surprised and impressed by the ability of children to think about effective and realistic ways of managing problems. When children develop their own plans of action with the guidance of parents, their sense of ownership and control is reinforced, as is their resilience.

10. Disciplining in a Way That Promotes Self-Discipline and Self-Worth

In our clinical work and seminars, parents frequently ask about discipline. To raise resilient children, parents must understand that one of their most important roles is to be a disciplinarian in the true sense. The word *discipline* relates to the word *disciple* and thus is a teaching process. We must appreciate that the ways in which we discipline our children can either reinforce or weaken self-esteem, self-control, and resilience.

While one of the main goals of discipline is to create safe and secure environments, another is to nurture self-control and self-discipline in children. This implies taking ownership for one's behavior. It is difficult to think of children with high self-esteem who do not also possess self-discipline. Family meetings, as suggested in the previous guidepost, can be used to engage children, within reason, in the creation of household rules and consequences so that they are less likely to experience rules as impositions.

Our Children, Our Future

While children come into this world with their own unique temperaments, parents and other caregivers strongly influence whether children will develop the characteristics and mindset associated with resilience or whether they will be burdened by low self-worth, self-doubt, and a diminished sense of hope. Developing a resilient mindset is not a luxury but an essential component of a successful future.

Subsequent chapters plumb the mindset of resilient children and the ten guideposts for parents to develop and reinforce this mindset. Chapter 12 looks beyond the home environment to the importance of parents and teachers working closely together so that the school setting can also reinforce resilience in youngsters. Raising resilient children must become a cornerstone in preparing ourselves and our children for the future.

2

Teaching and Conveying Empathy

*E*mpathy is popularly defined as the ability to identify with or vicariously experience the feelings, thoughts, or attitudes of others. Thus, to be empathic with our children requires us to "walk in their shoes." Taking the time to understand and experience our children's perspective is recognized as an important component of parenting, but it is often difficult to accomplish. Why is this the case? In our work with parents, we have found more often than not that they have formulated their opinions and definitions of their children's problems with scant attention paid to the child's view. In many ways, we as professionals may unintentionally have fostered this one-sided perspective.

When parents consult with us about their children's problems, we routinely ask questions to obtain the history, nature, and severity of the problems. Our focus traditionally was on the parents' view: "What interventions have you attempted? How effective have these interventions been?" We were not trained to ask parents, as a matter of course, what they believed their *children* thought or felt. During our years of clinical work, however, we have come to realize the one-sidedness of this approach.

Now, in addition to gathering history from the parents' perspective, we ask a series of questions to assess and hopefully foster the process of parental empathy. For example: "Make believe you are your child. Describe a typical day in your child's life, but through your child's eyes. How does your child feel when he or she gets up in the morning, gets on the school bus, gets to school, receives a poor grade, interacts with other students, and sits down to do homework? What words would your child use to describe you as a parent?" Many parents tell us they find these questions thought-provoking, illustrating a point of view they had not previously considered.

We pose these kinds of questions because they reflect our appreciation of empathy. Parental empathy, the capacity to be empathic and assume the perspective of our children, sets the foundation for fostering resilience. The first set of questions we ask provides factual information. The second, however, provides insight. These exploratory questions help us to assess the ability of parents to place themselves in the shoes of the child. They also highlight for parents the importance of practicing and teaching empathy.

In particular, many parents tell us that they have never considered how their children might describe them. They find this a puzzling and difficult question to answer. As parents, we readily agree that typically we do not consider what our children would say about us and the things we do. In fact, in many circumstances, we do not consider this to be important. The operative philosophy instead is "If I say it is time for bed, I'm not really concerned whether you think I'm being unfair; I just want you to go to bed." Yet, it is essential that in all of our interactions with our children we make an effort to understand the child's view and perspective.

This chapter examines the importance of empathy in raising resilient children and creating a resilient mindset. You'll learn about the obstacles that make it difficult to be empathic in so many interactions with our children as well as guidelines to nurture empathy in ourselves and in our kids.

The Role of Empathy

Empathy has been touted as an important component of "emotional intelligence." The capacity to be empathic facilitates communication. Empathy provides the strength to change negative scripts and to love our children in ways that allow them to feel listened to and appreciated. Empathy is the starting point to helping children locate islands of competence and success in their lives, to develop responsibility, compassion, and a social conscience. The modeling of empathy helps children feel comfortable to learn from their mistakes and to view mistakes as opportunities rather than failures. Most important, empathy creates a relationship with our children, letting them know that we hear them. This sets the stage for them to listen to and truly hear us.

The better able we are to assume the perspective of our children, the better we can understand, communicate, teach, and even love our children. Empathic parents are guided by the following kinds of questions:

- Am I saying or doing things in a way that would make my children the most receptive to listening to what I have to say and learning from me?

- Would I want anyone to speak with me in the way I am speaking with my children?
- What do my children think about the choices I make for them?

Posing these questions promotes many of the goals of parenting. What we must accomplish with our children to build a resilient mindset would be weakened if our words and actions led our youngsters to tune us out, resent us, or act in disruptive ways to let us know how they feel.

Sally, the shy eight-year-old from Chapter 1, exemplifies how the well-intentioned goals of parents can backfire if they are not guided by the question "Would I want anyone to speak with me in the way I am speaking with my child?" The parental messages to Sally that she communicate with others and maintain eye contact became lost in the tone of the parents' voices and their exhortations. Lacking empathy, this piece of parental guidance served to increase Sally's anxiety and hesitation. If Mrs. Carter were equally shy, how would she feel if her husband or boss harshly told her to look people in the eye? Would she learn from their harshness? Would she thank them for their concern? Most likely, she would not. Most likely, she would be more self-conscious, ill at ease, and ultimately angry at their lack of understanding.

Gregory, a fifteen-year-old whose room would never be featured as a model in *House and Garden* magazine, was constantly directed by his parents, Mr. and Mrs. Smith, to clean up the mess that seemed to proliferate in every inch of his living space. The Smiths' frustration often led them to bring up a litany of concerns that began with the condition of his room but soon encompassed his choice of clothing and friends, his unfinished homework, and the blare of his stereo. By the time they had voiced their second concern, Gregory was no longer listening.

To be empathic and to model empathy, Gregory's parents must ask, "How would we feel if we had not completed several household or work responsibilities and our family or boss confronted us with a long list of our shortcomings and lack of responsibility?"

Finally, what did twelve-year-old Michael hear when he experienced difficulty completing the radio kit? His father's words, tinged with sarcasm were, "I told you it wouldn't work. You don't have enough patience to read the directions carefully." Mr. Burton's outburst was based on his frustration as well as his anxiety about the impact Michael's style might have later in his life. A more empathic stance on his part would have been: "If I were having difficulty with a task, would I want to be greeted with anger and a demeaning comment? Would this help me learn?" If the answer is no, then the parent should refrain from directing those comments toward the child.

All parents naturally want their children to listen and respond to them, but while most parents can articulate goals that they hope to accomplish in their interactions with their children, all too often these parental objectives are sabotaged by a lack of consideration of the child's point of view. If we fail to be empathic, not only with our children but also with spouses, coworkers, and neighbors, our words and actions are likely to trigger negative reactions that minimize a willingness to listen, respond, and cooperate.

A popular saying is that children don't do what we *say*; they do what we *do*. For better or worse, we are models for our children. If we are not empathic, if we become blinded by our own agendas at the expense of not taking even a moment to listen to what our children tell us, then it will not be easy for *them* to develop empathy.

In a family therapy session, fifteen-year-old Lucy commented that no one liked her and she had few friends. Her mother, Mrs. Sailor, piped up, "You don't have friends because you don't know how to treat people. You think you can just boss other kids around and they will continue to want to be with you."

Lucy slouched in her chair, appearing sullen and angry. She murmured, "You always have to tell me what I'm doing wrong. You never listen to what I have to say. You make it seem that everything is my fault."

Mrs. Sailor's intentions were good. She wanted her daughter to assume at least some responsibility for her lack of friendships. However, the tone of her voice, her choice of words, and her lack of empathy led her away from this goal and served simply to increase the tension between them. If Mrs. Sailor had reflected on how she would have felt if *she* had told someone that she was unhappy and had few friends and the response she received was "You just don't know how to behave. You really have a major problem," it is more likely that she would have responded to her daughter in a less accusatory way. By responding in an aggressive fashion, by not initially acknowledging her daughter's distress, Mrs. Sailor did not model empathy, nor did she validate her daughter's point of view.

Lucy's brother, Simon, was frequently reprimanded for teasing Lucy and making demeaning comments such as "You never do anything right. You're such a loser. That's why no one likes you." Understandably, Mr. and Mrs. Sailor were also quite upset by these comments, especially as they witnessed their daughter becoming more sullen and her relationship with her brother becoming more distant. As we worked with this family, we observed the ways in which Mr. and Mrs. Sailor spoke to each other. Right off the bat, Mr. Sailor offered the opinion that family life would be more harmonious if his wife were better at setting limits and that she "lacks the courage to do so."

Mrs. Sailor burst into tears as she blurted, "All you do is put me down in front of the kids. You never say anything positive. You're such a critical person."

At this, Simon angrily said to his father, "And you tell me to speak in a nice way to Lucy, but look how you talk to Mom."

Mr. Sailor appeared surprised by his son's statement. He started to defend himself, asserting, "What I say to your mother . . . ," but then caught himself in midsentence and said, "I shouldn't talk to your mother that way."

This dramatic moment, in which Mr. Sailor realized that Simon's treatment of Lucy paralleled *his* treatment of his wife, was a catalyst for all family members to develop empathy and change their behaviors toward each other.

The ease with which a child can relate to others, form friendships, and find comfort and support in relationships is integral to the child's resilience. When parents practice and model empathy, they provide the foundation for the development of skills necessary to form satisfying and gratifying interpersonal relationships. Such skills include accurately interpreting social cues, engaging in comfortable and productive dialogue with others, listening actively, being encouraging and supportive, and learning to resolve differences of opinion and conflicts. Each demonstration of empathy by parents toward their children, each effort to genuinely understand and validate what their children are communicating, and each time a power struggle is avoided by taking a moment to appreciate a child's perspective plants the seeds necessary for interpersonal success.

These actions teach children that empathy is a major pillar for the establishment and maintenance of friendships and a means to resolve conflict through negotiation and compromise. The power of actions that teach important lessons to children about how to relate to others should not be underestimated. This empathic quality of parenting has been demonstrated to contribute significantly to adjustment among children.

As Simon could tell you, a parent's efficacy in teaching interpersonal skills can be undermined by the child's observation of the parent's own interactional style. Parents often naively assume that their children do not have opinions about how they interact with each other, yet this could not be further from the truth.

When asked about his parents, Jeffrey, an astute ten-year-old, commented, "They always argue. They never listen to each other. They always tell each other they are wrong. It's as if one of them always has to win." Adding an exclamation point to this description, Jeffrey continued, "They never hold hands or kiss each other like my friend Manny's parents do. Every time I play at Manny's house, I notice that his parents really act nice toward each other and kid with each other."

One of the reasons Jeffrey was referred for evaluation was his difficulty in getting along with peers. Jeffrey's teacher observed, "He always has to have the last word and make certain he wins the argument. He constantly turns his classmates off." Sometimes the acorn does not fall far from the tree. In this case, however, the similarity between parent and offspring appeared to be the result not of biology and genetics but rather of parenting style and observed behavior.

In contrast, Belinda, also ten, described her parents as being "lovey dovey," often holding hands and kissing. Typical of a preadolescent, she said this with a feigned sense of embarrassment, but it was evident that she found comfort in their "lovey-doveyness." She also noted that when her parents had disagreements, they tried to resolve their differences in an amiable way. Belinda explained that her parents "treat each other with respect." They did not interrupt or insult each other. By watching and listening to her parents and observing the way they modeled empathy, Belinda was learning important interpersonal skills.

We continue to be impressed by the insightful observations that children make of their parents. Ask your children about your interpersonal style, and you too likely will be surprised.

The Challenge to Be Empathic

Going back to the problem posed at the beginning of this chapter, if we as parents know that empathy is necessary and important for raising resilient children, why do so many of us find it difficult to be empathic? The better we understand the roadblocks to becoming empathic, the better equipped we are to clear the path. This section outlines four principal obstacles to empathy, then the section that follows offers strategies to change unproductive actions and strengthen an empathic view.

Obstacle One: *We Often Practice What We Have Lived, or History Has a Nasty Way of Repeating Itself*

Parents lament on countless occasions, "I promised I would never say that to my own children since I hated it so much when my parents said it to me. So, why did I say it?" If one grows up in a home in which parents are not very empathic, in which children are told how they should feel and think, in which communication is limited, one-sided, and often invalidated, then it is more difficult to develop and practice empathy as a parent. Whatever the process, our present behavior is in part shaped by our past experiences.

Of course, having empathic parents does not guarantee that a child will be empathic. Many biological as well as environmental factors contribute to human behavior. However, having empathic parents can't hurt.

Mr. and Mrs. Branston consulted us about their eight-year-old son, Seth. Mrs. Branston described Seth as oppositional: "He knows how to push my buttons. He is always trying to get me angry." She became especially upset when Seth and his ten-year-old sister teased each other. Mrs. Branston would respond by yelling at Seth and blaming him for all of the confrontations.

Mr. Branston demurred, saying that it was his impression that Seth was more cooperative than his wife described but that she and Seth often locked horns. Implicit in his message was that his wife was a contributor to Seth's behavioral problems, particularly their confrontations. Over time, this led Mrs. Branston to the position that her husband was unsupportive and didn't understand. At one meeting, she angrily said to him, "You wouldn't take Seth's side if you were home more often and could see how he behaved!"

To their credit, Seth's parents had made an effort to change things at home. First they attended a parenting class suggested by their family physician. They agreed that they obtained many good ideas from the class but that the parent trainer was too rigid. They came away convinced that in the trainer's eyes there was only one right way of dealing with Seth's behavior, one they felt was incompatible with their personalities and beliefs. Next, Mrs. Branston read one of the popular books on dealing with noncompliant, disruptive children. Once again, although some of the strategies were helpful, Seth's mother reported being somewhat saddened by this book because the author suggested that children like Seth were born difficult and that, short of controlling or containing his behavior, there was not much that could be done to actually change the status quo.

Nonetheless, here were Seth's parents seeking out another professional. They truly cared about their son and, with our input, were willing to look at the problem from a different perspective. We asked Mrs. Branston to examine her reactions to her son, and when she did, she began to realize that she was overreacting to his behavior and clearly not responding, even in small part, with empathy.

When asked what she thought was interfering with her ability to be empathic, she said with a pained look, "I really don't know."

However within a few weeks, she linked her lack of empathy to her childhood experiences. She remembered that her older brother, with whom she got along quite well in their adult years, continually taunted her when they were children. When she sought protection from her parents, their typical retort was, "You're too sensitive. You can't always be such a baby. You have to learn to take care of yourself." Whatever her parents' intentions might have been, she had felt betrayed by their response. It hurt that her parents did not appreciate or validate what she was saying and feeling.

Thus, when Seth and his sister engaged in teasing, their heated words unleashed memories of the teasing she had received from her brother and the perceived lack of support from her parents. Her parents' failure to empathize with her distress robbed her, in part, of opportunities to learn empathy. Years later, this negatively impacted her parenting skills. The difficulty was more pronounced when she was faced with a situation that paralleled her own experiences. With this insight, Mrs. Branston returned to some of the strategies she had learned in the parenting class and in the book she had read. Weeks later, she reported that things were better for all family members.

Obstacle Two: It Is Difficult to Be Empathic When You Are Angry

It is also difficult to be empathic when you are upset with, annoyed by, or disappointed in someone else. At many of our workshops, we ask parents to raise their hands if they consider themselves to be empathic. Typically, after a few brave souls have the courage to do so, thereby breaking the ice, the vast majority of those in attendance follow suit. It is not unusual to hear "I always attempt to place myself inside the shoes of my children and see the world through their eyes."

It has been our experience, however, that while many caring parents judge themselves to be empathic, empathy is more apparent when the actions of those around us suit our preferences. It is easy to be empathic with our children when they do what we ask them to do, when they go to bed and get up on time without problems, when they finish their chores and homework without being reminded, when they obtain good grades in school, when they say "hello," "please," and "thank you" to others without being reminded, and when we convince ourselves that it is not just how they act but also who they are that makes us feel proud as parents.

It is much more challenging to be empathic when our children's actions don't meet our expectations. Anger and disappointment have an insidious way of reducing empathy and of blinding us to the pejorative power of our words and actions. Each of us can provide a personal example of having said something in anger to our children or to others that we would like to retract. When anger is our pilot, we are less likely to be reflective. We are less likely to consider our choice of words. We are more likely to act to relieve our annoyance rather than to teach our children. When Michael, discouraged by his mistakes, decided to quit building the radio, his father responded by saying, "I told you it wouldn't work. You don't have enough patience to read the directions carefully." Michael's father later realized that what he said served to relieve his frustration but, in doing so, weakened his son's resolve and motivation to return to the activity. He'd allowed himself to become annoyed and frustrated because Michael's quitting did not meet his expectations. The upshot was that he spoke impulsively, failing to consider Michael's likely perception of and reaction to his unkind words.

In a family therapy session, fifteen-year-old Rachel reported to her parents, Mr. and Mrs. Sterling, that she was feeling depressed. Words such as these typically evoke anxiety in parents.

Mrs. Sterling immediately countered, "But there's no reason for you to be depressed. We give you everything you need, and we are a loving family." On hearing this, Rachel slumped in her chair and grimly vowed not to speak again.

It was stressful for Mrs. Sterling to consider that her daughter might have a problem that could lead to a self-destructive act. While her response to Rachel was rooted in part in a desire to reassure her daughter, as well as herself, that things were not so bad and could be better, it was a statement lacking in empathy.

In many ways, Mrs. Sterling's response was similar to that of Mrs. Sailor when Lucy commented that she had few friends. Mrs. Sterling failed to empathize or to validate what Rachel was trying to communicate. During the course of the family counseling visit, she remarked that if Rachel was in fact depressed, then *she* must have failed as a parent. She also harbored anger toward Rachel for what she perceived to be her daughter's playing the martyr to gain attention. All of these beliefs contributed to the absence of empathy in her words. Although this was a relationship problem that would not be solved in one visit, we suggested that she give thought to a more empathic response to Rachel's statement such as: "We know that you have been depressed, and we're glad that you can tell us. That is why we are here, to figure out how we can all be of help."

During another family therapy visit, we asked Joshua's parents, Mr. and Mrs. Rogers, to describe a typical day in their teenage son's life, but through his eyes.

Mr. Rogers responded, "He sets his alarm for 6:30 A.M., shuts it off immediately, and falls back to sleep. We have to come into his room at 6:45 to wake him up so he can get ready for school. He yells at us, 'Get out of my room. It's my space.'"

As Mr. Rogers continued his description of Josh's difficulty in getting ready for school, we politely interrupted him. We explained that he was not answering the question as it had been posed; rather than placing himself inside the shoes of Joshua, he had responded to the question from his own perspective. That response was influenced in great part by his anger and frustration. He could not understand why his once happy, pleasant, successful son was now failing in school, angry, withdrawn, and depressed.

Seeing things solely from our own vantage point is human nature. These examples highlight the difficulty we all share in being empathic, particularly when anger and frustration are the dominant emotions fueling our behavior.

Obstacle Three: "My Child's Goal in Life Is to Make Me Angry"

If this were the game show "Family Feud," it is likely that the number one reason that parents would give for why your child engages in negative behavior would be, "He does it on purpose to bother me." When *we* make a mistake, we can usually attribute it to some factor beyond our control. However, when someone else makes the same mistake, we often are quick to point it out as an example of that individual's shortcomings.

Almost automatically, we tend to believe that our children can control the majority of their negative behaviors "if they choose to." It is difficult for parents to be empathic when they read a negative motive into a child's behavior that has little if any basis in reality. For instance, John, the seventh-grader with a history of reading problems described in Chapter 1, was viewed by his parents as "not putting enough effort into school and being lazy." They further questioned whether John's behavior represented a way of getting back at them for the rules they set in the household. It's no surprise, given this interpretation of John's behavior, that the Kahns spent the day angry, faultfinding, and repeatedly reminding John to "try harder." In actuality, in many situations John was trying hard. His seeming lack of effort was rooted in his frustration and sense of hopelessness, caused by a then undiagnosed set of problems, including a learning disability and attention deficit hyperactivity disorder.

As long as Mr. and Mrs. Kahn adhered to the opinion that he was a lazy child, their words and the tone of their voices were accusatory. Empathy was nowhere to be found. When John's problems were finally diagnosed, his parents realized the errors of their past behavior and, in their own words, "felt awful."

In a related case, Mr. and Mrs. Ashlund sought help because of their four-year-old son Robert's difficult bedtime behavior. When it was time for bed, he would run through the house; when his parents attempted to restrain him, he would scream and yell, sometimes for hours. This behavior, they explained, had occurred for at least six months. Prior to that time, Robert had not exhibited bedtime problems.

When we asked about their understanding of this scenario, it was apparent that they viewed Robert's behavior through a lens of opposition and a need for attention. Since the Ashlunds felt that Robert received a great deal of their attention in the course of the day, they responded angrily when he resisted going to bed. Their perception of his behavior often prompted them to respond to his screaming with loud, angry words. Several times, out of frustration, they resorted to spanking. Although they reported being unhappy about having to use corporal punishment, they also said that the spanking typically worked. Robert would remain in his bed afterward, often crying himself to sleep.

Since Robert's behavior persisted night after night despite their actions, we questioned if that approach was actually successful and one that would achieve long-lasting results. Their view of the problem as an indication of opposition and hunger for unwarranted attention appeared to increase their anger and diminish their capacity for empathy. A vicious cycle had been set in motion. The Ashlunds, now lacking empathy, were led to viewing their child's behavior only one way, keeping them in a punitive mode of response. As we spoke further, it was clear that rather than improving conflicts at home, their behavior served to heighten Robert's anger and tantrums, which in turn further depleted their capacity for empathy.

During our interview with Robert, we asked whether he ever had "scary dreams." He looked surprised and responded, "How did you know?"

We explained that many children his age have nightmares and that we wondered about his. A sense of relief softened his face as he talked about bad dreams, with monsters pursuing him and his family. We then suggested that Robert draw a picture of one of these dreams so that we could show it to his parents. As we casually asked more questions about the dreams, Robert revealed that he was afraid to go to sleep because then he would have those "bad" dreams.

Although Robert's parents saw his bedtime behavior as oppositional and manipulative, Robert's comments during our interview pointed to the conclusion that the onset of his bedtime problems resulted from a young child's attempt to avoid the anxiety associated with nightmares. Robert's parents, after seeing his drawing, were willing to consider this alternative hypothesis. This shift in their thinking immediately led them to be more empathic and to appreciate the near desperate feelings that their son had been experiencing each evening.

Robert offered two suggestions himself to help ease his anxiety. He asked for a night-light, which his parents had previously refused. He also asked to have a photo of his parents placed by his bed; if he felt afraid, he said, he could look at their picture. These recommendations were met with agreement by Robert's parents. They also agreed to read him an extra story each evening and to leave his door open. Robert's tantrums and resistance to going to bed ceased. The household atmosphere, especially at bedtime, improved markedly. A major factor in the improvement of Robert's behavior was the ability of his parents to understand his perspective and to shift their view of the cause of his tantrums.

Finally, consider the relationship between five-year-old Cindy and her mother, Ms. Peterson, a single parent. From Ms. Peterson's description, it appeared that Cindy had been temperamentally difficult from the time she was born: "Cindy never seems satisfied and always wants more. I can never give her enough. From the moment she gets up in the morning, she wants to provoke a fight, and her favorite saying is 'You're not fair.' I feel that she has a personal vendetta against me."

This statement was not offered with humor. Ms. Peterson seemed convinced that her daughter was "out to get" her. Guided by the "personal vendetta" explanation, she viewed nearly all of Cindy's behavior as manipulative. She used this interpretation to justify her harsh and overly punitive response. Empathy on the part of Ms. Peterson had long since departed their relationship, if in fact it had ever been present.

We realized that if Ms. Peterson were going to change her relatively entrenched view of the source of Cindy's behavior, we had to begin by displaying empathy toward *her*. We had to offer an alternative explanation that she was willing to consider, and we have found that we cannot expect parents to become more empathic toward their children unless we first practice empathy toward *them*. All people are more open to hearing new ideas if the ideas are expressed in respectful, nonaccusatory, and, most important, empathic ways.

We told Ms. Peterson that we could understand why many parents would interpret Cindy's behavior as manipulative and within her control but that we wondered if she had considered any other explanations for Cindy's behavior. She had not. We then explained that the different temperaments that children bring into the world affect their behavior and how they respond to experiences and events in their lives. We offered a number of simple examples, such as children who are excessively shy, anxious, or hyperactive. We also provided her with reading material about childhood temperament.

At our next meeting, it was evident that her anger and frustration regarding her daughter had lessened significantly. As we sat down to begin the session, she immediately asked, "What are the best ways to parent a child with a difficult temperament?"

The information we had provided Ms. Peterson helped to shift her view toward being more realistic and more empathic. She realized that frequently Cindy did not choose her behavior. To mitigate Cindy's insatiability and inflexibility, we suggested that Ms. Peterson set a special time to be with Cindy each evening and that she build many more choices into the child's routine (e.g., what to eat, what to wear). A new understanding of Cindy's behavior enhanced Ms. Peterson's ability to be empathic. She was then able to use this skill repeatedly to manage her frustration and anger. This not only led to an improvement in their relationship but also increased Ms. Peterson's ability to manage Cindy's behavior.

Obstacle Four: Believing That Empathy Interferes with Parenting

At one of our workshops, a father asked, "Won't being empathic keep me from setting limits? Isn't it another way of advocating that you let kids do whatever they want and spoil them?" While this concern is shared by most parents, the explanation of "spoiling children" is wielded like a giant hammer by some so-called parenting experts advocating one-sided, unilateral discipline in which children speak when spoken to and their feelings are unimportant. Empathy, however, has nothing to do with giving in to children, spoiling them, or refraining from setting appropriate limits. In fact, children will learn better from us and accept our limits when we practice empathy and try to understand their point of view.

We can be empathic and yet disapprove of what our children do. We can validate our children's feelings and beliefs but not necessarily agree with them. For example, twelve-year-old Julie told her parents they were unfair for not letting her accompany her friends to "hang out" at the mall. Instead of responding angrily, lecturing, or engaging in a power struggle with their daughter, they began by validating her feelings, saying, "We know that you think we are not being fair, and we know that unless we said you could go, you would still think we were not being fair. We're sorry about that, but we don't feel comfortable with our twelve-year-old daughter hanging out at the mall all afternoon."

We would not expect Julie to thank her parents for setting this limit. However, the fact that they acknowledged her feelings made it easier for her to listen to what they had to say. When Julie learned that her friends' parents had similar reservations about their children spending an afternoon without adult supervision at the mall, an alternate activity was explored and chosen.

Also illustrative of this obstacle is our work with seven-year-old Evan and his father. Mr. Dooley resorted to slapping Evan's backside when he continued to whine about wanting to watch a particular television program that his father thought was inappropriate for someone so young. When we first discussed with Mr. Dooley the concept of placing himself in Evan's shoes, he retorted, "I don't care if he wants to watch that show; he can't! And he has to learn that if he whines, I'll give him a reason for whining."

But the response of corporal punishment to Evan's whining did not solve this problem and added stress and tension to the household. We explained to Mr. Dooley that his actions led Evan to view him through a negative, punitive lens. We emphasized that empathy could be used to create a climate in which his son would be more inclined to listen to and learn from him.

Consequently, when the situation arose again, Mr. Dooley responded in a calm voice, "I know you want to watch this show, but it's not a show for kids. You can keep whining, but it won't change my opinion. However, if you want to watch television, there are two other shows you can choose from."

When parents are upset, frustrated, or angry, it is difficult for them to be empathic. The process of empathy does not come easily or naturally for most of us. It is likewise true that by our simply being empathic, all of our children's problems will not miraculously disappear. In many circumstances, even when parents are empathic, children continue to respond with difficult behavior. Nonetheless, empathy is the best place to begin changing our children's behavior, building solid parent-child relationships, and fostering resilience. It is certainly a more promising solution than the alternative of escalating stress and anger.

Becoming an Empathic Parent

A parent's goal must be to be empathic at all times, good times and trying times alike. Always strive to begin with your child's perspective, recognizing that empathy is a crucial skill in raising resilient children. As you've already realized, the capacity to be empathic requires thoughtfulness together with the powerful belief that to be heard and understood one must first listen and seek understanding. The following three guidelines will help you to begin to strengthen and maintain this process.

Guideline One: Begin with Empathy

Empathy is more than a fad or a flavor-of-the-month approach to parenting. Parents are bombarded by experts with new and often conflicting ideas of how to raise their children. We believe these approaches fall short in preparing our children for life in the new millennium. Some experts recommend that children be allowed to cry themselves to sleep so as not to spoil them, while others disagree. One child development specialist may advocate selective spanking as a form of discipline, while another contends that spanking represents child abuse. One expert may perceive any form of competition as harmful to a child's psyche, while another endorses the virtues of competing and learning how to deal with winning and losing.

Parents have repeatedly told us, "Every new book or article I read about raising children adds more confusion and insecurity to my life." Thus, we realize with a modicum of anxiety and trepidation that your response to the guidelines we present may be, "Here are two more child experts with their own particular views to confuse us even further."

There are honest differences of opinion among those of us who have studied and lectured about the process of raising children. Your reading this book implies that you share our concerns about the future and our conviction that the manner in which parents raise their children and prepare them for the future must emphasize resilience. In this endeavor, empathy must assume a central role.

If you want to strengthen your capacity for empathy, begin accepting and appreciating that empathy must play a part in every aspect of your relationship with your children. This acceptance requires you to become clear about the definition of empathy. Don't confuse it with giving in, spoiling your children, or being indecisive. Empathy should be thought of as a foundation for effective communication. By relating effectively with our children, we shape and reinforce their resilience. As you appreciate and practice empathy, this skill will become a natural part of your repertoire.

Guideline Two: Let Experience Be Your Guide

As we have discussed, many parents are frustrated by the fact that they often speak ineffectively in the voices of their own parents when they encounter problems with their children. You'll find strategies and suggestions for changing these negative scripts in Chapter 4. At this point, however, we suggest the following empathy exercise in which you think about your own childhood experiences and use them as a guide in shaping your interactions with your children.

Many parents fail to take advantage of this resource. Let it work for you. This exercise in recalling our childhood experiences reinforces empathy since it requires that we think back to when we were children and then use those memories to place ourselves in our children's shoes.

Ask yourself the following questions:

- What was one of the most wonderful experiences I ever had with my mother? What was one with my father?
- What was an experience I resented with my mother? What was one I resented with my father?
- How did my parents respond when I made a mistake?

Considering these questions sets the stage for parents to examine their childhood memories and use them as guideposts. These are not just street signs directing one kind of behavior or another but road maps to modify and guide behavior. When parents reflect on these questions, our capacity to empathize with our children is reinforced. These thoughts prompt us to think about how our children experience us.

Thirteen-year-old Mary complained that her parents, Mr. and Mrs. Brewster, put too much pressure on her to earn good grades. She also said that while they frequently criticized her, they offered only minimal positive feedback and, for that matter, a minimal amount of their time. When we asked the Brewsters to think about their own positive and negative memories of their parents, Mrs. Brewster reported having similar memories of her parents. She recalled that she had frequently felt that all they cared about were her grades. However, as she reflected on positive memories, she immediately recalled a number of noteworthy occurrences, including a message written by her mother to her on a birthday card expressing how much her parents loved her and how much they enjoyed the time they spent with her during outings.

The Brewsters used their own memories to begin to change and guide their interactions with Mary. They spent less time thinking about her homework and made an effort to write a note telling her how much they loved her. Mary at first questioned their actions.

They told her, "Sometimes we forget to tell you how much you mean to us and how much we love you." Mrs. Brewster began to spend more time with Mary in a number of activities, including working on a charity drive. Mary thoroughly enjoyed this time with her mother. Her parents' capacity to become more empathic noticeably improved their relationship.

Guideline Three: Put Empathy into Action

At the beginning of the chapter, we presented this question as a tool: "What words would your child use to describe you as a parent?" Take a moment now to consider how you would respond to the following:

- Describe your mother.
- Describe your father.
- When you were a child, how would your mother have described you? How would your father have described you?
- If you could have changed one thing about your mother, what would it have been? What would you have changed about your father?

As you answer these questions, remember that just as you have certain words and images to describe your parents, your children have words and images to describe you. Each time you look into the eyes of your children, each time you talk and interact with them, they form thoughts and images to describe you. If we are to raise resilient children, we must reflect on how we would wish our children to describe us.

Keeping this in mind, take a sheet of paper and divide it in two. On one side write down all of the words you *hope* your children would use to describe you. Think about why you chose those words. Consider what behaviors on your part would contribute to their using these descriptions. After completing this list, on the other side of the page, write down all of the words you think your children would *actually* use to describe you. What experiences might lead your children to use these words? Then compare the two lists. How close are they? The further apart, the more work you have ahead of you. We even suggest in many cases that you share these lists with your children.

When we think seriously about how our children would describe us, we are engaging in empathy. As testimony to the benefit of sharpening our empathy skills, one father announced in a session, "I have changed the way I speak with my children. I find that I focus much more on the positive than the negative, and even when I correct something, I do it in a way that makes them actually listen to me." With his wife sitting next to him, he added in a humorous tone, "I even think more about what I say to my wife."

We conclude this section with the story of fourteen-year-old Jay and his strained relationship with his father, Mr. Parsons. When we asked Mr. Parsons to describe his own father and mother and how he thought they would have described him, he squirmed and faltered.

A week later, after being given time to reflect, Mr. Parsons commented, "Those questions triggered a lot of emotions." He explained that as he thought about how he would describe his own father, what came to mind was "inflexible, overly demanding, rarely positive, a poor listener who always had to be right and who could never say 'I love you.'" He added, "When I was

Jay's age, I think my father would have described me as "bullheaded, inflexible, won't take no for an answer." He continued, "What dawned on me was that history was repeating itself in my family. I would describe Jay the very same way that my father would have described me, and I bet Jay would use the same words to describe me that I used to describe *my* father." His voice was tinged with sadness, and his distress was evident. "I don't want history to repeat itself any longer."

This was a turning point in his relationship with Jay. We began to identify steps that family members could take to change and rewrite their negative scripts. In family therapy, we began to examine and reinforce everyone's capacity for empathy. Jay, his sister, and both parents worked to improve their relationships. The empathy exercise was a major impetus in this process.

The Drought of Empathy

Families function better, communication improves, and children are more resilient when all members of the household make an effort to begin with and practice empathy every day. A helpful first step in improving the somewhat frightening future described earlier in this book is for all of us to begin to use empathy in our communications with our children, neighbors, coworkers, and even elected officials. We must seek and practice empathy among religious and ethnic groups, even among countries.

The time and effort we spend as parents in strengthening our capacity for empathy will pay many dividends. These actions will help us develop positive, lifelong relationships with our children and will serve as a guiding principle in shaping and reinforcing resilience in our children. And perhaps producing a generation of empathic individuals will significantly affect the future for all of us.

3

Communicating Effectively

To Listen, to Learn, to Influence

The questions and comments that parents raise at the close of our workshops invariably follow a consistent theme, one that reflects problems in parent-child communication. A recent workshop was indicative of this:

One father asked, exasperated, "How do I get my son to listen to me? He tunes me out!"

Another echoed, "When I ask my son any question, he has the same answer, 'I don't know!' How do I get him to talk to me?"

Still another parent remarked, "My daughter says that the only thing I tell her is what she is doing wrong, that I never say anything about all of the things she does right."

And, "Is being monosyllabic a condition of adolescence?"

In response to each of these parents, we emphasized the importance of communication. Finally, one brave parent stood up and said, half jokingly, "If I hear one more parenting expert use the word *communication*, I'm going to scream! I *am* communicating, but my child is not!"

What steps are necessary to climb the stairway to effective communication with our children? How can we help our kids learn to communicate better? Why do we often feel that we are communicating and they are not?

Although the importance of communication is frequently emphasized in response to parents' questions about problems with their children, effective communication is easily discussed but much more difficult to implement. Knowing what to do is not the same as doing what you know. Communicating effectively requires narrowing that gap between what we know and what we do.

As children grow, they experience thousands upon thousands of verbal and nonverbal communications from their parents, teachers, other adults, siblings, and peers. How we hear and respond to the communications of our children is critical in the process of fostering resilience. This chapter is devoted to communication and the obstacles and steps necessary to incorporating what we know into our everyday interactions with our children.

Communication and a Resilient Mindset

Rarely in our workshops have parents risen to comment about the wonderful level of communication they experience with their children. This is not surprising, given that many parents attend workshops because they are experiencing problems. However, developing effective communication skills is more than communicating about problems between our children and us; it encompasses the quality of our communication minute-to-minute, hour-to-hour, day-after-day, across all types of situations. It is these daily communications that foster resilience.

If we have a clear understanding of the major components of the mindset of resilient youngsters, then every interaction with our children can be guided by the goal of strengthening this mindset. We can use our communications with them to model and reinforce such qualities of resilience as empathy, hope, optimism, problem-solving ability, reflection, coping ability, ease in interpersonal situations, self-worth, appropriate risk-taking, and a sense of control or ownership over one's life. Communication is a foundation for developing and strengthening all of these qualities.

As we stressed about empathy in the previous chapter, parents' communications with children should be guided by questions such as "Am I saying or doing things in a way that would make my children the most receptive to listening to what I have to say and learning from me?" and "Would I want anyone to speak to me in the way I'm speaking to my children?"

For a variety of reasons, even well-intentioned parents communicate in ways that at best have little chance of nurturing resilience and at worst actually chip away at a child's resilient mindset. For example, when Jane's mother jumped in and told her daughter how to behave with girls who did not want to sit with her at school, rather than encourage and help Jane to arrive at her own solutions to problems, she communicated in a way that negated a resilient mindset. When Gregory, the fifteen-year-old with a messy room, heard a litany of complaints from his frustrated parents, he quickly tuned them out, and their message fell on deaf ears.

The challenge of simultaneously keeping our goals in mind and communicating effectively, free of the emotion that often accompanies problems with our children, is daunting. When we're frustrated, we bring our own excess baggage from the past into the current situation. On the other hand, the more successful we become at examining our goals and motives, and questioning whether the means by which we are communicating are advancing or inhibiting these goals, the more likely we are to foster resilience in our children.

Thus, in our communications we should often ask ourselves:

- Do my messages convey and teach respect?
- Am I fostering realistic expectations in my children?
- Am I helping my children learn how to solve problems?
- Am I teaching empathy and compassion?
- Am I promoting self-discipline and self-control?
- Am I setting limits in ways that permit my children to learn from me rather than resent me?
- Am I truly listening to and validating what my children are saying?
- Do my children know that I value their input?
- Do my children know how special they are to me?
- Am I helping my children to appreciate that mistakes are part of the process of learning?
- Am I comfortable in acknowledging my own mistakes and apologizing for them?

Guided by these kinds of questions, let's examine how the parents of Jane and Gregory might have communicated differently had they understood that the resolution of a particular problem can extend far beyond the immediate solution in fostering problem-solving skills. These examples also introduce the concept of rewriting negative scripts, or changing the means by which we communicate and interact with our children to enhance our relationship and develop their resilience. The next chapter goes into greater depth on how to employ this strategy. Keep in mind that although the following dialogues appear obvious now, in the heat of the moment it is much more difficult to stay the course and do what you know.

Let's Do Lunch

Jane came crashing through the front door, slamming it open and slamming it shut. She threw her book bag on the floor and in tears cried, "I hate them! They're so mean! They wouldn't let me sit with them at lunch."

Her mother came rushing downstairs, worried that Jane had been injured. Relieved to see that her daughter was physically unharmed, Mrs. Jones shouted impulsively, "Don't slam the door!" She continued, "You scared me half to death. What's wrong? Hate who? Who wouldn't let you sit with them?" Variations of this exchange had played out before. Mrs. Jones was of the opinion that Jane was simply too sensitive and created many of her problems.

"I thought they were my friends," Jane blubbered.

"Stop crying," said Mrs. Smith.

Jane sobbed quietly for a moment while her mother waited. She then explained, "Lily, Allyson, and Abby. I thought they were my friends. I don't know why they're so mean to me. I didn't do anything to them."

At that moment Mrs. Jones realized that although Jane was not physically injured, she was emotionally hurt. It mattered little that these appeared to be trivial events to Mrs. Jones; they were major events to Jane. Deciding to try another approach, Mrs. Jones responded, "It hurts when our friends don't want us to sit with them. What do you think happened?"

Jane looked at her mother. By now the tears had stopped flowing. Usually her mother would have quickly told her what to do. This response caught Jane's attention.

"I have no idea," said Jane. "When I went to sit at the lunch table, they said it was taken. I told them there was room left, but they said Marsha was coming over to sit. They looked so annoyed at me. I didn't do anything to them." Jane wore a pained look.

"You have no idea why they acted that way?"

"No. I felt so stupid. I just walked away. I hate them, Mom. What should I do?"

Mrs. Jones opened her mouth to speak as she had done so many times before, but she recognized that offering a solution, telling Jane what to do about her problems with friends, was having little effect in improving Jane's social relations. She decided at that moment to enlist Jane's help in arriving at possible solutions. She knew that to develop a resilient mindset, Jane needed experience in learning how to deal with problems. Mrs. Jones replied, "There may be a couple of things to do. But first, I want to make sure I understand what you would have liked to have happened when you approached them at lunch. I also want to make sure you have some idea of what you want to do now."

"I don't know. I'm just so angry," Jane repeated. "I felt so stupid."

Mrs. Jones made an effort to validate Jane's feelings as well as convey the message that Jane had the ability to think of solutions: "All of us feel angry and hurt when we're rejected. I know you're not sure what to do, but maybe we can think about it together."

"Maybe tomorrow I should just go back to the table and see what happens," Jane said.

"That's a possible way of handling things," her mother answered. "It could work, but what if they do the same thing?" Her intent here was not only to help Jane arrive at a plan of action but also to encourage her to think about the prospective outcomes.

Jane answered, "If they did the same thing, I would feel really stupid, and then it's so tough to say anything with other people around."

"So, what else can you do, Jane?"

"Maybe I can call Allyson tonight. She is my closest friend, you know. Maybe I can ask her why they didn't let me sit with them. I can tell her that it hurt my feelings. But what if she says they just don't want to be my friend anymore? I couldn't face that. I just wouldn't go back to school."

"If she said that, would you feel comfortable asking her why she didn't want to be your friend?"

"I'm not sure," answered Jane. "Well, probably. She has always been nice to me."

Mrs. Jones asked, "Would you rather call Allyson tonight or just ask the girls at the lunch table tomorrow?"

"I think I would rather call Allyson tonight," Jane responded. "I would feel really stupid if I asked all of them tomorrow and they just said there wasn't enough room, or if they didn't want to talk to me."

"That makes sense," Mrs. Jones said with a smile. Then, to encourage her daughter to think of possible responses from her friend so she could be prepared, she prompted, "What if you call Allyson and she says there just wasn't enough room?"

"I think it would be easier for me to say to Allyson alone on the phone, rather than at the lunch table, that last week there were enough seats for all of us, so how come there aren't enough seats now? Or maybe," continued Jane, "I'll ask why they wanted to sit with Marsha and not me."

Mrs. Jones put her arm around her daughter. Her efforts now were directed at supporting Jane's decision and helping her understand that if a solution doesn't work out, you can learn from it and think of another option. She told her, "That seems to make a lot of sense. You should try it, and if it doesn't work, we can think of other possible things to do."

Some parents may think that this style of interaction is artificial. Others may adhere to the axiom that if children ask you what to do, you should tell them. "That's what parents are for; they have more experience than their children."

Our response is that parents can engage in such discussions without having it sound artificial. Likewise, while there are many times that we should offer specific suggestions to our children, particularly when safety is involved, we will better serve our children's growth and resiliency by using our knowledge and experience to teach them to think and to encourage them to arrive at their own solutions. This type of encouragement reinforces problem-solving skills, a sense of ownership, and a feeling of control over one's life—vital ingredients of the mindset of resilient children.

Mission: Control

Now let's apply similar guidelines to a hypothetical communication between Gregory and his parents. In the past, Gregory's parents, wilted by his lack of organization and his messiness, repeatedly and angrily recited a list of complaints. They viewed Gregory's behavior as within his control and thus labeled him as willful and stubborn. As noted earlier, however, Gregory suffered from learning and attentional problems, which contributed to his lack of organization. Over time Gregory tuned out his parents because he was tired of their message. Gregory's parents maintained that their goal for Gregory was for him to be more responsible and organized, and to keep a reasonably clean room, one that "would not be condemned by the health department."

Although Mr. and Mrs. Smith were very clear about their goals, they neglected to consider the gap between those goals and the means by which they were attempting to reach them. They failed to ask themselves whether the ways in which they were speaking with and acting toward Gregory created an environment in which he would want to listen and respond to them.

Following is one possible example of a dialogue between Gregory and his parents that is more likely to lead to success for both parties.

Mr. and Mrs. Smith realized that the majority of their conversations with Gregory about responsibility, organization, and the condition of his room occurred in the heat of the moment when they became annoyed, frustrated, or angry at his behavior and actions. They decided to try a different approach, so during a rest on a family bicycling outing they initiated a conversation with him about these problems.

"Gregory, we want to talk to you about something important," Mrs. Smith said as she handed her son a water bottle and a snack.

Gregory looked worried, concerned that perhaps there was a serious family problem.

"Dad and I feel we have been nagging you quite a bit lately," Mrs. Smith continued, hoping that this opening would reduce the probability of his immediately becoming defensive. She made it clear that she was willing to bear some responsibility for the tension in their home.

Greg looked relieved and responded somewhat sarcastically, "I'm glad you finally realized that you're always on my back."

Mr. Smith did his best not to be goaded by Gregory's sarcasm. In the past such a comment from Gregory would often have invoked an equally sarcastic rejoinder from Mr. Smith. Instead, he smiled and said, "We really don't want to be on your back, but sometimes we feel we have no choice."

"Then why do you keep nagging me about everything?"

"We would really prefer not to keep reminding you about things," responded Mrs. Smith, "but we feel there are certain responsibilities we all have. When you don't meet yours, we start to remind you, and before long it comes across as nagging."

"You can say that again!"

"We want to figure out how we can all work together to avoid the battles we're having," said Mr. Smith. "Maybe we should focus on a few of the important things we would like to see done at home and develop a plan to get them done. That includes what you think Mom and I should be responsible for."

By attempting to involve Gregory in the process of problem solving, making him an active rather than passive participant, Mr. Smith hoped to reinforce his son's belief that he had some control over what transpired in his life. This is an important quality linked to a resilient mindset. By including himself and his wife as part of the problem-solving process, he also hoped to lessen the tension between Gregory and them.

"What do you think are the most important things?" asked Gregory as he sat up and looked at his parents.

"Are there things that you want Dad and me to do differently?" Mrs. Smith asked.

"Yeah, stop getting on my back all the time."

"OK, we will," Mr. Smith responded, "but that means there are some things that you have to take responsibility for also."

The conversation continued. Gregory was more willing to listen to what his parents had to say because of the way they communicated their concerns. Their message was couched in words that reinforced a problem-solving attitude. They were neither judgmental nor accusatory. When this kind of attitude is established, our children are more willing to engage in a process that reinforces resilience. In Gregory's case, the process permitted him to examine various options to problems, to develop a plan of action with his parents, and ultimately to be successful.

Obstacles to Climbing the Stairway to Successful Communication

Three key obstacles can prevent even well-meaning parents from communicating effectively with their children. They follow the same pattern as the obstacles that compromise empathy outlined in Chapter 2. Let's examine each of them.

Obstacle One: We Practice What We Have Lived

History, both good and bad experiences, shapes our behavior. If a parent grew up in a home in which the family communication style did not promote resilience, it is typically more difficult, but certainly not impossible, for that parent to spontaneously communicate in ways that nurture a resilient mindset in children.

Mr. Roy consulted us because of the struggles he was having with the misbehavior of his nine-year-old son, Danny. In several family meetings, we saw evidence of Mr. Roy's stern voice, preoccupation with what his son did wrong, and lack of positive feedback when he did something right. In Mr. Roy's eyes, correct behavior was expected and did not require reinforcement.

In an individual meeting with Mr. Roy, we asked him to describe his own father. He responded that most of his recollections of his father were of anger and yelling, often directed toward him. When we asked if his father ever communicated words or gestures of affection toward him, Mr. Roy thought for a moment and then teared up.

"When he was dying," Mr. Roy responded. "He told me he loved me. On the one hand I was glad he said it, but on the other I wondered why he couldn't have told me that years ago." He then added, "I also remember that whenever he spoke to me, he constantly pointed his finger at me. It almost felt as if he was stabbing me."

Mr. Roy began to recognize how many of his communications with Danny paralleled those between his father and him, exchanges filled with anger and a lack of warmth. This recognition helped motivate him to change his perspective and enhance his capacity for empathy, thereby impacting the way he spoke with his son. He worked at being less harsh and more positive and reinforcing. These changes were difficult for him at first, given the limited exposure he had as a child to more positive communications. However, he was determined not to let history repeat itself with his own son.

This situation is common in sports. Zach's father, an athlete all of his life, was extremely competitive. Although he praised Zach in many situations, while coaching him during sporting events, he was stern, often angry and accusatory. This was how his own father had interacted with him. Although he recalled not liking it, he was of the opinion that it had made him a better athlete. Unfortunately, it was having just the opposite effect on Zach. Zach began to withdraw from sporting activities in which his father was serving as a volunteer or coach. Zach's father slowly realized that what had seemingly worked for him when he was a child was not working for his son and that a change was necessary.

Obstacle Two: Anger Clouds Effective Communication

In the best of all possible worlds, when we become angry or upset, an automatic system would call into play our most sophisticated communication skills to help defuse our emotions and direct our attention to a search for reasonable solutions. Having this ability would greatly minimize power struggles with our children. Unfortunately, it is precisely when we are angry and frustrated that our communication skills, which are closely interwoven with other resiliency skills such as empathy and problem solving, are noticeably weakened. The style of angry communication that results often exacerbates rather than ameliorates a problem situation.

When Michael became discouraged and gave up building a radio, his father's sarcastic comments only fueled the fire. Words of encouragement might have made a positive difference. Similarly, when seven-year-old Evan whined about not being allowed to watch a television program, his father's response initially was a swat on the backside. Obviously, striking a whining child does little to serve the development of resilience. Although it may stop the whining, it doesn't solve the problem. What does help, he learned, is to say in a steady voice: "I know you want to watch this show, but it's not a show for kids. You can keep whining, but it will not change my opinion. However, if you want to watch television, there are two other shows you can choose from." In this way, Mr. Dooley is much more likely to temper his son's anger and reinforce the notion that life presents different options and choices, many of which will lead to satisfaction and success.

If we adhere to the goal of nurturing a resilient mindset in our children, then every interaction can be guided by this goal.

Obstacle Three: We Sometimes Believe That Our Children's Goal Is to Wear Us Down

All children at times test their parents. One of our roles as parents is to set expectations and limits for our children. While they will not respond by saying, "I'm so glad you set these limits since it shows me that you are concerned, loving parents," if limits and goals are established in an atmosphere free of anger and tension, children likely will feel safe and secure. However, if we view our children's questioning of our authority as evidence that they hold a "personal vendetta" against us, like five-year-old Cindy's mother, our communications reflect and reinforce this negative perception and breed power struggles.

This parental dynamic was evident in thirteen-year-old Alicia's battles with her parents. Both Mr. and Mrs. Grimes grew up in controlling homes and were afforded few opportunities to offer their opinions or engage in discussion. They carried this style of upbringing into their parenting practices and quickly interpreted any disagreement voiced by Alicia as her attempt to control and anger them. Consequently, almost all of their communications were based on the belief that they had to make certain Alicia understood that they were in charge. This mindset was reflected in their angry comments, including "You'll do what I say since I'm your mother" and "You're always trying to get your way; you never show any respect."

Since Mr. and Mrs. Grimes were constantly poised to expect stubbornness, they rarely said anything positive to their daughter. The combination of their negative remarks and lack of encouraging statements contributed to an increasingly tense, often explosive family environment.

Ten Steps for Effective Communication: To Listen, to Learn, to Influence

We are much more likely to influence our children in positive ways when we listen, learn, and understand their point of view, when we have our goals and priorities clearly in mind, and when we know how to communicate effectively. Achieving the goal of effective communication begins with the following strategies for listening to and validating what our children say, and responding honestly, consistently, and proactively.

Step One: Begin at Birth

Is it really possible that the style by which we talk to our children from the moment of their birth sets the stage for effective communication? Yes! Although it may not seem so obvious to some people, it quickly becomes so when a child is fourteen and parents feel the need to discuss important topics such as sex and drugs but have never taken time over the years to sit down and have a conversation with their child. A comfortable atmosphere for communicating, let alone communicating about important issues, has never been established.

Parents in these families often feel uneasy when they want to "have a talk" with their kids. Unfortunately, neither side has any experience in the activity, so both parties feel uncomfortable. As one parent told us, "It was like an unnatural act. I felt awkward. My daughter felt awkward. We went back and forth from silence to interrupting each other to finishing each other's sentences. In the end, each of us wanted to get the discussion over as quickly as possible. Not much was accomplished."

Attempting to enter into discussions about serious matters with our children without having set the foundation over the years of communicating about a variety of issues is similar to deciding to begin an exercise regime by jogging five miles the first day, never having jogged before. In this scenario, the jogger is likely to quickly become exhausted or collapse. It's common sense for novice joggers to build up their stamina by running a much shorter distance and slowly increasing to five miles. A similar approach is required to strengthen healthy communication with our children.

Don't infer from this that if communication was less than ideal during the early years in our children's lives, then it cannot be strengthened and improved. The point is that if we begin to refine patterns of communication when our children are young, they are more likely to speak with and listen to us as they grow. Even before our children possess language, we have countless opportunities to communicate verbally and nonverbally with them. Cuddling, holding, and playing with them; speaking to them; responding to their first sounds; and asking them questions are all actions that create a climate in which the seeds of effective communication are planted and nurtured early in life.

Step Two: Be Proactive

Many families in today's hectic, fast-paced world have developed a reactive communication style. They catch each other on the run and barely find time to discuss all of the important issues facing their family, let alone engage in friendly discussion. We must strive to move toward a proactive style. In addition to taking advantage of spontaneous moments for communication, it helps to schedule specific family times. For example, when our children are young, we should ensure that we have opportunities to play with and read to them. These activities not only provide wonderful moments to communicate a wealth of information, to let our children know how much we love them, and to take them on imaginary adventures about characters in books but also stimulate their language and cognitive capacities, shaping their abilities to learn new ways of coping and solving problems.

As children grow, it is important for families to establish a weekly time to discuss family issues and problems as well as possible solutions. We worked with a family in which parents and their two sons scheduled a regular weekly half-hour meeting, longer if necessary. They often set up an agenda beforehand. While an agenda may appear somewhat formal, it worked for this family. Both sons developed a greater sense of ownership since their agenda items carried equal weight with their parents' items.

Keep in mind, though, that communication should not be confined to a scheduled, once-a-week event. Parents should communicate with their children every day. In addition, families should strive to eat at least one meal together each day, during which each family member can discuss topics of interest with everyone listening.

Finally, being proactive means that we accept the responsibility of communicating with our children about important subjects *before* they become problems. Many parents avoid discussing issues such as drug and alcohol use until they are concerned that their child may be at risk. Parents have told us that they want to discuss these areas with their children but don't know what to say. Others are concerned that bringing up certain topics may make their children more curious about them and apt to experiment. The fractured logic of the latter position is that if we don't talk about it, it doesn't exist!

Step Three: Become an Active Listener

Closely tied to empathy is the importance of being an active listener. Too often when we think of effective communication, we think of the best ways to express ourselves. While expressive language is a major component of communication, we must begin, as author Stephen Covey reminds us, by making certain that we understand before seeking to be understood (Covey 1989). It is difficult, if not impossible, to engage in effective communication with our children if we fail to first listen to what they have to say.

To be an active listener implies that we begin without assumptions. On a crowded airplane we recently observed a family separated by a number of rows. Someone began listening to popular music through headphones quite loudly. Without giving it a second thought, the mother stood up and walked two rows down the aisle, telling her son to lower his music. The problem was that he wasn't the one with the music on!

Being active listeners implies that we truly attempt to understand the verbal and nonverbal messages conveyed by our children, that we perceive the feelings, thoughts, and beliefs that they are communicating, and that we do not let our own agendas or our need to get our own point across interfere with our ability to appreciate what our children are attempting to tell us. Active listeners also recognize that often unspoken messages or meanings are conveyed along with the spoken word. Active listening involves an effort to understand these meanings before seeking to be understood.

Chapter 2 introduced four-year-old Robert, who was having difficulty going to bed and instead would run through the house. His parents reacted by chasing him, yelling at him, and eventually restraining him. It was only when we interviewed Robert that we realized that his difficulty in going to sleep had its genesis in his frightening dreams. Once we listened closely and actively to what he had to say, once we were empathic, even this four-year-old was able to become involved in arriving at possible solutions to his problem. He did so with impressive sophistication, requesting a night-light and a photo of his parents to keep next to his bedside.

When the first author's older son, Rich, was seven, the family was set to fly to Florida for a vacation. Although Rich had flown a number of times, he approached Bob the day before departure and asked in a somewhat anxious voice, "What happens if I feel sick on the plane?"

Fortunately, Bob was neither too busy nor too preoccupied at the time and therefore didn't answer with a nonreflective, seemingly reassuring comment such as "Don't worry; if people feel sick on the plane, there are bags in front of each seat in case they have to throw up."

Instead he made certain that he understood the meaning *behind* the question. He asked, "Are you afraid that something is going to happen when we fly to Florida?"

With that, the floodgates opened. Rich relayed that he had just seen a report of a plane crash on the television news. Bob acknowledged that planes could crash and that that was a scary thought but that it rarely happened. He added that flying is very safe, especially since there are people who carefully check planes before they take off and pilots with many years of experience flying them. This discussion appreciably lessened Rich's anxiety.

In this instance, active listening allowed the parent to go beyond the child's stated worry about becoming sick to his real concern about a possible crash. Features of a resilient mindset, including empathy, problem solving, and learning to feel more in control of a situation, were reinforced.

Step Four: Make Sure You Say, "I Heard You"

It isn't enough to just listen. You must validate what your children are saying and confirm they have been heard. Effective communication will be derailed if we fail to validate what our children tell us. Validation does not imply that we agree with everything our children think or believe but rather that we acknowledge their perspective. Validation helps children believe that adults are listening to and respect their views. This creates a climate for ongoing communication.

If instead we immediately respond to children by telling them that they should not feel the way they do, we are effectively ending communication. We are telling them we are not interested in what they have to say. This occurred with fifteen-year-old Rachel when she commented during her family therapy session that she was depressed. Instead of validating Rachel's statement, her mother quickly responded, "But there's no reason for you to be depressed. We give you everything you need, and we are a loving family."

Although Mrs. Sterling's intention was to alleviate Rachel's sadness, her own anxiety and insecurity prompted a comment that only led Rachel to become even more withdrawn. The opportunity to be empathic and to search for ways to understand and ameliorate Rachel's sadness was short-circuited, as was the nurturing of a resilient mindset.

At one of our workshops, a mother commented that her ten-year-old son with attention deficit hyperactivity disorder constantly voiced the opinion that he was "dumb, stupid, and a real loser." She attempted to talk him out of his opinion by telling him that he was not dumb, stupid, or a loser and should not feel that way. She wondered why her son's typical response to these comments was to become more upset and angry and walk away.

Tearfully, she said, "I'm just trying to be of help. My son has so many strengths, but he refuses to notice them. What can I do?"

First, we counseled her to listen actively when her son spoke and to appreciate what he was telling her about how he was feeling. We pointed out that his willingness to communicate about his distress was a positive sign. Second, we urged her to validate what she heard him saying. For example, when her son expressed these negative beliefs, she could respond "I know that you feel dumb and stupid. I'm glad you can tell me how you feel, even though I see things differently. I know there are activities at which you're successful. I bet that together we can figure out what would help you feel better about yourself."

When parents acknowledge their children's feelings, children tend to be more willing to examine ways of working with their parents to discover options to improve problem situations. As a final illustration of our failure as parents to validate, let's revisit fifteen-year-old Lucy, whom we met in the previous chapter. In the family therapy session Lucy stated, "No one likes me."

Lucy's mother responded by observing, "You don't have friends because you don't know how to treat people." She continued in an accusatory tone, "You think you can just boss other kids around and they will continue to want to be with you."

"You always have to tell me what I'm doing wrong," Lucy angrily answered. "You never listen to what I have to say. You make it seem that everything is my fault."

Her mother's intention, impeded by frustration, was to have Lucy assume a greater sense of responsibility for what was transpiring in her life. While teaching our children to accept responsibility is a significant feature of resilience, imposing it on them when they are feeling sad and vulnerable is not. The manner in which Mrs. Sailor communicated provoked Lucy's anger and counteracted the goal.

What might she have said instead? One possibility is "It's not easy when no one seems to like us. Not having friends can be very difficult. Maybe together we can figure out why this is happening to you and how we can improve things." Such a statement would allow Lucy to feel less defensive about reflecting on her role in this problem.

Does your style validate your children's perceptions, or are you more likely to disagree with them and offer editorial comments that lead to their resentment? If we want children to learn from us, then we must ensure that we practice a communication style that helps them feel safe, secure, and validated.

Step Five: Do Unto Others . . .

We want and expect others to treat us with respect, to communicate clearly, and to respond fairly. Yet, in the heat of the moment we don't always treat others the way we would like them to treat us.

Joel's parents, Mr. and Mrs. Castle, consulted us because Joel constantly gave up when a task became difficult. They presented a list of examples of their son's quitting activities after short periods of time, including baseball, soccer, art, and piano. The pattern was always the same: Joel would voice great interest in the activity, but after a brief time any hardship he experienced, such as not scoring a goal in soccer or making slow progress in the art class, resulted in his voicing a hatred for the activity and resistance to continuing. As a consequence, Mr. and Mrs. Castle were nearing their wit's end.

This was apparent when Joel asked to play ice hockey. His mother responded, "Why should we buy you ice hockey equipment, when you keep quitting at everything you do! You seem to think that if you can't be perfect, you are just not going to do it. No one can learn anything that way."

Mr. Castle told us that one day when his frustration turned to anger, he said to Joel, "You are just a loser." The moment he uttered those words, he wished he could take them back.

They accepted the fact that their efforts at helping Joel stick with activities had failed, and they were perplexed as to why he behaved this way. When we discussed the importance of empathy in guiding their communication with their son, they conceded that they had not been empathic. They protested, "But we don't quit at things; he does."

We acknowledged the Castles' feelings and noted that we could understand their consternation. It is disappointing and painful to observe our children constantly giving up and to watch as they build a history of great expectations and then failed hopes. Endorsing their goal of teaching Joel to stick with things and to learn to enjoy the process of mastery, we emphasized that perseverance is an important component of a resilient mindset.

We asked the Castles to think about ways in which they could communicate with Joel to increase his willingness to persevere in the face of a challenge. We offered some basic guidelines for effective communication and prepared them for their first discussion with Joel on the subject. They did not have to wait long. A few days later, the opportunity arose when Joel informed his parents that he wanted to take saxophone lessons.

In the past the Castles would have initially responded with a sarcastic comment about Joel's quitting the piano, followed by denying his request. This time they attempted to engage Joel in a dialogue about his request but, more important, about his mindset concerning success.

"We're glad that you want to learn to play the saxophone," Mrs. Castle responded. "But before we make a decision together, we think it's important that we talk about something."

Joel looked angry. "Not another lecture!"

Mrs. Castle responded calmly, "I hope it doesn't come across as a lecture, but if it does, let us know."

With this seemingly simple comment, Mrs. Castle hoped to smooth the way toward more effective communication. She didn't respond defensively or angrily to Joel's provocation but instead invited him to inform them should they appear to be lecturing.

"I will certainly let you know," answered Joel with a somewhat surprised look.

"Dad and I support your desire to take saxophone lessons," Mrs. Castle said. "But before we say yes, we want to discuss a concern we have."

"I can guess what that is," Joel jumped in.

"What do you think it is?" Mr. Castle asked.

"You told me I was a loser," Joel said as he looked right at his father. "You think I'll just quit again."

Mr. Castle answered, "Joel, I know I said that, and I'm sorry. I was just so frustrated that you begin so many things with great hope, but then when the going gets rough, you quit. But you're right; this is what we're concerned about."

"Well, I won't quit at the sax," he stated.

"We believe you," added Mrs. Castle. "We know you wouldn't want to quit, but sometimes when you feel you're not making enough progress, even if you didn't plan to quit, that seems to be the only option you consider. Then Dad and I become upset and begin to yell, and soon we're all angry at each other."

"I know," responded Joel. "Just don't yell!"

"It is something Dad and I have to work on, but we also feel that you have some responsibility as well. If we make a commitment to rent or buy the saxophone, then you must make a commitment to stick with it, even if you become frustrated."

"Well, people can change their minds."

"We agree," said Mr. Castle, "but we're concerned that you're changing your mind too frequently and not giving yourself a chance to learn new things." He hoped not only to validate Joel's point of view but also to begin to articulate the problem, setting the stage to solving it.

"I do learn new things," insisted Joel. "I just know when I don't like to do something."

"We know when you say that you don't want to do something anymore that you don't like doing it," responded Mrs. Castle. "What we are saying is that you may not be giving yourself a chance to see if you would like it and could do better."

In a calmer, less defensive tone, Joel responded, "Well, what if I say I will stick with the saxophone?"

"That would make it easier for Dad and me to say OK to renting you a saxophone and paying for lessons," Mrs. Castle responded. "But let me ask, what if after a few weeks you decide you want to quit?" She was trying here to help her son think about possible options and consequences and how he might handle things differently this next time compared with the past.

"I won't quit," Joel insisted.

"Well, what if we have an understanding?" asked Mr. Castle. "Your mother and I will support your taking up the sax so long as you continue with the lessons and practice for a certain amount of time."

"For how long?"

"What do you think?" Mr. Castle answered. By encouraging Joel to provide a limit, he hoped to reinforce his son's sense of ownership in the agreement, an important feature of a resilient mindset. If he did not concur with Joel's time frame, then they could negotiate.

"Maybe for this entire school year," responded Joel.

"That seems fair," said Mrs. Castle. "I hope you enjoy playing the saxophone. But even if it turns out not to be as much fun as you thought, your commitment is to stick with it at least until the end of the school year. That means taking lessons and practicing. You could also play in the school band. Our commitment is to rent you the instrument and pay for the lessons."

With a smile and a high five to his dad, Joel responded, "I'll do it."

"I'm glad to hear that," answered Mr. Castle.

Obviously, not every interaction with our children will be resolved so positively, but we increase the probability of success when we are empathic and engage in discussions with our children that lessen defensiveness and allow each family member to listen to the other. A problem-solving approach thrives in such an atmosphere.

Step Six: Use Nonjudgmental and Nonaccusatory Communication

This step encompasses empathy and validation. In our research related to resiliency, several young adults whom we interviewed described growing up among parents and teachers who functioned like prosecuting attorneys. One young man stated, "I always felt that my parents were looking to catch me in a lie, in a transgression. I always felt on the defensive, and after a while I would bend the truth to get them off my back. I know I shouldn't have done it. It led them to mistrust me even more than they had. I just didn't know what else to do. They just didn't seem to be encouraging. I felt that they were on a mission to find my faults."

When we are upset with our children, it is easy to adopt an accusatory mode and to make assumptions about their behavior that prompt us to say and do things that are deemed by them to be critical and judgmental. Many of the children and parents described in this chapter illustrate the damaging effects of accusatory and judgmental communications. If we want our children to learn from us rather than resent us, we must minimize accusatory messages. The alternatives to judgmental comments offered here do not impinge on our authority as parents but rather increase the probability that our children will listen to what we have to say.

It is difficult to reinforce a resilient mindset in our children when the home atmosphere is filled with tension, anger, and mistrust. As subsequent chapters explain, to offset a negative atmosphere we must ensure that we offer our children an abundance of positive comments, including those that capture how much we care about and love them.

Step Seven: Communicate Clearly and Briefly

Many parents attempt to communicate so much information at one time that *any* rational human being on the receiving end, not just a child, would become overloaded. Our routine communications with our children should be brief and focused. Communication is a lifelong process; not everything must be accomplished in one discussion. If too much information is offered at once, children may become overwhelmed and incapable of processing any of it. This is particularly true if the text is laced with negative comments.

What defines brief? How many topics should we discuss at once with our children? There are no fixed answers. Basically, the younger our children, the simpler our messages should be. Even teenagers, however, are not thrilled when they feel that we are discussing the same issues repeatedly. Take cues from your children: if a conversation is becoming increasingly fruitless, if the same problems come up time and again, if problem solving is being replaced by tension and accusation, that's a sign to take a break.

At such times, we suggest you say to your children, "Everyone is getting so angry, but nothing is being accomplished. This is not the best time to continue this discussion. We all need a break." During the respite, consider how to change your script to facilitate better discussion.

Step Eight: Serve as a Model of Honesty and Dignity

Parents sometimes are indirect and not forthright with their children. While we are not suggesting that you discuss issues that are beyond your children's emotional or cognitive capabilities or that are highly personal, the fact is that children are extremely astute at recognizing when parents hide things from them or bend the truth. You must use your best judgment in what to share or not share. Too often, however, parents err on the side of fostering a cloak of secrecy in the household.

As one example, we received a call from Mr. and Mrs. Foster, the parents of eight-year-old twin sisters Stacy and Charlotte. The twins' maternal grandmother had recently been diagnosed with ovarian cancer, and the prognosis for her recovery was guarded. The parents limited their remarks to the girls because a relative had said that they were too young to be told the truth; it would upset them too much. The girls sensed by the sadness of their mother that something was wrong, but when they inquired what was happening, they were told only that their grandmother was not feeling well. Mr. and Mrs.

Foster were becoming increasingly perplexed about what to say, especially as their daughters asked more questions.

When they called us for a consultation, it was evident that these were caring, loving parents. They wanted to take the best course of action with their children but did not know what to do.

In our meeting with the Fosters, we discussed the importance of being honest with their daughters in a way that the girls could understand. We placed the issue of honesty within a framework of resiliency: When we are honest, it is easier for our children to ask questions, thereby allowing us to understand their feelings and worries so we can help them manage their distress. Attempting to hide or minimize the reality of a difficult situation conveys to children that we feel that they cannot handle the situation and that they should not approach us. The result is that we rob them of an opportunity to feel more in control, to learn techniques for coping with stressful conditions, and to learn to handle painful feelings.

Mr. and Mrs. Foster were receptive to our recommendations. They informed their daughters that their grandmother was very ill. Immediately Stacy asked if Grandmother was going to die. Her parents answered honestly that the doctors were doing the best they could but that Grandmother was not improving. They also verbalized their sadness, and as they did, they became tearful. By communicating and modeling their sadness, they allowed their daughters to share their anxieties and sorrow as well. This openness prompted the girls to express other worries, such as whether one of their parents might die, what would happen to their grandfather if he were all alone, and whether you could "catch" Grandmother's illness.

Mr. and Mrs. Foster skillfully answered these questions and found the tension in the household dissolving. Mrs. Foster noted, "It was as if we finally acknowledged the elephant in the room that had been there since my mother became sick." In subsequent weeks they helped their daughters to take more active steps to overcome their anxiety and sadness by encouraging them to draw pictures and design a get-well card for their grandmother. While they were helping their daughters to confront the likely death of a loved one, they were also nurturing in them a resilient mindset. By communicating sensitively and honestly, they modeled compassion, coping, and a feeling that even in the face of adversity it is possible to achieve a state of ease.

We also model honesty when our children ask us questions for which we do not have an answer and we respond, "That's a good question. I'm not sure of the answer, but let's figure out how we can find out." In addition, honesty is displayed when we make a mistake or do something that is questionable and are able to tell our children that we made a mistake or that we are sorry. Mistakes are teachable moments. They are opportunities from which to learn.

Step Nine: Accept Repetition

Communication is an ongoing process. Children may have to hear a message many times before they understand and incorporate it into their thinking. While this may seem obvious, comments from well-meaning parents frequently bespeak that they do not truly appreciate the importance of repetition. For example, at one of our sex education workshops, a mother commented, "My four-year-old daughter asked me about the differences between boys and girls. She wondered if girls were born with a penis and then it was taken away. I explained that girls were not born with a penis. She seemed to accept this, but two days later she asked if girls were born with a penis. I explained again, and she asked the same question a few days later. Did I say something wrong in the way I explained it? Why didn't she get it?"

From this woman's account, it was clear that she had handled her daughter's questions very well. We reminded her that in most situations when we are learning something new, particularly when we are young, we need to hear the message several times before it is incorporated into our thinking. Even as adults, when we learn something new, we tend to ask the same questions a number of times.

Parents must be prepared to answer the same questions from children repeatedly. Questions represent children's attempts to understand their world, develop and feel a sense of mastery, gain knowledge, and solve problems. All of these are qualities linked to a resilient mindset. In addition, the seemingly same question may have a different meaning to children as they get older and their cognitive skills improve. For instance, when a seven-year-old asks, "How was I born?" the answer will typically require greater specificity (often to the parent's discomfort) than when a four-year-old asks the same question.

If we are to raise resilient children, our words and actions must convey to them that none of their questions is silly or irrelevant. We must actively reinforce the curiosity of our children by responding with such comments as "That's a wonderful question." When they repeat the same question a few times, we may say, "I'm glad you asked me again. Some things take time to learn." If children develop the feeling that their questions and comments are silly or bothersome, they will refrain from asking them and, in the process, will be deprived of opportunities to learn.

One adult we met captured this feeling as she recalled her first-grade teacher's response to a question she raised. The teacher answered, "Weren't you listening? I just answered that question."

The woman attested, "After my teacher said that, I never asked another question in class."

Step Ten: Make Humor an Integral Part of Your Communication

Playfulness and humor are important ingredients in the communication process. While some parents find it easier to "lighten up" than others, keep in mind that the better able we are to call on humor at appropriate times, the more our communication will be facilitated. Many of us can think of times in our personal and professional lives when a laugh helped us to be less defensive and more willing to listen and learn. Since the ability to use and respond to humor is another component of a resilient mindset, our use of humor can help to develop this component in our children.

In multiple studies around the world, humor has repeatedly been found to help children cope with adversity. Tapping the ability of humor to "break the ice," the second author greets children brought for evaluation with the observation, "I know you're not here to find out what's wrong with you but to find out what's right with you and wrong with everyone *else*! We've got to help everyone, including you, understand your strengths. After all, when you finish school, they don't ask about your *worst* subject and assign you that job." This obvious levity quickly eases the apprehension of a child being brought to see the "doctor."

One caveat about calling on humor, however, is to think about how it will be received by others. If we are angry with our children and they are angry with us, jocularity can easily be experienced as sarcasm. Humor should be used to create a warm environment in which parents and children feel comfortable and in which children will more readily learn from us.

The first author recalls his response on those occasions when his two sons engaged in loud arguments. Bob told them that he knew that brothers fought, based on his own experiences with his brothers when he was growing up. However, he felt that their arguments were becoming too loud and said that if they wanted to argue, they should go to the field behind the house and argue outside. He added, "But don't use your names during the argument: I don't want the neighbors to know whose kids are yelling since it might hurt my reputation as a psychologist." This injection of humor helped to deflate the intensity of their emotions. They never did venture out to the back field.

Communication and the Resilient Mindset

If we listen and learn, we can influence. If, on the other hand, we make little time to communicate with our children, if we allow most discussions to take place in response to an emergency, issues will rarely be resolved, and what passes as communication will often result in an intensification of problems.

The manner in which we communicate with our children sets the foundation for the chapters that follow. Be sure to keep the points presented here in mind as you proceed.

4

Changing the Words of Parenting

Rewriting Negative Scripts

We are the authors of our lives. Our words and behaviors in raising our children, echoed again and again in similar situations and in similar ways with predictable outcomes, become the "scripts of parenting." When the outcomes are positive, parents should repeat these successful scripts. When the outcomes are not good, these "negative scripts" should be modified or abandoned. Yet, frequently they are not. In fact, these negative scripts often become the mainstay of the efforts of many well-meaning parents to raise resilient children. While we want our children to be flexible, thoughtful, and receptive to new ideas and approaches, we often fail to model these behaviors, and we fall prey to the seductive trap of negative scripts.

Many parents find that their words, though repeated to their children for weeks, months, and in some instances even years, fail to result in the desired outcome, but they nevertheless continue to follow these scripts, sometimes more forcefully than before. In fact, current use of these negative scripts appears to best predict future use. Certainly there are benefits to perseverance, but why is it that we experience so much difficulty recognizing, acknowledging, and changing our course of action?

No parent is immune. Although some of us may resort to these negative scripts more frequently than others, even the best parents can find themselves befuddled as they attempt to modify or impact their children's behavior.

Negative scripts contain words and actions of parenting that, rather than help foster resilience, are more prone to increase family conflict for all family members. This chapter helps you identify and understand the incorrect thoughts, ideas, and attributions that frequently lead to the use of such scripts. It also offers a set of essential principles to help you change your words and write positive scripts. Changing negative scripts is a cornerstone of raising resilient children. Learning to change your words of parenting will help you maintain the mindset of strengthening your child's ability to accurately understand and identify problems. As a result, when confronted with challenges, your child will reflect, analyze, and ultimately act on productive solutions.

Persistence and Predictability: The Good, the Bad, and the Ineffective

Why do parents persist in the face of repeated negative results? Typically, this is not how we approach our lives outside of our families. If a mechanic is unable to identify a problem with our car, we seek another mechanic. If we have a disagreement with a shop clerk, we take our business to another store. Yet, in our personal lives, with our friends and families, this is not always the case. Though it appears that it is easier to change a negative script with a friend than with a family member, hands-down the most difficult negative scripts to rewrite are those we have written with our children.

Although predictability can be a virtue in providing a sense of consistency and security when parenting children, it can limit one's vision and obstruct creative answers to problems. When predictability borders on rigidity, when it confines us to a narrow path that ends in stressful, unhappy destinations, and when we continue to walk down that path without considering alternative road maps, predictability becomes self-defeating. In most households, one can actually predict with great accuracy the responses of parents to their children and children to their parents. It is almost as if family members, over time, play the role of actors following a well-orchestrated script with little room for improvisation.

In our professional work, we have witnessed parents who, in response to long-standing problematic behaviors in their children, adhere to their own scripts, hoping that somehow their children will be the ones to change. These scripts and the scenes they play out are repeated over and over, unfortunately with minimal change. If children are to change their negative scripts, parents must first have the insight and courage to change their own. When we state emphatically at our workshops that "our children will outlast us if given the opportunity," all the parents in the room smile in agreement. Every parent can offer firsthand examples of having repeatedly told or, for that matter, nagged a child either to do or not do something with little, if any, positive response on the child's part. While this repeated pattern of negativity may appear obvious to the viewer, to the parent participant it is anything but.

Though we are professionals, we too are parents. The first author recalls with some humor (with the passage of years such events always appear humorous) how in his clinical work he counseled parents not to be so predictable and to take an active role in changing ineffective, negative scripts used repeatedly with their children. But did he follow his own advice? Of course not. When his older son underachieved in junior and senior high school for four years, doing just enough to pass his courses, a negative script was cast in stone.

Each evening upon arriving home from work, even before offering a warm greeting, he asked his son, "Did you do your homework yet?"

His son quickly and consistently answered, "Yes," although typically this was not the case. Even as the evidence piled up that his son was falling behind, the same script played out again and again.

Why would someone who knew better, in this case a professional parenting consultant, ask the same ineffective question over and over for four years? There certainly were other more productive and less intrusive ways to handle the homework problem. In great part, Bob's inflexibility was based on frustration and anger, captured by the following question he asked himself: How could a well-known professional who offers workshops on the topic of motivating students, which in fact have been attended by many of his son's teachers, have a son who was not doing his homework? It certainly did not look good for Bob's reputation.

Anger often clouds rational thinking. Bob assumed erroneously that the problem was his son's and that the son should change, not the father. In looking back, however, he realizes that he bore some responsibility for stress in the household, given his overreaction to his son's earning less than A or B grades. Of course, with hindsight it is always easier to accept responsibility, especially since his son graduated Phi Beta Kappa from college and today is a successful man running a business. Ironically, the beginning of his success appeared to coincide with Bob changing a negative script by ceasing to nag and instead finding ample opportunities to encourage and build on his son's many strengths.

Another example is that of a mother who attended one of our parenting workshops. The very next day, she called to report that as she listened to the lecture, she understood for the first time the predictable, negative scripts she had written and repeated each day with her two teenage sons. From the time she woke up each morning, she said, she had sounded like a broken record, harping on her sons about being ready on time for school, criticizing their eating habits, and pestering them about not making their beds. She added that for a long time she believed that "if only my sons did what I asked, the household would be a happier place." She was uncertain how these scripts came to be written and why they persisted in the face of failure. Nonetheless, she acknowledged that she must "rewrite" what she had been doing. She used the word figuratively and literally. That evening she sat down and wrote individual notes to each of her sons, telling them how much she cared about them and promising that she would work to stop being such a "nag." She laughed as she recounted her sons' reactions the following morning.

They approached their mother and asked warmly, "Are you looking for a nice Mother's Day present?"

She said that she had not had so much fun with her sons in a long time and felt so much better that morning. She wondered, as many other parents do, "Why didn't I think of doing something like this months or years ago? Why was I so blind to something so obvious?"

These are thought-provoking questions. How did we come to write these negative scripts? Why do we persist in parenting practices that are counterproductive? How do we change the words of parenting and rewrite negative scripts? Before tackling these questions, it is important to be clear about the two fundamental reasons for placing the responsibility of rewriting these scripts on the shoulders of parents.

First, it is the role of parents to create an environment at home in which children will be more likely to listen to what we have to say and be responsive to our requests. If such an environment does not exist, if a lack of respect has eroded feelings of trust, cooperation, and, in some cases, love, it is less probable that children will be motivated to change their scripts. Remember that seemingly small changes on the parts of parents can have a major positive impact in their relationships with their children. As the adults in the household, parents must pave the way for emotional and interpersonal growth. If parents wait for their children to say, "I see the light—all of your nagging, sarcasm, and badgering has paid off. I will now do what you have asked me to do. I will change my behavior," they will wait a very long time.

Second, when parents are willing to make reasonable modifications in their words of parenting and to rewrite negative scripts, they demonstrate the benefits of mastering problem-solving and decision-making skills. They help their children understand the value of not locking horns, avoiding power struggles, learning to negotiate and solve problems, and not exhausting energy on relatively insignificant themes.

Children are astute observers. They don't always do what we say, but they usually do what we do. If you refuse to modify your ways of responding to your children, then you are robbing them of opportunities that will help them change their own scripts for today and throughout their lives.

How Negative Scripts Come to Be Written and the Obstacles That Perpetuate Unhappy Reruns

The *reasons* negative scripts are written also stand as obstacles to changing the words and actions of parents. They take on a second life and become roadblocks perpetuating futile parenting actions. These reasons are often used by parents consciously or unconsciously as dogma to maintain negative scripts. Thus, if you can learn to understand the basis of this resistance, you are more likely to understand how negative scripts come to be written in your family and to overcome these roadblocks and move forward.

A set of myths, misconceptions, and excess baggage that each of us carries, beginning with childhood observations in our families, contributes to the reluctance of parents to modify the ways they approach their children. Let's run down these six obstacles to changing the words of parenting.

Obstacle One: One Size Fits All; All Children Are Basically the Same

This misconception by parents leads to the composition of many negative scripts. It prevents parents from changing futile practices. Parents who believe that all children are the same at birth and that what works with one child will work with all children are poorly informed. Chapter 1 introduced this point, and it is treated in greater detail in Chapter 6, which concerns developing realistic expectations and goals while respecting the individuality of each child.

The one-size-fits-all myth is played out in multiple ways. Variations include a lack of understanding on the part of parents as to the impact that age, developmental level, learning style, and temperament may have in shaping how our children will respond. This problem is particularly obvious in our work with temperamentally difficult children. For example, in the minds of many parents, hyperactive children have the capacity to change but refuse to do so. Failing to appreciate that this particular child may know what to do but not be able to consistently do it perpetuates the repetitive use of a negative script, such as cajoling the child to sit through a meal.

Remember Sally, the shy eight-year-old who was unable to assert herself? Her mother began each morning by exhorting her daughter to try to make friends and asked each evening, "Did you speak with other kids today? Did anyone invite you to their house? Did you invite anyone to our home?" Although Mrs. Carter was wise enough to not openly compare her two children, she often thought about her seven-year-old son, whom she dubbed "Mr. Popularity," and could not understand why her daughter was unable or unwilling to exert the effort necessary to develop peer relations. Mrs. Carter was well meaning, but her frustration prevented her from seeking out an explanation that would have helped her better understand the significant temperamental differences between her children. Lacking that insight, she felt that if she continued to remind Sally about the importance of friendships and encouraged her to make friends, eventually Sally would do so.

This mother's script was very predictable and, unfortunately, very unproductive. Finally, when Mrs. Carter stopped calling attention to her daughter's lack of friendships and instead, with support, made an effort "behind the scenes" by arranging for another child to come over to play, the situation began to improve.

Obstacle Two: Changing My Words Will Spoil My Child

Parents sometimes assume that once they have proceeded down a certain road, changing the script when things are not working is tantamount to "giving in to" or "spoiling" children. The sense is that if we change our usual way of doing business, it will be interpreted as a sign of weakness by our children, and as a consequence they will not learn responsibility. A case in point is Carl, the ten-year-old child we met in Chapter 1. Carl had trouble completing repetitive, effortful activities, such as preparing for school. He also had difficulty remaining seated throughout dinner each evening. His father repeatedly raised his voice, becoming louder and louder as the meal progressed, each time in response to Carl's slipping off the chair, dropping an eating utensil, or getting up on his knees. This scenario played out repeatedly each evening. Dinner, a time for family members to share each other's company and discuss their day, became an activity that other family members tried to avoid.

Mr. Thomas refused to consider changing his expectations or his negative script, arguing, "Carl has to learn to sit with the rest of the family at dinnertime. If we let him get up from the table before the meal is finished, this will be a message to him that he can do whatever he wants and so can his siblings. The stakes will get higher and higher."

The fact that this negative script had been played out unsuccessfully for years seemed to weigh little in Mr. Thomas's equation. Nor did he acknowledge the fact that the unpleasant climate created by this script added further family stress.

It is vital for parents to recognize that when a tense situation has existed for a very long time, when children constantly experience us as nagging or lecturing them so that our words begin to fall on deaf ears, changing our usual behavior does not mean spoiling the child. It also does not mean that you do away with all rules and expectations; parents have the right and responsibility to establish a clearly defined, nonnegotiable set of rules, especially those related to safety and security (e.g., riding a bicycle, obeying curfews). Changes of negative scripts should be guided by the goals of lessening anger and resentment, enhancing your relationship with your child, encouraging your child to change his or her behaviors, and promoting more responsible comportment.

We are in danger of spoiling children only when we do away with expectations and allow children to do whatever they want. Changing negative scripts does not imply abdicating our responsibility as parents.

Let's return to Carl's family. Mr. Thomas's concern was that if he permitted Carl to get up from the table before the meal was finished, Carl would interpret this as freedom to do whatever he chose. Mr. Thomas experienced difficulty weighing this concern against the fact that his course of action, which had lasted for years, had become counterproductive. It had not accomplished what he intended and had compounded family stress. Yet, in the heat of the moment, what may be obvious to others was not evident to Mr. Thomas. He had convinced himself that if he persisted in his course of action, his son "would eventually get the message."

Mr. Thomas simply did not understand that for Carl, knowing what to do did not always translate into doing what he knew. Even if Carl "got the message," it was not likely, given his hyperactivity, that he could stay seated without fidgeting, dropping something, or moving for an entire meal. It was important, particularly for Carl, to develop a sense of responsibility. It was also critical that the level of tension in Carl's home decrease.

We explained to Mr. Thomas that there were many ways to accomplish these goals. First, we helped him understand Carl's temperament and the difficulty Carl experienced following certain household rules. We suggested the possibility of changing the negative script, recommending that he tell Carl that he recognized that it was difficult for him to remain seated for an entire meal and that if Carl felt the need to leave the table, it would be accepted as long as he did not do so in a disruptive way. The agreement would be that Carl's meal would remain at his place for a set time before the table was cleared.

Mr. Thomas also decided that he would compliment Carl when Carl was sitting and eating appropriately. In other words, his attention would shift to what Carl was doing right rather than what he was doing wrong. In response to Mr. Thomas's question about fairness, we suggested that the same offer to get up from the table be made to Carl's two older siblings, neither of whom experienced problems sitting through a meal. In addition, we urged him, as discussed in Chapter 2, to practice empathy and model this more supportive behavior for Carl's siblings so that they might be more understanding of Carl's struggles as well as his strengths.

Mr. Thomas was initially hesitant to make this course adjustment, but we helped him to realize that harboring the belief that changing his approach would be giving in to his son ignored the fact that his standard operating procedure was not working. Much to his surprise, when he became more empathic and flexible with Carl, tension at the dinner table decreased. Mrs. Thomas immediately noticed the change. Carl now typically required only one brief departure from the table before returning and finishing his meal. Carl's siblings rarely left the table. Mr. and Mrs. Thomas reported a sense of relaxation at dinnertime; the meal became a source of pleasure.

This new atmosphere could be traced directly to the changes Mr. Thomas made in his negative script, changes that did not result, as he once feared they would, in his son's taking advantage of his father's "weakness."

Obstacle Three: It Was Good Enough for Me, or I Turned Out OK

The third myth, or misconception, that keeps negative scripts in place is the one that says, "My parents raised me this way. It was good enough for me.

Look at how I turned out." This tenet often is hauled out when the subject is discipline or the setting of rules.

John, the seventh-grade gifted athlete but weak student whom we also met earlier, was caught in this type of negative script with his father. Mr. Kahn believed that John's problems stemmed from the need for stronger, harsher discipline. He increasingly resorted to corporal punishment as the main way of "teaching" his son. He held a rigid and extremely high set of expectations and followed the practice that if John did something wrong, he would immediately be told, but if he did something right, praise was withheld lest the boy "become conceited."

This style of parenting is very similar to how Mr. Kahn was raised. Now he was experiencing difficulty seeing the forest for the trees. It was hard for him to understand how this parenting style had shaped his personality and in fact affected the way he related to family, friends, and coworkers. He had experienced only one style of parenting and thus relied on the behaviors to which he had been exposed and with which he felt comfortable. He resisted learning other approaches, having convinced himself that this was the most effective means of parenting and that those "parenting experts" didn't "know beans."

When his wife chided that he was too negative or harsh, he dismissed her comments with an angry retort, such as "If you were more consistent and firm, this problem wouldn't be as bad as it is."

John's parents came to see us when school personnel suggested that the increase in reports of John's behavioral problems at school, including a number of angry outbursts as the result of failed tests, might be related to an undiagnosed learning disability. In fact, an in-depth assessment revealed that although John was quite bright, he couldn't readily move ideas from his head on to paper. As the demands of school, particularly written language requirements, increased in the middle school years, John's struggles intensified.

As Mr. Kahn became more comfortable in a series of counseling sessions, his defensive style diminished. During one session he spontaneously commented that perhaps as a child in school he struggled with the very same learning disability as John. He recalled painfully that not only had the problem remained unidentified but also his father repeatedly accused him of being lazy in school and responded with an increasingly punitive set of interventions.

Mr. Kahn then asked to see us alone. In that private session he spoke about his upbringing and the emotional wall he had created to cope with this painful childhood environment. He mentioned specifically the "beatings" he received from his father and the resentment that they produced in him, abandoning the deception that these beatings had made him a better person. He also expressed how much he had desired recognition from his father for his accomplishments but instead had been flooded with criticism. The courage to face his past permitted him to begin to change his behavior patterns toward his son, and he was able to begin offering John positive feedback and encouragement.

But changing this negative script was not easy. John had become so accustomed to negative remarks that, at first, he dismissed his father's positive comments. Fortunately this did not deter Mr. Kahn, and eventually John became more receptive to his father's praise. Corporal punishment was abandoned in their home. Mr. Kahn also made it a point each evening to help his son take satisfaction in even small daily academic accomplishments.

The combination of special education assistance and the rewriting of a negative script from punitive sarcasm and anger to empathy and positive reinforcement resulted in a very positive change in John's outlook on life, school functioning, and relationship with his father.

Obstacle Four: Our Children Should Be More Appreciative of Our Hard Work and Parental Effort

This myth is powerfully responsible for parents' returning to negative scripts when their initial efforts to change are not met with immediate success. Note that when Mr. Kahn made an effort to change his negative script, John did not immediately respond in a positive way. His behavior was still angry and defiant, and he didn't even acknowledge his father's effort. Perhaps this is an aspect of the nature of parenting that we must learn to accept: children don't spend a large amount of time being thankful for the wonderful lives their parents have created for them.

Many parents state that when they attempt to change their parenting style by changing negative scripts, their children's behavior remains the same. Not only does it take courage on the part of parents to change, but much effort and energy must be expended as well. When this energy and effort are initially met with little, if any, sign of change or appreciation by their children, it is not unusual for parents to lament, "See, it doesn't work. They're not willing to take any responsibility on their own." Once this resentment is triggered, parents are likely to return to their former scripts and become even less willing to initiate changes in the future.

We are constantly reminding ourselves and the families with whom we work that change takes time. Whether it's a golf swing, dietary habits, or negative scripts, when a pattern of behavior has operated for years, when a negative script has been syndicated into reruns, change takes time. Although some youngsters respond quickly and positively to nuances in their parents' scripts, many do not. It is often difficult to predict a child's response. A change in script that involves parents' becoming more consistent about following through with consequences may cause some youngsters to actually behave *worse* to test the resolve of their parents. Then, once they are convinced that their parents are committed to this new order, their behavior begins to improve.

In scientific circles, this testing of resolve is referred to as *extinction*. Human beings, regardless of their age, respond in ways to which they have become accustomed. Even as the environment changes, they continue to respond habitually at first. Over time, however, the habit weakens, and the individual's response changes.

Keep in mind that when the change in script involves emotion or attention, such as spending more time with children, telling them you love them, or being more demonstrative, some children may not know how to respond. Some may not acknowledge the efforts; some may not appear appreciative and, in fact, may even wonder if their parents have an ulterior motive. We must remember that if we feel we have given careful consideration to our new scripts and behavior, we must not give up on them after just a few days. It takes years for patterns of behavior and negative scripts to develop. Hopefully it will take less time for our children to believe that things can really change.

Obstacle Five: A Goal Is Realistic—If I Say So

Parents frequently get caught in negative scripts when desired changes are unrealistic or difficult to achieve quickly. This fate almost befell the Garner family.

The family was well off financially, but Mr. Garner, an executive with a large company, worked long hours, and his three children complained that they rarely saw him. He was gone by the time they awoke in the morning and some evenings did not return until they were asleep. He often missed school and athletic events.

Mrs. Garner told us with a sense of exasperation, "We almost never eat dinner as a family. I often have no help getting the kids to bed. We never have time to talk."

Her husband countered, "I'm doing the best I can to earn a good living for you and the kids. I know, though, that I have to spend more time with all of you."

As we began discussing positive solutions, Mr. Garner promised to make an effort to be home by 6:00 each evening so the family could have dinner together. His wife looked at him with disbelief. Instead of responding that this would be great, she cautioned that his attempts to change his work schedule so drastically and quickly would lead to greater problems and resentment. Though Mr. Garner protested at first, he reluctantly concurred. They then agreed that as a first step Mr. Garner would arrange his schedule and commitments so that he could be home for dinner every Wednesday.

Even being home one evening a week on a predictable basis was much more of a challenge than he realized, but he was able to manage it. Once Mr. Garner experienced this initial success, he not only increased his dinner commitment to a second evening but also arranged his schedule so that on two or three days a week he could depart for work later in the morning, allowing him to have breakfast with the kids. Had he attempted to make drastic changes in his schedule all at once, we concur with his wife's prediction that this would have been a prescription for failure.

While we are all aware of the sage advice, "Don't bite off more than you can chew," many of us continue to do so. We may understand the need for change but sometimes underestimate the amount of time and effort, as well as the cost, necessary to effect realistic and long-lasting change. Unfortunately there are few choices in our lives that carry only potential benefits with no possible liabilities. If we establish unrealistic expectations that cannot possibly be met due to their liabilities, we move further from, rather than closer to, our goal of rewriting negative scripts.

Obstacle Six: Carrying Around Excess Baggage from the Past

Most airlines now have a rule: only two carry-ons allowed. This may be a good rule for life as well.

As discussed earlier, when we become parents we bring all of our lifetime experiences with us. Although our behavior is certainly shaped by our genetics, our day-in-and-day-out experiences shape the choices we make and the scripts we write as we raise our children. Hopefully the majority of these experiences help us to create positive interactions with our children, interactions that will foster their resilience. However, many of us are burdened by experiences from the past that not only influence our parenting practices in negative ways, reinforcing negative scripts, but also blind us to recognizing these scripts and rewriting them.

Mr. Kahn, for example, had relied on corporal punishment and an absence of positive feedback to discipline John. His belief—in essence, "My parents did this to me. It was good for me; look how I turned out"—captured a man who brought unresolved anger and pain into his relationship with his son. His excess baggage negatively influenced how he interpreted and responded to his child's school problems and behavior. This attitude contributed to a narrow-minded and rigid style that did not allow the parent to step back, recognize the negative scripts he had written, become more empathic, and reflect on other approaches to use with his son. In his mind the problem was his son's and not his; it was therefore his son who had to change.

Sally's mother, Mrs. Carter, tearfully came up to us after one of our workshops. She had been touched by our discussion of the different temperaments that children experience from birth (a topic developed further in Chapter 6). This was an important revelation for Mrs. Carter since she had erroneously believed that although behavioral problems such as hyperactivity could result from genetics and temperament, shyness does not. Learning that some children are born shy and cautious, and are in many ways victims of their hesitation, had a profound impact. In her words, she realized that she was "ruining" her daughter's life by constantly telling Sally in front of others to say hello, to be more polite, and to look at people.

The distress Mrs. Carter experienced was evident as she said, "I couldn't understand how I could have a shy child. I was very shy growing up, and I told myself I would not let the same thing happen to my daughter. So, from an early age I told my daughter not to be shy, and I went out of my way to remind her when she was."

Sally's shy behavior was rooted in her temperament. She was born to respond to her environment this way. But the problem was exacerbated by Mrs. Carter's own ghosts from her childhood. Her attempts to raise an outgoing, gregarious daughter served only to increase Sally's anxiety in social situations.

Mrs. Carter became more optimistic when we explained that, as eminent child psychiatrist Dr. John Werry has noted, "biology is not destiny." It does, however, affect probability. Genetically, a child like Sally is more likely to respond to a given environment in shy, retiring ways, but this doesn't mean that the child cannot learn to be more assertive and outgoing. Sally's mother accepted our referral to a child therapist. She called several months later to report that the situation was much better. She and her daughter were learning strategies to cope with anxiety, and there was a noticeable improvement in their relationship. More important, Sally's teachers had started to observe a change for the better in Sally's behavior in the classroom.

Reading these reasons for and obstacles to changing negative scripts may be painful. In our professional and private lives, we have yet to meet a parent unable to identify at least one of these reasons and obstacles that has led to the writing of a negative script. Our emphasis on articulating the myths, misconceptions, and excess baggage is not meant as a criticism of parents; it is meant as a comment that parents are people, and people are not perfect. It is not our purpose to stir up anger, guilt, blame, or shame. We do want to help you understand the process by which negative scripts come to be written and the impediments to change. That understanding is the beginning step in replacing negative parental scripts and behavior with more adaptive, positive ones.

Before proceeding, think about three particular negative scripts that you use with your children. Remember, negative scripts are defined as expressions used repeatedly that are ineffective in bringing about the desired behavior and often create increased family stress, tension, and impaired relationships. You can note your three scripts simply as titles or themes (e.g., the dinner table problem) or, if you are sufficiently motivated, actually write out the exchange of words that takes place. For example (Carl gets up out of his seat):

Mr. Thomas: Carl, sit down.
Carl: I'll be right back.
Mr. Thomas: Carl, come back here now!
Carl: I'm coming!
Mrs. Thomas: Don't yell.

When we finally hear ourselves saying and doing the same things repeatedly with negligible beneficial results, we discover our negative scripts. Use the three examples that you cited to begin changing your words and actions of parenting.

Five Principles to Writing Positive Scripts

What may appear to be an obvious course of action to take toward more effective parenting practices, in this case the writing of positive scripts, is often filled with roadblocks. Understanding the origins of negative scripts and the obstacles to changing them is a critical first step. With this step behind you, you are ready to begin rewriting your own scripts. Although the journey down this path may be difficult, to be successful, the writing of positive scripts must be directed by five principles. These principles will help you develop a constructive mindset and are very similar to a basic problem-solving model. Our premise here is that to develop the mindset of resilience in a child, parents must model that mindset in their own behaviors. This model appears again in Chapter 10 as a means of teaching children to solve problems and make decisions.

Principle One: Accept Your Responsibility to Change

This chapter has emphasized the importance of reflecting on what you can do differently when problems exist with your children. Parents possessing a resilient mindset recognize that they must first look at what they can change in themselves before expecting their children to change. Constructive changes that parents undertake will encourage their children to make positive changes as well. Thus, when a problem is ongoing, a first step toward resolution is for parents to ask, "What is it that I have been doing or not doing that has contributed to this negative script, and what is it that I can do to begin to lessen this problem?"

The emphasis is on what the parents can do. Although this too may seem straightforward, many parents proceed down the wrong road when they fail to acknowledge this feature. When parents immediately assume that it is the child who must change, the probability of change is dramatically reduced.

Review the three negative scripts that you identified as your personal examples, and choose one for a reference as you read about these five principles. Have you accepted the fact that for this negative script to change, you must begin by asking yourself what you can do differently? Do you understand the reasons this script developed and the obstacles that thus far have prevented you from realizing your need to change? If not, take the necessary time to work through these questions. If you can answer affirmatively, you are now in a position to change.

Principle Two: Know the Problem—Know the Goal

This principle is more complex than it may seem at first. The initial directive must be to *define* in observable terms the nature of your child's problem. This is not to minimize the importance of determining the *roots* of the problem. The drawback with expending energy on efforts to ascertain what "caused" a child's problem is that you may well arrive at erroneous beliefs that then distract you from defining and solving the problem.

The most productive course is to first articulate in concrete terms what the problem is and then to strive to understand some of its underpinnings. The statements "My child is stubborn, and that's why she never listens to us" and "Our son is lazy, and that's why he always quits at things" reflect parents' *perceptions* of what causes or drives a problem and are not very helpful in solving it.

Placing primary stress on the perceived cause rather than the definition of the problem is often exasperating and fruitless for our children. This is especially true when we are angry and out of patience, prompting us to express to them what we believe is the cause of their problems: "You're just so lazy!" Naturally children often experience such remarks as judgmental. For instance, one parent told us that when she accused her child of dawdling in the morning and thus not being ready for the bus, he responded, "You just don't give me enough time." Here, the mother's focus on the assumed cause rather than the definition of the problem—"You are not ready when you need to be"— only fueled the conflict. Defining the problem in a clear, nonjudgmental way as a first step invites the child to engage in a problem-solving activity rather than arousing resentment and anger.

This principle requires that you know the goal as well. The goal should also be defined in operational, practical terms, such as "We want our son to finish things that he starts in a reasonable time" or "We want our daughter to respond when we ask a question."

Obtaining a comprehensive view of the problem and the goal may be difficult initially, but once you develop the mindset to do so, with practice the process becomes increasingly automatic. Once the problem and the goal are defined, it is important for you to ask yourself questions such as the following: How long has the problem existed? How severely does the problem affect our family? How much does it interfere with day-to-day functioning? How has the problem progressed to its current status?

In addressing these questions honestly, you'll find that the status of your child's problem becomes clear, and then you can work on gaining a better picture of its underpinnings. You may even discover that the problem resides more in your perception than in reality. For example, parents who overreact when their child brings home a number of Cs on a report card may hold expectations that place too much pressure on the child. At other times, a child's difficulties, while seemingly intense, prove to be developmentally appropriate and, with parental support, short-lived.

For instance, we received a call from Mrs. Vance about her four-year-old son, Adam, who had begun to have nightmares. During these incidents Adam seemed quite distressed and was difficult to arouse. In the morning he could not remember the nightmares. Mrs. Vance thought that he must have experienced some sort of trauma that led to these terrible dreams. However, no trauma had been reported nor had Adam's behavior changed in any other way.

We explained that at this age many youngsters experience nightmares. This is typically a sleep-related problem, not caused by life trauma or experience, and usually does not last very long. We suggested that rather than writing a negative script in which Mrs. Vance launched a desperate search for Adam's "trauma," beginning with repeatedly quizzing him during the day, she and her husband calmly and patiently support him during the night. We counseled the Vances to refrain from raising the subject with Adam and, if he awoke during the night because of a nightmare, to soothe him until he fell asleep again.

Identifying the problem early allowed an accurate assessment concerning its existence, severity, and impact on day-to-day functioning. The problem was defined as a normal developmental issue related to sleep. The goal was defined as supporting Adam as needed, preventing this problem from taking on more significance than it deserved.

This chapter described earlier how parents magnify children's behaviors by concluding that if behaviors such as leaving the dinner table or being timid were not met head on, they would lead to serious life consequences. In fact, it is this fear of later life consequences that brings many parents to our offices. Although they come in with a list of current problems, their primary concern quickly becomes apparent: rather than viewing these incidents as part and parcel of raising children, they have begun to anticipate that the situation may speak to a dire future outcome. Again, this is not to deny the child's problems; it is to call attention to the impact of parents' reactions to the problems.

Being empathic and listening to our children facilitate the process of understanding how a problem developed and how a negative script came to be written. In many instances problem behaviors represent a youngster's ways of coping with stress and pressure. They may in fact be a signal to parents to look beyond the behavior and recognize the underlying stress as the true problem.

Thirteen-year-old Jennifer was exceptionally bright but not when it came to organization. From her room to her school desk, the three-dimensional world around her always appeared to be in chaos. Because she was such an accomplished student, during the elementary years, her teachers often overlooked this disorganization problem, providing support and encouragement. However, as Jennifer entered middle school, the level of organization, planning, and, for that matter, length of assignments increased. Despite her intellect and achievement, Jennifer struggled with these demands. She began to receive warning slips from teachers concerning missing assignments, sloppiness, and lack of preparation. With the insight of a supportive school psychologist, Jennifer's family realized that the solution lay in not prodding her to work harder but providing her with assistance for organizing and completing assignments.

A related "success story" concerns a family in which a ten-year-old son with significant physical problems required a great deal of support and time from his parents. His thirteen-year-old sister, who had been an excellent student, over time began experiencing increasing problems at school. As her parents discussed her declining grades with her, they sensed a very clear message to the effect of "Maybe I will get some of the attention now."

Although parents may question why their daughter would resort to failing grades to gain some of the attention she felt her brother was receiving and why she just didn't tell them directly about feeling left out, the purpose of this principle is to define the problem and the goal. In this case the problem was not poor school performance but this girl's diminished sense of belonging and acceptance within her family. The goal was also clear. Her parents set aside time each evening to spend with their daughter and, in a humorous, loving way, told her that she no longer needed to receive poor grades to attain their attention and love.

As for your own negative script, can you clearly define the problem? Do you have a specified goal in mind? Do you understand how the problem developed and how the script came to be written? Can you place this problem within a realistic perspective in regard to the impact it has had on your family and your relationship with your child? Make certain these answers are clear before proceeding to the next principle.

Principle Three: Know What You Have Done So Far and Why It Hasn't Worked

Having now defined the problem and the goal, we must also clarify why our approach thus far has been ineffective. This entails assessing our current parental scripts.

At one point, Carl's parents decided in response to his difficulty in getting ready for school to wake him thirty minutes earlier than usual. However, waking Carl up earlier did not seem to help. Carl used the extra time to daydream or play with his toys and was still not ready when the school bus arrived. His parents nevertheless continued to wake him thirty minutes early, and when he was still not ready, they reprimanded him, turning breakfast time into a tense battleground. Obviously this script was not working.

Natasha's parents, Mr. and Mrs. Eastman, in response to their unhappiness with Natasha's high school grades, began restricting privileges. In turn she became increasingly belligerent. They observed that they had taken so many things away from Natasha (stereo, phone, social contact) that practically all that remained in her room was her bed. They recognized that their course of action was not having a positive impact on their daughter and that their interactions with her were becoming increasingly strained. They decided instead to speak with Natasha in a nonaccusatory way about the importance of schoolwork, thus setting the stage for her active participation in finding solutions.

Mr. and Mrs. Whitman felt that their son, Tyler, made insatiable demands on their time. They could spend fifty-nine minutes out of an hour with him and he would remind them of the one minute they were not there. Their negative script was composed in an effort to convince their son how much time they actually spent with him. Yet, he was never satisfied. If the Whitman's expected their son to thank them for their observations about all of the time they spent with him, they were disappointed. He instead accused them of not caring about him, which only served to trigger further anger and resentment on their part.

Similar to many other parents, the Whitmans felt that they had exhausted all strategies and now it was their son's responsibility to change his perception. As we have learned, this stance leads to the writing and repeated use of a negative script. If our children are to modify their view of the world, if they are to abandon *their* counterproductive scripts, then *we* must create new scripts that make it easier for them to change. Our flexibility often encourages flexibility and problem solving in our children, which then reinforces a resilient mindset.

In this case Mr. and Mrs. Whitman realized that the problem was not that Tyler was being unfair but that temperamentally he had a strong need for attention; the negative impact that this need had on the family was the problem. The goal therefore was to help Tyler meet this need in functional ways. Rather than repeatedly reminding him about the amount of time they had spent together, Tyler's parents began engaging him in activities outside of the family in which he could make a contribution and, thus, feel needed and important. They also provided "special times" for him with one of them.

To help you critique your own negative script in light of this principle, make a list of the ways in which you have attempted to resolve the problem. Then assign a score based on the success of each solution. Have some worked better than others? Can one be modified to improve results?

Principle Four: Seek and Ye Shall Find—Every Problem Has a Positive Solution

A *positive* solution begins as a *possible* solution. We rewrite the negative script, defining the problem and setting our goal. If we move away from blame and shame, if we recognize that changing our scripts will precipitate our children to change theirs, we begin the process of exploring possible solutions and ultimately finding a positive solution. Parents must always remember that when they are willing to entertain new scripts, even if they previously felt that they had exhausted all possible approaches, good things can happen. For many parents this is an invigorating process, in which despair and stagnant perspectives are replaced with realistic hope and creative solutions.

We suggested to Mr. and Mrs. Thomas, for instance, that they assume a more empathic stance and accept that Carl's temperament made it difficult for him to be ready regardless of the amount of time available. We also pointed out that all of us work harder and are ready sooner when we are looking forward to something. Therefore, if Carl were more successful in class or had a special job in school in the morning, getting ready might become easier.

The Thomases collaborated with Carl's teacher to find a motivating activity to offer him each morning at school. Like most other children, Carl loved to help others, so he was invited to come in a few minutes early and assist the secretary in the office. This was a highly motivating task that energized Carl to get ready for school on time. The activity also served to boost his self-esteem. He began to feel that school was a place where his strengths were highlighted. He eventually developed such a positive relationship with the principal that he was assigned the title of "assistant to the principal" and given a diploma. The diploma was displayed with pride in his room at home.

This entire solution was predicated on parents' changing from a script that was ineffective, attempting to harass their son to be ready sooner, to one that boosted his self-esteem and provided a highly motivating reason to be in school.

Tyler, the insatiable child who reproached his parents for the one minute they were not available to him, provides another practical lesson in changing scripts. This insatiable quality became less problematic when it was accepted as a feature of Tyler's temperament. The gist was not that the Whitmans failed to provide enough time and love but rather that he had not experienced his parents' actions in this way. Recall that to remedy the situation, Mr. and Mrs. Whitman not only identified outside activities that would help Tyler feel needed and accepted but also established special times alone with him. They highlighted this time by saying, "This is a special time, so even if the phone rings, I am not going to get it. The answering machine can do that." As children get older, they still require special times with one or both of their parents, whether that takes the form of going out to eat each week, attending a sporting event, or even jogging.

Having a special time with one child does not preclude doing things as a family. Keep in mind that the dynamics are different. A time that a parent establishes to be alone with a child serves several functions: it emphasizes that the parent feels the child is important, provides an opportunity for the parent to get to know the child better without the distraction of siblings, and helps to minimize the child's feelings of not getting enough attention and love.

Now for the problem that *you* flagged for this section, try to come up with three possible solutions. These should be ones you have not yet attempted.

Choose the one that best appeals to you and mentally outline a positive script that would help you introduce this solution and put it into action with your child.

Principle Five: If at First You Don't Succeed, Try Again

It would be unrealistic to believe that in every case, the solution you have chosen and the new script you have carefully planned will be successful. If a new script does not yield a positive outcome, do not let yourself become frustrated, angry, or, for that matter, helpless. If, as often happens, the situation does not improve, the rekindled hope heretofore offered by the new script can degenerate to a sense of false promise and pessimism. In this climate, many parents throw up their hands and say, "We have tried everything, even what you suggested, and nothing works!"

It is exactly for this reason that we must accept the principle that if a new script does not work, we try again. The reality is that some solutions that look foolproof on the drawing board fall flat when implemented. To counteract those feelings of failure that can ensue, it helps to ask, "What if it doesn't work? What is our backup plan?" Posing these questions is not a self-fulfilling prophesy for failure. We anticipate that the new approach *will* be successful, but in case it is not, it is prudent to have one or two backup strategies. That's why we suggested that you think of three solutions to the problem in question.

If we want to teach our children that when an approach is not successful, when mistakes are made, we can learn from these mistakes, then we must model this philosophy. One of the most salient features of a resilient mindset is the belief that mistakes are experiences from which we can learn. Chapter 8 sets out the principles to help children develop this critical capacity.

We Write the Scripts . . . We Can Edit Them

Almost every theory on the development of healthy self-esteem and resilience emphasizes that individuals need to focus on what they can control. When people expend much time and energy trying to change circumstances that are beyond their control, they become more exasperated and hopeless.

Rewriting negative scripts is inextricably interwoven with this notion of personal control. If we can assess the effectiveness of our behaviors as scripted, many of which are very predictable with our children, then we can move forward. We can begin by distinguishing those behaviors that are productive from those that are not. We can then target the latter by understanding the processes that led to their development and the obstacles that prevent their change. By employing a set of principles, we can define problems accurately, set realistic goals, and rewrite our words.

We are the authors of our lives. If we do not like the script, we are not condemned to follow it. The guidepost of rewriting negative scripts is basic to helping our children develop a resilient mindset. Instead of searching for our happiness and the happiness of our children by having them change their scripts, we can be empowered with the knowledge that as authors of our own lives we will benefit most by examining what we can do differently. The process of creating new scripts is based on identifying *possible* solutions that hopefully will become *positive* solutions. These scripts give our children incentive to change theirs.

A difficult lesson for many of us is that we have control over only one person: ourselves. We should not attempt to control our children, but through our courage to change our words and actions we *can* guide and teach them. In doing so, we serve as models of resilience and hope.

5

Loving Our Children in Ways That Help Them Feel Special and Appreciated

For at least a thousand years, writers and philosophers have questioned the meaning of love. Some people have even built a career on the topic. Scientists study the hormones of love. Child developmentalists study the bonds of love. Marital experts examine the process of love. Through it all, there has been a consensus that "loving our children" is one of the most significant tasks of parenting. Feeling loved every day, knowing that parents hold a special place in their hearts for him or her, provides a child with a wellspring of strength to face daily challenges and to develop a resilient mindset.

Though we recognize the importance of loving our children and helping them feel special and appreciated, we are sometimes blocked from conveying this love to them. The problem is not, "Are we loving them enough?" Of course, it would be hard to imagine too much love as a bad thing. Rather, the challenge is to convey our love to them in ways that build a scaffolding for the development of a resilient mindset. We wonder, is it our words or the number of times we say those words, the tone we use, or the physical proximity to our children that truly tells and reassures them that we love them?

In a park not long ago, a mother and her three-year-old child were playing a game they had obviously played many times before:

Mother, smiling, repeatedly asked, "How much do I love you?"

Each time, her child responded differently: first by spreading his arms and saying, "This much," then each successive time by providing an answer that clearly had been modeled on previous interactions between them. "More than all the stars in the sky," the child responded.

Mother leaned forward and hugged her son. There could be no doubt that this child felt loved.

So, is love a product, the end point of our daily interactions with our children, or is love a process, a means by which we provide them with support every day of their lives? For purposes of this chapter, it's the latter. Feeling loved is a process. It is a style of interaction that we constantly display toward our children. Offering empathy, changing negative scripts, and teaching our children to communicate effectively are some of the ways in which we convey our love. Responding appropriately to our children's emotional needs helps them to feel safe, secure, and loved. By assisting them to experience success, nurturing responsibility, providing consistent and appropriate discipline, and teaching them to handle adversity, we demonstrate how much we love them.

This chapter shows how the process of love is shaped and molded day in and day out with our children. The assumption here is that parents love their children. Even in cases of parents promulgating horrific acts on their children or expressing ambivalence about them, we hold that the seeds of love were probably once planted. Unfortunately, left unnourished, they never grew or, in some instances, were trampled upon. The process of loving their children is derailed for some parents when they allow their children's behavior to interfere with helping them feel special and appreciated. It is in precisely those situations, however, during those stressful times that our children most need to feel loved and accepted for who they are and not necessarily for who we would like them to be.

The Feeling of Being Loved

What does the feeling of being loved encompass? In the wonderful play *Fiddler on the Roof*, after twenty-five years of marriage Tevye asks his wife if she loves him. In response, she recounts their shared experiences over the years, bringing children into the world and working together side by side. She asks how after twenty-five years of her cooking and cleaning for him, he can question whether or not she loves him. In the end Tevye sings, "and I suppose I love you too."

Tevye raises an important question: How do you know that someone loves you? Common themes are observable in the behavior and comments of children who feel loved and accepted. Acceptance provides them with the courage to try new things and with parental support to engage in discovering their identity. The process of love allows parents to express acceptance to their children in the absence of intimidation or humiliation.

The feeling of being loved is not tainted by what is commonly referred to as "conditional love." Such love is conceived of as contingently offered when children conform to the standards and behaviors established by their parents. Sally's anxiety around others and her inability to be assertive led her parents to exhort her to say hello; in her mind the message was that they would love her more if she were outgoing and talkative, behaviors that were difficult for her to exhibit, given her temperament. Mary's parents pressured her to obtain good grades, suggesting at one point that if she loved them, she would work harder in school; this led her to believe that their love and acceptance were dependent on her performance.

When children feel loved and accepted, they feel special and appreciated in their parents' eyes. They believe that they hold a special place in the hearts and minds of their parents. They sense that their parents enjoy being with them. These youngsters know that their parents appreciate them. This feeling of specialness, which has nothing to do with being self-centered, is a key component for children to believe that they are loveable and worthwhile.

One ten-year-old girl perfectly capsulized it for us: "I know my parents are busy, but they always find time for me and my sister. When I'm having some trouble with my homework, one of my parents always seems to be there to help. They are patient and explain things carefully when I'm having problems. Although we argue sometimes, I feel that they really listen to me and love me." From this young girl we learn the important lesson that feeling loved is a process that we convey to our children day in and day out.

Love and the Charismatic Adult

We had the occasion some years ago to interview a young teen referred to us because of problems with depression, anxiety, and a learning disability. As we talked, it became clear that his worried, hopeless feelings were deep-seated. He had performed poorly in school for seven years and, despite receiving help, continued to lag far behind his classmates in basic academic subjects. He was not so much depressed as demoralized. He had few friends, and in his eyes there was precious little he could do well.

The conversation turned to his view of the future. We asked a standard question: If you could be anyone for a day, who would you choose to be? (In many cases the choice is a famous athlete, movie star, etc.) The goal is to generate some idea of the child's hope and optimism by soliciting his view as to whether and how he might achieve this revered status in the future.

Without hesitation this young man responded, "My dad."

Surprised, we inquired, "Why would you choose your dad?"

He looked back at us and answered, "You just have to know my dad. He really loves me."

The image of his father that this young man held in his heart and head represents our working definition of what the late author and psychologist Julius Segal called a "charismatic adult," as noted in Chapter 1. Such adults need not necessarily be a parent. They are individuals who in their interactions with a child convey love and acceptance and help that child feel special. With the young teen we just described, despite the adversity he was facing, his sense of security and belonging as well as his optimism about the future were bolstered by the love that his father communicated daily and the strength of their relationship.

Segal defined the role of a charismatic adult in the life of children as "a person with whom they identify and from whom they gather strength." Segal's ideas are supported by several studies of adults with childhood histories of risk, including abuse, neglect, and school failure. Researchers found that a number of these individuals had risen above the adversity; they had met significant challenges and were now leading successful and satisfying personal and professional lives. One of the most important factors the subjects cited as helping them to become successful was having at least one adult in their lives who generally cared about and loved them. There was at least one adult who was an advocate for them, especially in times of need. This finding is reported repeatedly in populations of individuals across multiple continents.

Segal's image of "gathering strength" provokes important questions about the effect we have on our children. When you interact with your children, do you ask yourself if they are gathering strength from your words and actions? When you put your children to bed at night, do you think about whether they are stronger people because of the things you have said or done that day? Have they gathered strength from you that will reinforce their sense of self-worth and resilience? Or, regrettably, are they weaker? These questions cannot help but spark reflections about our relationships with our children, as well as the true process of love and helping them gather strength.

Recently we met with Mr. and Mrs. Rawley about their four-year-old son, Austin, their first child. They had another child, now six months of age, who possessed a very even temperament. Austin unfortunately did not. Though they loved him dearly, the Rawleys were sorely frustrated by their perceived inability to manage and "shape" his behavior. Austin was affectionate and loving but extremely hyperactive. He had already been asked to leave one preschool and was starting another. His parents expressed deep feelings of inadequacy, not only because of their defeat in trying to shape his behavior each day, but also because of the pain they experienced over the reaction that his behavior garnered from others. A number of other families in the neighborhood would not allow Austin to come into their homes. His former preschool teacher likewise was exasperated after a year of attempting to modify and change Austin's behavior to help him become "part of the group."

Austin was also feeling the consequences of "his problems." He had commented to his parents several times that other children did not like him and that his teacher did not think he was smart. It was clear that on many days Austin went to bed "in the red," having received much more in the way of anger and criticism from those around him than support and encouragement. He was not gathering strength from the important adults in his life.

We discussed with Mr. and Mrs. Rawley what might happen to a child over many years of experiencing these thoughts and feelings on a daily basis. We suggested that what Austin needed most was their constant, unconditional love and support despite the difficult nature of his behavior.

It's also relevant that during a visit to our playroom, Austin's behavior, though impulsive and restless, was in fact very normal, as was his emotional response. Without hesitation he provided a hug at the end of the hour. This was not a troubled child but a child, owing to his difficult temperament, destined for trouble.

Carl's parents faced a similar situation when Carl had difficulty getting ready for school on time and sitting through dinner. Mr. Thomas was able to change his negative script with his son by understanding that Carl's problems were driven by his temperament and that he could modify his approach to Carl without "giving in."

Our discussion about the importance of being a charismatic adult helped Mr. Thomas to find the courage to make these changes. We asked him to consider whether Carl gathered strength and developed positive qualities from him. We asked the same questions of Sally's parents: Did their responses to her shy behavior build her up or further tear her down? It was only when these parents recognized the futility of attempting to help their children in the absence of a loving process that they became sources of strength for them.

Now meet Allen, an eight-year-old whose parents, Mr. and Mrs. Norton, also loved him dearly. Allen's disabilities extended into the area of social relations. Just as he had difficulty learning to read the printed word, he also experienced difficulty learning to read and track the verbal and nonverbal cues of others. He was not shy, but his attempts to be part of the group were poorly received. He did not know when to stop talking and had trouble taking turns. He would frequently act silly to gain attention. Though he thought his actions made him just like everyone else, he was shunned by most of his schoolmates and teased by others. Allen could not understand the role his behavior played in this outcome and thus felt sad and mistreated. His parents frequently spoke to him about his interactions with others, but they were disturbed by his seeming lack of progress, prompting them to bring him for counseling.

Allen was thrilled when he was invited to the birthday party of a classmate. He had not been invited to a school birthday party since kindergarten. He poignantly told his mother, "They finally like me." Allen didn't know that every child in the class had been invited to this party, but even if he had, it is not likely that this knowledge would have dampened his enthusiasm. He was excited as his mother drove him to the party. In a low-key manner, Mrs. Norton endeavored to reinforce appropriate social skills, reminding him to give other children a chance to speak, to not brag, and to offer compliments to his peers.

After being greeted by the mother of the birthday child, Allen found himself alone. He tried to join a group of boys jumping on the trampoline, but it was as if he were invisible. When he tried to take a turn, they told him it was not his turn. Eventually they moved off and left him to jump on the trampoline by himself.

During the party, several of the more aggressive boys told Allen that he should not have been invited. Then, according to Allen, one of his classmates slipped while carrying a piece of cake and the cake landed on Allen's head. This was met by laughter by some children and pity by others. Two girls in the class helped Allen clean cake out of his hair. All of his hopes to be accepted vanished as he wiped his face and retreated into the hallway by the front door to wait for his mother.

When Mrs. Norton arrived and saw Allen sitting by himself, she intuitively knew that something had happened, but she was so frustrated by his continued difficulties and seeming resistance to "getting better" that her sadness and anger got the best of her. She said something that later she wished she could retract: "No wonder you don't have any friends. You just sit and mope around. How can you have friends by sitting there by yourself?" Allen looked as his mother, began to cry, and walked out the front door.

During our discussions of charismatic adults, Mrs. Norton acknowledged, "I was anything but a charismatic adult when I said that to Allen. If anything, I was the opposite of a charismatic adult. What little dignity he may have had left, I took from him." What Allen had needed most at that moment was his mother's unconditional love and respect.

Our discussions with Allen's mother helped her to manage her feelings and expectations and to be guided by the goal of helping her son to gather strength from her. We revisited the birthday party scene and reflected on what Mrs. Norton could have done to change the script in a way that would enable her son to learn and gain strength from the humiliation he experienced.

"What he needed to hear from me was not anger and criticism," Mrs. Norton concluded. "He was feeling so down that he needed some words of encouragement, some hope that we could try to figure out some ways for him to learn to get along with kids and ways that he could respond when they insulted him. He needed to feel loved."

Think of your daily interactions with your children. Place yourself in their shoes. Now ask yourself: If someone responded to me the way I responded to my children, would I walk away from that interaction feeling stronger, would I feel loved, would I be a more resilient person, or would I feel more defeated? The answer to this question defines the very process of loving our children.

Feeling Loved and a Resilient Mindset

Feeling loved, special, and appreciated is a cornerstone of a child's resilient mindset. Resilient children feel hopeful and possess high self-worth. They set realistic goals and expectations for themselves and those around them. They learn to solve problems and to view mistakes as experiences from which to learn. Children with resilient mindsets use productive ways of coping with adversity. They don't deny their vulnerabilities but are able to capitalize on their strengths. They learn to relate well to others, are comfortable in seeking assistance, and, most important, learn to focus on what they have control over rather than on what they can little influence.

These characteristics are most successfully nurtured and reinforced in the context of the relationship with a charismatic adult. Such an adult communicates acceptance and love and provides a climate in which children can learn the attitudes and skills that form the core of a resilient mindset. When we feel unconditional love we are less defensive and more willing to listen and learn from others. In the context of a safe and secure relationship between parent and child, both parties are more apt to set realistic goals, to solve problems and make decisions effectively, to take appropriate risks, and to request assistance when necessary.

It is difficult to imagine a resilient child who has not experienced this type of loving relationship. It is little wonder that adults who have overcome great childhood adversity quickly attribute their success to at least one adult who was there for them during their childhood and adolescent years. While it is our hope that all children encounter many charismatic adults in their lives in addition to their parents, we have been impressed with the power that even one such adult, parent or not, can have in promoting hope and resilience in a child.

The Lake Family: The Process of Love Is Difficult if You Haven't Been on the Receiving End

Many parents are hard-pressed to demonstrate unconditional love and are at a loss to demonstrate to their children how special they are to them. As with the Lake family, more often than not, the ability of parents to overtly engage in the process of loving their children is complicated by their personal experiences. When children grow up in a home in which the expression of love is minimal, in which they rarely feel special in the eyes of their parents, in which they do not witness displays of affection between their parents or are not recipients of such displays themselves, it is difficult to engage in the process of loving when *they* have children. This does not imply that change is impossible, just that the axiom that "we tend to raise our children the way we were raised" may hold more truth than we sometimes wish to acknowledge. Having parents who comfortably demonstrate love and affection provides children with a model of how to relate to their own children.

Mr. and Mrs. Lake consulted us about their thirteen-year-old son, Brian, who had a history of misbehavior and, as he was getting older, was becoming increasingly disruptive at home. They described Brian as "selfish, self-centered, not willing to help around the house, and always expecting others to do things for him." Their frustration and anger toward Brian were obvious from the moment they entered our office.

In the course of taking a history, we asked the Lakes what words Brian might choose to describe them.

Mr. Lake responded, "Brian would say I'm always on his back. But the only reason I am on his back is that he is so oppositional and uncooperative." Anger and frustration were evident in his facial expression. He continued, "If I weren't on his back, he wouldn't do anything but play video games and talk to his friends on the phone."

Mrs. Lake stated, "When he was little, I didn't mind doing things for him like making his bed or waking him up in the morning. But he's old enough now that he shouldn't expect us to continue doing these things for him."

This was the first personal observation Mrs. Lake made during the interview. For the most part, she deferred to her husband, allowing him to provide most of the history. To shift away from the markedly negative focus on Brian, we asked the Lakes to reflect back to a time when they were Brian's age and to recall what, if any, positive comments they heard from their parents. While this request surprised them, they were willing to try. What followed was revealing.

Mr. Lake said, "My parents weren't ones to show affection or to compliment me, but I knew that they cared about me."

We asked, "How did you know that? In what ways did they demonstrate their care?"

"I just knew," he responded.

"And what about you, Mrs. Lake?"

Mrs. Lake said that her mother had been somewhat distant for reasons that she never quite understood. But as she described her father, she commented, "He always seemed to have something nice to say to me. When he came home from work, he always gave me a kiss and told me he loved me." Tears welled in her eyes as she mentioned that her father had recently passed away. "When I helped out, he always thanked me."

Mr. Lake quickly added, "But Brian never helps out."

Based on this depiction, it appeared to us that at least part of the problem was the Lakes' inability to demonstrate their love for Brian. We decided to first address Mr. Lake's perception that Brian was never cooperative or helpful, which we believed was rooted in his own experiences with his parents. We asked, "We know it feels as if Brian never helps out, but can you think of any instances when he was more cooperative?"

"Yeah, but they were not big deals," Mr. Lake quickly responded. "He cleaned his room, and he helped his brother do an art project for school. I *expect* Brian to clean his room and help his brother. My wife and I have taught Brian the importance of responsibility. Besides, he hardly ever helps out."

"What might happen," we asked, "if either of you said something positive to Brian when he met these expected responsibilities, such as cleaning his room or helping out?"

Once again it was Mr. Lake who responded. "I don't think it would make a difference. He is really a selfish kid."

"What do you think, Mrs. Lake?" we prompted.

Still musing about her experiences with her father, she answered, "I remember how special I felt when my father said something nice to me. Even if it was just something small. Once when I was nine or ten, he came over and gave me a big hug after I put away some toys. I still remember it vividly today."

Mr. Lake's negative scripts, however, were well entrenched. He practically bellowed, "But, dear, Brian doesn't help out!"

We asked, "Would Brian be more likely to help out if he heard some positive comments?"

For whatever reason, perhaps our patience or perhaps Mr. Lake's perception that we truly empathized with his frustration, he responded, "I don't know."

"Did you ever want to hear something positive, something encouraging, from your parents?" we asked him.

His answer was brief. "They weren't into that kind of stuff."

We persisted, "Based on what you have told us, we know that about your parents. But did you ever wish that they would offer you encouragement or tell you how much they cared for you?"

"I never thought about it," Mr. Lake responded. "I don't know. I don't know if Brian, or most kids these days, will change if we tell them how much we care about them. I just don't know if it makes that much of a difference when people compliment you."

Mr. Lake's remark and his failure to appreciate the importance of encouraging and demonstrating love toward one's children are not unique. There may be many reasons why this occurs. Unfortunately, there are many Mr. Lakes, deprived of parents who served as models of encouragement and love, unable to express positive feelings toward their children, unable to express unconditional love and support. To help him relate to being on the receiving end of positive attention and to become more comfortable in his interactions with Brian, we asked Mr. Lake to think about a recent experience in which he was complimented.

He smiled and said, "It just happened today. I was in charge of a project for a new product, and we came in a few days early and under cost. My boss made a special point of coming by my office to thank me."

Here we used a touch of humor to help guide him to understanding, "And of course you told your boss, 'Please don't compliment me; I was just doing my job.'"

He laughed and conceded, "I actually liked it." Then he ventured, "Maybe I liked it even more than some others would have since I almost never heard these kinds of compliments when I was growing up. OK. You've made your point."

Mr. Lake agreed to make an effort to be more encouraging with Brian and to offer positive feedback, even for everyday activities. Mrs. Lake was very supportive of this goal.

At a memorable meeting that followed, Mr. Lake recounted, "I told Brian something that I wanted to say for a long time. It's something I would have loved to hear even once from my parents: I told him that even when he did not clean up his room, I still loved him." Mr. Lake added, "I think Brian was stunned. He just looked at me as if I had arrived from another planet. But I could tell it was important to him."

With some guidance, Mr. Lake was now able to model for his son what had not been modeled for him: truly communicating to his son that he was special and loved. As with any activity, practice leads to improvement. For Mr. Lake, the positive feelings generated from this particular activity were something he had not experienced very much in his life and were almost intoxicating, motivating him to redouble his efforts to maintain a positive relationship with his son.

The Holt Family: Confusing Love and a Lack of Discipline

The fear of spoiling our children has bearing on several subjects in this book. More often than not, this fear is based on the mistaken assumption that if parents express too much love, they will raise self-centered, narcissistic children. This assumption is extended to the erroneous conclusion that by displaying affection and love, we may in fact be taking the first step toward spoiling our children. Yet, just the opposite appears to be true: children are more receptive to accepting limits, developing compassion, and taking responsibility when they feel loved and respected by their parents. When children feel unloved, they are less likely to listen and are more likely to engage in obstructive behavior. When parents exert more energy controlling their children than loving them, the number of problems gets bigger, not smaller.

Mr. and Mrs. Holt relayed to us that their nine-year-old daughter, Mimi, was difficult to please from the moment she was born. Mimi was hypersensitive to touch and sound. Even as an infant, she appeared to dislike being held; her body would tense. As a toddler, she was "strong willed," and when she didn't get what she desired she would scream and cry. As she developed language, words were added to these outbursts, including accusations that her parents didn't love her because they wouldn't accede to her demands. Mr. and Mrs. Holt said that when they acquiesced to Mimi's demands, she became even more demanding.

Mrs. Holt tearfully and angrily told us, "Mimi is insatiable. We show her love, and she takes advantage of it."

The Holts' nine-year adventure of raising a daughter with a difficult temperament led them to believe that Mimi might equate their attempts to love her as spoiling her. This resulted in their offering fewer expressions of love and affection, which only reinforced Mimi's feelings that she was unloved. When she felt unloved, she became more demanding. A negative script and destructive cycle had become the hallmark of the Holts' relationship with their daughter.

We discussed with Mimi's parents the trials of raising a seemingly "insatiable" child. Mimi's temperament was difficult to understand and parent. Her behavior often left the Holts feeling angry, bewildered, and exhausted, as it would any parent in this situation. They had little energy or inclination to communicate positive emotions to her.

We counseled the Holts that their attempts to satisfy and love Mimi might take on all the features of a tightrope balancing act. That is, they would have to find ways to demonstrate their love for their daughter while setting limits on her demands and not being thrown off balance by her subsequent anger. We emphasized that Mimi's demandingness was rooted in her temperament and did not stem from a failure on their part. We asked the Holts to set aside a special time with Mimi each night and to even label it "special." At first they were resistant.

Mr. Holt, feeling burned out by his daughter's unreasonable demands, conjectured, "If we give her another half hour of undivided attention, she'll want three hours. She will become even more spoiled and self-centered."

We responded that "special" time, in our experience, actually decreases a child's demandingness. The concrete nature of a regular time helps to offset for many children the feeling that they do not receive enough of their parents' time and love. Although Mimi's parents voiced lingering reservations, they also realized that what they were doing was not working, and they were becoming increasingly annoyed and less positive with their daughter.

It was our hope that this special time would provide the Holts with the opportunity to express their love on an unconditional basis. The Holts told Mimi that they wanted to make certain that one of them had time to spend with her alone each evening. They explained that this would be a time during which they could play games with her or engage in any other activity that was mutually agreed upon.

The Holts also had a younger child whose behavior much more easily fit their expectations and for whom they experienced little difficulty expressing their love and support. We urged them to set aside time for this younger child as well to minimize sibling jealousy.

To the Holts' surprise, Mimi responded well to her special time. It did not produce demands for more time but actually served to reduce Mimi's insatiable requests. Although Mimi's behavioral problems had been fueled by her early childhood temperament, the ideas and beliefs that she had formed about herself and the world around her over the years were a significant force in shaping her daily behavior—in particular, her view that she was not appreciated by her parents.

Mimi's awareness that she would have regular time with her parents appeared to ease her feelings that they did not love her or did not want her. On several occasions she requested longer periods of time with them or asked for new toys or games, but the Holts also found that Mimi was more reasonable when they set a limit. A positive cycle began to develop in which Mimi's more acceptable behavior made it easier for the Holts to express their love, which reinforced Mimi's feelings that she was loved, which further influenced her behavior.

In essence, the presence of the special time made change possible, but the true impetus for this change was the Holts' courage to examine their behavior and choose a different path.

Six Steps to Helping Your Children Feel Loved, Special, and Appreciated

Every interaction with your children is an opportunity to engage in the loving process. Every interaction is an opportunity to help your children feel special and appreciated. Granted, in some situations it may be more difficult, but those are the very situations in which it is vital to reinforce a resilient mindset in your children. Regardless of whether you perceive yourself as doing a good or a mediocre job in meeting this important goal, the following six steps will help you to strengthen your resolve and modify your behavior.

Step One: Let Your Memories of Childhood Be Your Guide

In our workshops and clinical activities, we ask parents to think about a childhood experience in which their parents made them feel special and appreciated. We also ask them to reflect on an experience that left them feeling unappreciated. We must incorporate into our parenting practices those experiences that helped us feel loved and special as well as understand those that did not. We should strive to avoid saying and doing things that led *us* to feel less worthy and less loved as children and, in many cases, as adults. We also suggest that parents think beyond their own families and consider other adults they knew while growing up who made them feel special and appreciated.

When parents describe the experiences that reinforced a feeling of being special and loved in the eyes of others, many seem to be of surprisingly minor importance. These seemingly minor events nevertheless had a strong personal impact on the tellers. Sometimes these events involved parents spending a little extra time with their children, writing a note, or reading at bedtime. One adult told us, "It wasn't just one occasion; it was the general feeling that when my parents were with me, all of their attention was focused on what I was doing. When they spoke to me, they never were distracted by listening to the radio or television or reading the paper. To have their undivided attention and praise made me feel that I was really special to them."

This recollection bears out the importance of encouraging and praising our children. Unfortunately, many children experience what one psychologist called a "praise deficit." All too often we forget to acknowledge and appreciate the people who are closest to us, including our spouse and children. Do your children experience a praise deficit? Do you voice more negative than positive comments during the course of a day?

The childhood experiences of the first author were a powerful impetus in writing this book. Bob's parents, both of whom were immigrants with little formal education, kept a "file" about him and each of his three brothers from the time they were born and continuing into their adult lives. They recognized the importance of helping their children feel special and loved. Keeping a file was one of the ways in which they did so.

Bob tells audiences, "Everything went into the files. Birthday cards, report cards, even my drawings. I know it may sound a little crazy, but as I was growing up, I felt special because of those files. I had no idea if anyone else in my neighborhood in Brooklyn had files, but I knew I did, as did my brothers. I felt that my life was in those files and that my parents enjoyed building them. It was a wonderful feeling."

Bob's mother died nearly twenty years ago. After her death, Bob's father told him, "I know that the file was very important to your mom, but it is just as important to me. So if it's OK, I would like to keep it going in her memory."

As Bob recounts, "I was in tears. Here was this seventy-six-year-old man who was saying to his sons that they were still important to him and he wanted to keep the files going. He had a wonderful way of making us feel special and appreciated in his eyes."

Ten years later on almost the exact anniversary of his mother's death, Bob's father passed away. Just before his death, Bob and his wife visited his father in Florida. When it came time for them to return to Boston, as his father always did, he gave Bob a warm hug and kiss good-bye; then he said something that seemingly was so simple and yet so powerful.

In describing what transpired, Bob comments, "I hope that all individuals, at least once, experience the joy of having a parent say something to them equivalent to what my father said to me. On the way back to Boston that day, I was so moved that I must have said a hundred times to myself, 'I am so fortunate that he is my dad. I am so lucky. I am so blessed.'"

As events transpired, Bob never had another conversation with his father. A couple of days after Bob returned from Florida, his father became seriously ill. When Bob flew back to Florida, his father was comatose in a hospice and was not expected to live through the night. Bob said his farewells and believes that his father heard what he said. The next morning, his father died peacefully.

What were the words that Bob's father said to him as he was leaving to return to Boston, words that he did not know would be his last to his son? Mr. Brooks said, "Now, Bob, remember, when you get back to Boston, if you have anything that you can send me for the file, please do. I always enjoy receiving things from you and hearing from you. You are so special. I love you dearly." To his dying days, the words and actions of Bob's father have helped Bob to feel special and appreciated. What a wonderful gift he provided to Bob and his brothers.

Step Two: Create Traditions and Special Times

Creating traditions and times set aside each day, week, or month as special times with our children establishes an atmosphere in which they feel loved and appreciated. When we designate these moments as special, we convey the message to our children that they are important to us and that we enjoy having uninterrupted time to spend with them. We should make every effort to adhere to these schedules. Obviously, this should not preclude having other, spontaneous moments, and there may be circumstances in which special times have to be moved. However it's arranged, time set aside each week for all of our children together as well as each child alone emphasizes that they are important to us and that we love them.

Unfortunately, for some families, events that constitute a reason to change a special time may be trivial. Often, well-intentioned parents permit other demands to compromise times with their children, such as we witnessed with Stephanie and her parents, Mr. and Mrs. Grant. Although the Grants set aside times to play with their child, these times were constantly interrupted by phone calls. To Stephanie, their actions communicated that the calls were more important than she was. In these circumstances, interrupted time often generates disappointment, frustration, and anger on children's parts.

Although many families set aside times each week when all family members are present, often during dinner or a family outing, you may find that setting aside times for each child individually is the most powerful way of communicating appreciation. A popular myth is that if families are in close proximity, family closeness will develop. On this point, we are reminded of the parents who stopped their car on the beginning of a family outing and threatened to return home because the siblings were fighting. In response to the threat, one of the children answered, "Good. We were having fun playing at home until you told us we had to do something as a family."

When children are young, special times often consist of outings to the playground or reading before bed. Regrettably, while parents may see this time as special, many children do not. To change that impression, you can highlight the importance of the activity by telling your child, "When I read to you, it is such an important, special time that even if the phone rings I won't answer it."

One six-year-old told us with excitement and joy, "I know my parents love me." When we inquired how he knew this, he responded, "When they read to me and the phone rings, they let the answering machine answer it." Sometimes the simplest gestures bring far-reaching results.

When the first author's son Rich was three years old, he was greeted with the birth of brother Doug. Rich's status thus was changed; he was no longer the only child in the household. To highlight that Rich was special, Bob established a tradition of taking him out to a local restaurant once a week. Bob and his wife always ensured that they had other special times with Rich as well, such as reading to him at bedtime, playing games, and taking him along on errands. The weekly dinner out, however, appeared to be one of the strongest indicators to Rich of how much he was appreciated. The tradition continued even when Rich and Doug were teenagers. Bob alternated weeks taking one of his sons out to eat and found it a wonderful time to have the child's undivided attention. Special time does not have to involve going out, although Bob found that it was pleasant to alter the normal routine and do something beyond the boundaries of the home. The second author and his son, Ryan, established a tradition of playing Ping-Pong each evening, an activity they have continued for the past eight years.

It has also been our experience that scheduled, special times for each child limit sibling rivalry. It highlights for the child that he or she will have time alone with Mom or Dad. With younger children it may be helpful to display a calendar, making note of the designated day or time with a colorful sticker.

Mark was an exuberant five-year-old when his parents brought him in because "he does not listen to what we tell him." Mark's exuberance frequently bordered on dangerous impulsivity. Often he acted without thinking, displaying his curiosity by taking appliances apart, leaving his seat, wandering away in public places, or bolting out into the street.

In one of our first meetings with Mark, we were somewhat surprised when this five-year-old said, "I think my father hates me."

We asked why he felt that way.

Out of the mouth of this young child came an obvious though insightful response. "He gets angry with me all the time."

Mark was quite perceptive. Mark's father, Mr. Stanton, who was the president of a large company, acknowledged that on many occasions he "disliked" his son. In contrast, Mr. Stanton enjoyed being with Mark's eight-year-old sister, Susie, noting that "Susie enjoys the things we do together. She is fun to be with." He added, "I have more than 300 people in my company who listen to me. My own son doesn't. I find it difficult to be with him."

Although there was a hint of humor in his comment, the tone was also laced with frustration and sadness.

This sadness was more apparent when Mr. Stanton said, "I feel that I'm growing more and more distant from Mark, and he's only five years old."

We empathized with Mr. Stanton and shared Mark's comment that he knew that at times his father did not want to be with him. We talked about ways that he could help his son feel special in his eyes. We suggested scheduling time alone, which was something that father and son had not had. To avoid Susie's feeling left out, we also suggested a special time for her as well. Mr. Stanton wondered what he could do alone with Mark that would not be stressful. We recommended a short activity that could be expanded if successful.

A few weeks later, Mark's father reported that this small investment in his son had reaped huge benefits. Mark came into the office and with great excitement and a big smile, said, "Guess what? Me and my dad, we have a private time each week. No one else, just me and my dad."

"What do you do in this private time?" we asked him.

"Every Friday," Mark responded, "before school my dad takes me to the Dunkin' Donuts, just me and my dad."

Mark's father indicated that the outings lasted only about twenty minutes and that he enjoyed the time alone with his son. For those twenty minutes, while eating donuts and drinking milk, Mark was able to keep his behavior reasonably focused. Although the private time at Dunkin' Donuts was not the only source of improvement in their relationship (Mr. and Mrs. Stanton were actively involved in a parenting class), it set the ball rolling.

After several months, Mark's father commented, "Once I learned to appreciate Mark's style and could accommodate him as much as possible, it was a pleasure to be with him. Although he can be exasperating at times, he can be a lot of fun."

Establishing special times provides opportunities for parents not only to spend uninterrupted moments with each child free of typical distractions but also to place the child in a more positive light, thereby building up a solid relationship. These special times foster a feeling of being loved and appreciated.

Step Three: Don't Miss Significant Occasions

This step is akin to the previous step of establishing special times and traditions. There are, however, some differences. A parent in the course of explaining the resentment and anger he still felt toward his father recalled, "Between the time I was five and thirteen years old, my father was home for only two of my birthdays. His job required him to travel a lot, but I can't understand why he couldn't arrange to be home for my birthday." As his eyes filled with tears, he confided, "I never felt that he cared about me."

If we are not present at the important events in our children's lives, they are likely to feel the same way as this man. In today's fast-paced world in which both parents may work, if one of our goals is to raise resilient children, we must make time available for them. While many of us have heard the adage "Quality time is more important than quantity time," the reality is that

if time spent with our children is limited and we are not present for important events such as their birthdays, first Little League game, first piano recital,
or first day of school, then quality time is significantly compromised.

At a workshop one father with grown children sadly told us, "Work consumed so much of my time that I missed out on many of my children's day-
to-day activities. When both of them went off to college, I felt as if I was a
stranger to them." Reminiscent of the song "Cat's in the Cradle" by the late
Harry Chapin, he mused, "Now that they are older, they don't seem to have
any time for me either."

Time invested in our children also pays future dividends in the time they
will invest in us as adults, allowing us to share in their adult lives as well.

Step Four: Be Demonstrative with Your Love

Some parents find it difficult to display affection. It may be that little if any
affection was shown to them when they were children and/or their temperamental style makes it uncomfortable for them to express feelings of warmth
openly. If you are this type of parent, it is important for you to take steps to
become more comfortable in hugging your children, holding their hands, sitting close to them while watching television, and communicating words of
endearment. If you are not accustomed to such actions, change does not
have to come all at one time. Set a pace that is comfortable for you, and begin
with activities that you enjoy. Changing any script in too rapid a fashion or
too pronounced a way dooms you for failure.

Mr. and Mrs. Lozen consulted us about their two children, eight-year-old
Lana and five-year-old Justin. Mr. Lozen explained that he felt the children
were "very needy." As examples, he offered that they would interrupt him and
his wife when they were on the phone or would jump onto his lap when he
was trying to watch the news on television. He stated, "They can be really
bothersome when I'm trying to do things."

To our surprise, Mrs. Lozen said to her husband, "Maybe they just want
to be with you and want you to show them that you love them. You hardly
ever hold them. And even when you kiss them you do it as if it were a duty
rather than a pleasure."

Mr. Lozen responded in defense, "The kids should know I love them. I
don't know why it's important for me to hug and kiss them all the time. I have
never been the demonstrative kind."

His wife then told him, "I realize you have difficulty showing affection toward me or any of our family members."

Frustrated, Mr. Lozen responded, "I'm sure the kids know, as you do, that I love them. I love you too."

We asked, "How do you think the children know this?"

Mr. Lozen replied honestly that he was not sure. We explained that it was not easy to change one's style of showing affection, but we asked Mr. Lozen to consider what might happen if he began to hold and hug his children more often. We said, "We don't want you to do anything that is uncomfortable. Perhaps you could consider a small first step."

Mr. Lozen thought for a while and said, "I enjoy reading to the kids before bedtime." He said that he usually sat on the edge of the bed rather than stretching out and making physical contact with the children, then added, "I think I would feel comfortable having them rest against me when I read to them."

During several subsequent meetings, Mr. Lozen's facial expressions and body posture changed appreciably as he described his interactions with both Lana and Justin. He had appeared annoyed and somewhat detached at our initial meeting. However, as he began to have the children sit by his side or on his lap while reading to them, play board games with them while stretched out on the floor, and kiss them in a more than perfunctory way, his joy and delight were apparent. We no longer heard the description "bothersome." Lana and Justin were somewhat startled at first by his behavior, but they soon came to enjoy their "new" father. As they felt increasingly loved by him and knew that he would give them time, their apparent "demandingness" decreased. Secure and appreciated children are rarely demanding.

Why would a seemingly intelligent man such as Mr. Lozen be so unaware of the importance of displaying affection toward his children? As we learned of Mr. Lozen's own childhood, the answer unfolded. He recalled that his parents rarely hugged or were playful with him. Phrases such as "I love you" were notably absent from their repertoire. Though he had been following the same script with his children that his parents had used with him, it was clear that there was a part of Mr. Lozen that wanted to change. With just a few sessions of coaching, his interactions with his children improved. Smiling, Mrs. Lozen commented that her husband had become more demonstrative toward her as well. The process of demonstrating love forged a new script for Mr. Lozen with his family, one that fostered and supported a resilient mindset.

Step Five: Build Up, Don't Chip Away at Your Children

A beautiful statue can be created by either starting with a large piece of marble and chipping away or starting with a small lump of clay and building up. Although in the art world either method may produce a beautiful work, in the parenting world the chipping method is unproductive. Some parents report their frustration after having exerted "so much energy" in raising their children. Unfortunately, the majority of their energy is directed at chipping away, attempting to shape the child into something they perceive as desirable. Instead, we advocate the building model: building up rather than chipping down. Our children must end each day with their emotional bank accounts "in the black." They must leave school each day the better for their experience. They must go to bed each evening having heard words of support, love, and encouragement, words that build up rather than chip away.

This book has portrayed many examples of the chipping style of parenting. Michael's father yelled at him and employed disparaging remarks when Michael gave up building a radio. Danny's father dwelled on his son's shortcomings, rarely offering positive feedback—a style he had acquired from his own father. Mary's mother pressured Mary to obtain good grades, resulting in her feeling criticized and unappreciated. Gregory's parents, exasperated by his disorganization and messiness, fired off rounds of complaints at the expense of more encouraging comments. Sally's parents attempted to "cure" her shyness by exhorting her to say hello to others.

As parents, we routinely engage in this chipping process without realizing it. We pronounce what our children are doing wrong rather than what they are doing right. We correct rather than teach. If the majority of our messages to our children ring negative, if we adopt the attitude that "If we don't tell them what they are doing wrong, they will never improve," our children will resent us and not learn from us. When we chip away at our children, we erode or fail to reinforce the features of a resilient mindset. It is difficult to develop a sense of self-worth, security, and confidence in the face of people who are unappreciative.

Chipping at our children, even with a loving tone, is likely to pose more risks than benefits. It is difficult for our children to feel loved when they perceive that we have chisels in our hands ready to attack their dignity and self-esteem at a moment's notice. If parents employ the chisel with regularity, they will weaken whatever confidence remains in their children. In contrast, parents who build up and offer positive comments will help create a strong foundation of love on which resilience will be constructed.

Step Six: Accept Your Children for Who They Are, Not What You Want Them to Be

Accepting children for themselves is a major theme of this book and is the substance of Chapter 6. Many of the foregoing case examples center on well-meaning parents expecting behaviors from their children that the children could not demonstrate. Ask yourself, "Am I willing to accept my children?" Acceptance does not mean allowing them to engage in whatever behavior they choose, or not disciplining or holding them responsible. It's recognizing and appreciating their unique qualities and not berating them for behaviors or emotions that may be part of their unique makeup and often beyond their control.

The best way to help our children change self-defeating behaviors or those that may not fit well in today's world is to create an atmosphere in which they feel safe and secure. In such a climate they are able to recognize that what we are attempting to teach them is based firmly on our unconditional love. Acceptance of our children, helping them understand how special they are in our eyes, exemplifies the process of love.

6

Accepting Our Children for Who They Are

The Foundation for Setting Realistic Goals and Expectations

To truly nurture a resilient mindset requires that we love our children unconditionally. To do so, we must accept our children for who they are and not necessarily what we want them to be. Troy and his parents, Mr. and Mrs. Summers, exemplify this dilemma. Troy, a sixteen-year-old high school junior, fell short of meeting his parents' academic expectations. His skills were average, but his parents, both college graduates, expected him to excel. Although Troy was quite athletic and was successful in high school sports, his B-average performance in classes never met his parents' expectations.

Although Troy's parents professed to us that they accepted Troy's level of abilities, his father submitted, "Everyone can work harder; everyone can do better. I started out as a poor student, and look at me now." This argument reflects a common trap into which many of us fall not just with our children but also with friends, colleagues, and coworkers. The trap of "I accept you but . . ." is seductive. If I begin by telling you that I accept who you are and what you can do, for some reason I believe that I can follow that up with "but" and add further expectations. Perhaps we all believe that simply stating the words "I accept you" greases the wheels, allowing us to then set the bar higher. Unfortunately, it is the level of the expectation bar, not the introductory statement of acceptance, that establishes the tone for our relationships with our children.

What then, exactly, does it mean to accept our children for who they are? More important, why is acceptance integral to effective parenting? How does it affect the goals and expectations we have for our children? Finally, why do many caring parents find acceptance difficult and find themselves in the "I accept you but . . ." trap? For example, parents will tell us they know that each of their children possesses a different temperament, then a moment later they will add, "But we treat each child the same and expect the same from each of our children." Fairness and acceptance are not synonymous with treating each child the same or having the same expectations and goals for each child. Fairness is shown by responding to each child based on that child's particular temperament and needs.

This chapter uses temperament, the inborn qualities of behavior that children bring into the world, as a format to explain the process of acceptance. We could as easily have chosen other strongly biologically driven qualities, such as language, motor, or academic development. Of course, all of these qualities can be affected by actions in the environment, but building resilient mindsets in our children requires an understanding and acceptance of their temperament and development. The chapter concludes with four steps to guide you through this process of acceptance and help you develop and maintain an accepting mindset.

Accepting Our Children: A Foundation for Resilience

The knowledge that we're accepted for who we are brings an inestimable feeling of safety and comfort. Acceptance is rooted in unconditional love and provides an environment for the reinforcement of a resilient mindset. Children who are accepted feel secure in reaching out to others, in seeking support, and in learning how to solve problems. They understand what they have the ability to change in their lives and do not become preoccupied with issues beyond their control. They are willing to take appropriate risks, to change their own negative scripts, to manage mistakes and failures, and to develop an optimistic view of life. Again, acceptance does not equate to letting our children do whatever they want or not setting limits on their behavior. If anything, when children feel accepted, it is easier for them to respond to our requests and limits. They experience these directives in an atmosphere of love and support. It is hard to imagine the emergence of a resilient mindset in a child who does not feel accepted.

The process of acceptance mandates the recognition that from birth, each child is unique. Although each child shares qualities that are similar to all other children, as well as qualities similar to only some, it is the recognition, acceptance, and nurturance of the unique qualities of each child that form the foundation for a resilient mindset. Once you can understand the process of acceptance and the role it plays in nurturing a resilient mindset, you can better develop realistic expectations and goals for your children.

Temperament consists of the inborn qualities that children bring to the world. Just as children have different physical features, they have different temperaments. Temperament influences the means by which children relate and respond to their environment, their styles of learning, and their strengths and vulnerabilities. Some are born, so to speak, more difficult to please, comfort, and satisfy than others. Some adapt well to changes in their immediate environment, while others are easily upset by any modification in routine. Some children demonstrate obvious pleasure at being held or cuddled, while others appear tense and uncomfortable. As children grow, these differences are manifested in the ways they learn, the activities in which they engage, and their ease in making friends. Even their abilities to reflect, to solve problems, and to view the world as being fair or unfair are in part shaped by temperamental qualities.

Acceptance and the Unique Temperament of Each Child

Given the dramatic variations in children's temperament, acceptance takes on an especially important feature for effective parenting. When we were trained as psychologists in the mid-'60s and early '70s, we were taught by our professors that every child was the same at birth, a common theory in those days. In our practice, when parents came to see us about their children, our first assumption used to be "You must be doing something wrong. You must be doing a poor job of parenting." In fact, the second author devoted his doctoral research to examining what exactly it was that mothers of four-year-old children with difficult behavior were doing that was creating "little monsters."

Our training was based on a belief that every child enters the world as a blank slate. Their daily experiences with parents are written on this slate in permanent marker, leading to pleasant, happy personalities and normal behavior for some children, while leading to emotional and behavioral problems for others. In this model, then, parents and other significant adults in the child's life are either given credit for the good work they have done or accused of writing incorrectly on this blank slate.

As a result, many of the first families we worked with received subtle and sometimes not so subtle messages from us of blame and accusation for their children's problems. Then, when our own first children were born, we recognized that "there is more to parenting than meets the eye." When each of us had a second child, we realized how different children are from birth.

The work of two pioneering researchers, Drs. Stella Chess and Alexander Thomas, contributed significantly to the field of child development, temperament, and parenting practices. In their studies of infants, Chess and Thomas discovered that even from birth the temperaments of infants differed noticeably. These differences were evidenced in the ways in which children responded to their parents as well as to their immediate environment. For example, some infants were overactive during the course of the day, while others were calm. Some seemed happy and pleasant throughout the day, while others were often irritable and difficult to comfort. Some infants were at ease, while others were seemingly tense. Some were hypersensitive to touch or sound, but others were receptive. Some rapidly developed predictable routines for eating and sleeping, while others experienced difficulty.

Observing these variations consistently in the infants they studied, Chess and Thomas noted a pattern for three kinds of temperament. They labeled these the "easy" child, the "slow-to-warm-up" child, and the "difficult" child. Although these were not precise categories since not all children fit neatly into one or another of the groups, most children could be classified by general type.

The point is not to pigeonhole our children into categories—a child may display characteristics of one type of temperament in some situations and different characteristics in other situations. The lesson to take from the important work of Chess and Thomas is the recognition and acceptance that children are different temperamentally from birth. Unless we are aware of and respond appropriately to these differences, as outlined here, we will have a very hard time raising a resilient child. If we do not learn to appreciate temperamental differences, we may hold expectations for our children that they cannot meet, leading to further stress, frustration, and conflict.

The Easy Child

Easy children are typically delightful to raise. Parents of easy children often feel excessively competent. In their actions and behavior, these children from birth seem to say to their parents, "Don't worry, I'm going to make you feel like the best parent in the world." Parents may proudly take children with an easy temperament to restaurants, to stores, and on trips. It is as if to say to those around them, "See, this is how you raise children." As children with easy temperaments grow, parents enjoy attending school conferences, predictably hearing the wonderful descriptions of their children offered by teachers. As parents often report, such children are socially adept, quick to learn the rules of behavior, easy to please and satisfy, even-tempered, and good sports. It is little wonder that children with this pattern of temperament, regardless of their intellectual abilities or academic achievement, bring joy to the adults in their lives. We all want to be with people who help us feel competent—temperamentally easy children star in that role.

Although being blessed with an easy temperament does not guarantee success, children with such a temperamental style will typically have an easier time relating to people, developing friendships, functioning at school, learning to solve problems, coping with adversity, and managing stress in comparison with other children. Thus, while biology isn't destiny, certainly for children with easier temperaments, biology powerfully shapes probability.

The Slow-to-Warm-Up Child

As the name implies, children in the second group require additional time to acclimate to new situations or people. Their behavior often prompts observers to refer to them as shy or cautious. These children display a certain hesitancy when confronted with new situations. For example, they are likely to remain physically close and hold on to a parent when entering a store with which they are not familiar. They are likely to remain in the background rather than interact with their peers at a birthday party or Little League game. They are apt to look away when greeted by strangers. They can create the impression that they are aloof and not interested in making friends, but in fact typically this is not the case. Rather, they are somewhat anxious about social interactions. They may spend time just watching others handle a particular task before undertaking it themselves.

Some parents of children with this temperamental style report that they are rarely risk takers. A change in their routine often elicits anxiety and retreat, as was true of Sally, the shy eight-year-old described earlier. Telling a child with this makeup to speak to people and make friends is often experienced as stressful. It is equivalent to asking a child who is unable to float to swim in ten feet of water. Over time, repeated requests such as these result in anger as well as anxiety on the child's part and in frustration on the part of parents, as with Sally's mother.

Researchers such as Dr. Jerome Kagen have demonstrated that slow-to-warm-up children appear to show signs of physical arousal, or what we sometimes refer to as the "fight or flight" phenomenon, over even minor events in their environment. Although the arrival of someone at the front door or entering a new store may not cause a marked level of arousal in most children, it tends to trigger this response in children with a slow-to-warm-up temperament. It is almost as if they stand on the threshold of being stressed, with any out-of-the-ordinary experience pushing them over the edge.

The Difficult Child

Children with difficult temperaments are the most challenging to raise. In contrast to children with easy temperaments, children in this group appear to enter the world telling their parents, "You are in for it!" Such children are often moody and intense in their reactions; in fact, they may overreact to many situations. They appear to experience little pleasure in most activities, are slow to develop consistency in sleeping and eating habits, and may be hypersensitive to touch or sound. Children with this pattern of temperament may complain that labels in their clothing are annoying. Parents of such children often report that their children complain that they are yelling at them when in fact they are not speaking in a loud voice at all.

Children with difficult temperaments often display another characteristic that is particularly problematic for parents and that impedes the process of acceptance. This is the quality of insatiability. Parents of these children often remark that they can spend fifty-nine minutes out of an hour with their child, and the child will remind them of the one minute when they were apart. At one of our workshops, a mother said, "I feel as if my daughter is sucking me dry. I can't satisfy her." The child's insatiability and demandingness drained her mother's energy and impaired her efforts to be supportive and encouraging.

During a family session, Mr. and Mrs. Post described their eight-year-old son, Jeremy, as insatiable. "Jeremy has been difficult from day one. We love him, but nothing we can do will ever satisfy him," commented Mr. Post.

Clearly stung by his parents' statement, Jeremy angrily rebutted, "My father was working late last night, and my mother didn't spend much time with me."

"But, honey," Mrs. Post protested, "we spent nearly the entire evening together until your father came home."

"But you were on the phone with Aunt Ellen."

"I only spoke with Aunt Ellen for ten minutes."

Mrs. Post's words appeared to land on deaf ears. Children with a difficult temperament often have problems with self-regulation and time estimation. In Jeremy's case his insatiability as well as his difficulty estimating time led him to believe that this short phone call comprised much of the evening.

We said to Jeremy, "It sounds as if you feel that your parents sometimes are too busy to spend enough time with you. What could we do to help you with this problem?" Our goal here was to validate Jeremy's perception—not to agree but rather to communicate that we heard, understood, and accepted his point of view. We added, "We've learned that some children need more time, and others less time, with their parents. It sounds as if you're someone who likes to have a lot of time with your parents."

Jeremy immediately broke the tension by responding, "Yeah, I like to be with my parents."

We suggested a regularly scheduled "special time" as an antidote for the experience of insatiability and to help create in Jeremy's mind the expectation and belief that he would receive "enough" of his parents' time and attention.

One of the most poignant descriptions of parenting a temperamentally difficult child was offered by Mrs. Paige. Her six-year-old son, Mitch, was particularly hyperactive. During his first therapy visit, Mitch's poor self-control made it a strain for him to "take a seat" as directed by the well-meaning therapist. Like a tornado, Mitch proceeded to whirl throughout the room. He knocked books off of a shelf. He moved so rapidly from one activity to the next that it was hard to engage him in any type of extended play or conversation. When something tipped over or fell, he was quick to apologize, a behavior he had learned and repeatedly practiced. His insatiability led him to ask to take every toy and game home from the therapist's office, and he became annoyed when told he could not. Unable to engage this child, the therapist was exhausted and frustrated; an hour appeared like three. He could readily empathize with how frustrated and exhausted the parents were.

We began the session with Mr. and Mrs. Paige by asking how their son made them feel. Mrs. Paige tearfully responded, "My son makes me feel like the most inadequate mother in the world. This isn't something new. This is a feeling I had from the moment he was born."

"Why do you say that?" we asked. "What was so difficult about him from birth?"

She relayed, "After Mitch was born, the nurses would bring him in for feeding. I always knew he was coming; I could hear him, like a police siren, wailing down the hall. I watched as my roommate cuddled, played with, and nursed her child. They seemed to be having such a good time. Do you know what it feels like to hold your newborn and he tries to squirm out of your arms?"

"It sounds as if that made you feel that you were doing something wrong."

"I was confused. It seemed to me that I was doing all of the right things, but nothing was working. I started to doubt everything I was doing. Do you know what it feels like to dry off your child with a soft towel after you give him a bath and he begins to scream?"

Mr. Paige attested, "At first I thought it was my wife's problem. If she just tried a little harder or was a little more patient, I thought, Mitch would be better. In fact, there were many times when I blamed my wife for Mitch's behavior. But when I became involved and I also experienced the same difficulty, I realized that Mitch had a problem."

Clearly the Paiges were anguished.

"Do you know what it feels like when the front doorbell or phone rings while your child is sleeping and he wakes up every single time crying and then won't go back to sleep?" Mrs. Paige continued, "I thought that maybe this was how most children behaved. However, when we had our second child and I had the opportunity to experience what my roommate experienced when I had my first child, I realized that something wasn't right. Though I can't help but believe it is my fault, I hate to say this, but part of me also looks at Mitch as damaged goods. Part of me believes there is something wrong with my child that makes it impossible for him to respond to me and to behave well."

It was evident from this admission that Mr. and Mrs. Paige were not aware of the significant temperamental differences among infants and that they had become frustrated and angry with their son at a very early age. As they raised their second child, they began to realize that there was something not right between them and their first child, but they still could not understand what prompted Mitch's behavior. Their lack of understanding compromised acceptance and led to the belief that their child was "damaged goods." Mrs. Paige's description of feeling like "the most inadequate mother in the world" indicated that from the moment she first held Mitch, she and her son had sadly become psychologically estranged.

We tackled the problem first by giving Mr. and Mrs. Paige reading material on children's temperament and asking them to complete a parent temperament questionnaire. Their responses to the questions allowed us to generate a profile of Mitch's temperament. In the next session we delved more into temperament and the coercive power that a child with a difficult temperament wields in shaping the parents' views of their inadequacy. Engaging the Paiges in this discovery was the first step to increasing their recognition and understanding, thereby enabling them to begin the process of accepting their child.

Think about the temperamental patterns of your children: are they easy, slow-to-warm up, or difficult? Have you already recognized these patterns? How have you responded to them? Remember that it is not so important for you to label these patterns of temperament one way or the other as to accept the concept of temperament—and, more important, to accept the temperament of your children.

Acceptance and the Concept of Mismatches: "Goodness of Fit"

We have been intrigued by the differences among the thousands of parents with whom we have worked in accepting the temperamental and developmental qualities of their children. Many of the examples in this book reveal well-meaning parents engaged in a tug-of-war to accept their children for who they are and not what they envision or want them to be. Some parents are caught in the trap of "I accept you but. . . ." In addition to Sally, who was slow to warm up, there was Austin, the child with a difficult temperament; Cindy, whose mother felt she had a "personal vendetta" against her; Mimi, who was seen as insatiable; and John, athletically gifted but whose learning and attentional problems were barriers to school success.

That brings us to George, who was thirteen years old when we first met him. George was referred to us because he had set a fire at school. He was shy, had few friends, and was doing minimally passing school work. George experienced both fine and large motor problems. It was difficult for him to write and read. George's sixteen-year-old sister, Linda, was a seemingly easy child temperamentally, with excellent interpersonal skills, a star athlete and an A student. It was obvious when we met George's parents, Mr. and Mrs. White, that they not only were angry with George but also had inadvertently set into motion the "good child–bad child" family process: for every negative description they provided of George, they offered a positive, loving description of Linda. In a nutshell, they were asking, "Why can't George be more like Linda?"

In a parent session, we asked Mr. and Mrs. White to describe their childhoods and adult lives. It quickly became apparent that their lives and personality styles were a script that Linda appeared to be following.

Mr. White stated, "I was on two teams in high school and still found the time for my studies. George does nothing extra and still can't seem to find enough time to complete his schoolwork."

Mrs. White pointed out that she too had been involved in many activities outside of school. "In college I was the class president one year. Although I had many additional responsibilities, I not only found time for school but also pledged a sorority and worked part-time. George was fired from his only part-time job after just a week because he was late every day."

"If George wanted to, he could turn his life around," Mr. White asserted.

It was clear the Whites had difficulty understanding the challenges that George faced. They viewed themselves as responsible for Linda's successes but were less willing to assume even partial responsibility for George's lack thereof.

"George is lazy and always has been. He never assumes responsibility. He blames everyone else for his shortcomings," commented Mr. White, who did not seem to realize that he was engaging in the same process of blame.

"What is it George does well?" we asked.

The Whites shrugged.

"Well, what does George really enjoy doing? What would he choose to do over any other activity?"

The Whites glanced at each other somewhat uncomfortably. Mr. White responded, "We're somewhat embarrassed to tell you. We just don't think it's the kind of activity that a thirteen-year-old boy should be spending much of his time doing."

Mr. White's discomfort implied that he was referring to some type of antisocial behavior. Fortunately, this was not the case.

His reticence in describing what his son enjoyed doing captured the difficulty he and his wife were having in accepting George's temperament. He bit the bullet and continued, "He likes to garden and take care of plants. That would be OK if he did well in school and was involved in other activities. How can a thirteen-year-old boy be so interested in plants?"

We told the Whites that we could see how upset they were but that George's interest in horticultural activities was not as unusual as they believed and that, if anything, there might be ways for them to join George in these activities. Our intent was to avoid embarrassing or distressing the Whites and to begin to change their mindset and facilitate the process of acceptance.

Rather than finding fault with the Whites' reactions to their son or with George's behavior, it was important to help them understand how they were trapped by their experiences and biases. This trap restricted the process of acceptance. The Whites were blinded by an image that they had of an "ideal" son. Because of this they were unable to accept him. They never allowed that George's feelings, thoughts, and actions were limited and determined by his temperament. By the same token, it was easy for them to accept their daughter because her temperament and behavior matched their own.

The negative scripts of George and his parents were entrenched. Given their histories, the Whites ridiculed George's interests while lamenting his lack of academic and athletic strengths. They balked at accepting their son for who he was. His setting a fire in school was figuratively and literally fueled by the anger and resentment that he harbored toward his parents, as well as a cry for recognition and help. It was telling that George carefully set the fire in a wastepaper basket so that it would not get out of hand.

In our sessions with the Whites, we helped them analyze their unrealistic expectations for George, the source of those expectations, and the frustration and anger that those unmet hopes had bred. Slowly the Whites formulated more realistic expectations and were able to accept George's interests without viewing them as a form of pathology, inadequacy, or failure on their part to instill good values and behaviors in their son.

We can take heart from the fact that a difficult temperament does not always lead to difficulty in parenting. While certain temperamental characteristics define the difficult child, some parents may not experience these so-called difficult qualities as beyond their abilities to manage. The parents' temperamental styles, interests, goals, life history, and expectations influence their perceptions of and reactions to the child's unique style.

Clifford's parents, for example, Mr. and Mrs. Hanover, could not understand why the neighborhood was distressed with the behavior of their extremely hyperactive four-year-old. Clifford's father, a successful businessman, had been extremely hyperactive as a child as well. Clifford's parents viewed this behavior as difficult but tolerable. They recognized that the behavior caused some trouble for their son but did not see his immediate problems as predictive of significant future life problems. Thus, they were more accepting and, accordingly, more effective in parenting Clifford. While their view sometimes made it hard for them to understand why the neighbors were so upset with Clifford's behavior, it also made it much easier for them to accept Clifford and develop a nurturing relationship with him.

Alex, another child with whom we worked, demonstrated many similarities to George's pattern of temperament and history. Instead of taking care of plants, however, Alex found enjoyment in pottery. And in contrast to Mr. and Mrs. White, Alex's mother, an artist, supported and encouraged his creating pottery, looking at it as a way for him to develop self-esteem. She set up a work space in the house with a potter's wheel and a kiln for Alex to create and develop his artistic skills. She recognized that to have a satisfying relationship with Alex, she must reasonably accept and accommodate her son's style, an approach that yielded positive results.

It's common for parents of multiple children to find it easier to relate to one child than to another, as these examples demonstrate. This is the concept of "goodness of fit." Our history, mindset, interests, and temperament dictate how easy or difficult it may be for us to accept any one of our children. Outgoing, gregarious parents may experience stress and tension raising a cautious, reserved child, yet feel quite competent with a child whose temperament is more like theirs.

But the dynamics of accepting our children are not predicated on just similarities in temperament. Goodness of fit is much more complicated. For example, a parent with a history of shy behavior, rather than being empathic with a shy child, may be especially pained and embarrassed by the child's demonstrating characteristics that are to some extent shaming for the parent. Similar tension may exist when achievement-oriented parents, such as the Whites, are raising a child who has difficulty with organization and attention. Children may be accused of laziness and lack of motivation when in fact they are expending a great deal of effort but lack the necessary cognitive skills or temperament to meet parents' expectations or, for that matter, to be more successful in certain life arenas.

These mismatches between parents and children, or the failure of parents to establish a goodness of fit between their style and that of their child, often result in anger and disappointment for all parties. In these situations, some youngsters feel that they have let their parents down. Their sense of failure leads to low self-esteem, poor problem-solving skills, and, ultimately, feeling unloved or unaccepted. This pattern sets in motion the antithesis of the development of a resilient mindset.

A mismatch between parent and child unfortunately can last a lifetime. We met Mr. and Mrs. Larsen, both forty years of age, when they were referred to us by their family physician for marital problems. They were raising two teenage boys. As we listened to their histories, it was evident that Mr. Larsen had been rejected at an early age by his father.

"My father was abusive," he said. "He called me a wimp or a sissy because I didn't like to fight. He told me that if I didn't get into a few fights each year, I probably wasn't sticking up for myself."

When we asked about his mother's stance, he said, "My mother was afraid of my father. He yelled at her too. But if she would come to my aid, he would tell her that she was raising a mama's boy."

Mrs. Larsen listened as her husband spoke. She commented that she had been aware of his childhood but that they had never talked much about its impact on him.

"On one occasion," Mr. Larsen continued, "when I was eight years old, I was beaten up at school. I don't know why it happened; it was just one of those playground things. I told my mother when I came home from school. When my father came home after work, he sent me out to look for this boy and told me not to come home until I had beaten him up. I'm still ashamed at what I did: I found a stick, came up behind this boy, and began hitting him. I had to be pulled away by an adult."

Tears came to Mr. Larsen's eyes as he concluded the story. "The boy's father brought me home and was pretty angry. My father told him to stop complaining, that boys would get into fights. As he closed the door, he told me it was about time I didn't act like a sissy. That's all he said, and then he walked away."

Mr. Larsen explained that he never felt comfortable in conflict, and although he had desperately wanted acceptance from his father, he never achieved this goal. As a teenager, he turned to alcohol, perhaps to dull his psychological pain. Though he graduated from high school, he moved from one job to the next.

"When I met my wife," he said, "I finally found someone who could provide the love, acceptance, and support I hadn't known. I found a job I liked, stopped drinking, and got my life together."

During this period, Mr. Larsen's mother died, and he continued to have little contact with his father. As his own sons reached their adolescent years, the normal stresses of raising teenagers awakened much of the pain he had experienced in his relationship with his father. He began to worry that his sons would grow apart from him as he had done from his father. He turned to alcohol to deaden his worries, but as a consequence his interactions with his wife and children were marked by anger. Fortunately, with the support of his wife, he sought our help.

What soon emerged were Mr. Larsen's unresolved feelings toward his father and his realization that he still wanted his father's acceptance. He resolved to stop drinking. In several family therapy sessions, family members aired their grievances and set in place solutions. Mr. Larsen, however, felt that the only way he could truly remove the burden of his unresolved feelings was to let his father know how he felt and to see if there was an opportunity for possible reconciliation.

We discussed various ways of approaching his communication with his father. After much consideration, Mr. Larsen decided to write his father a letter. Although they had had minimal communication in the previous fifteen years, Mr. Larsen made an effort to change his script toward his father. He took an active role to rid himself of the ghosts of his past. The letter was not accusatory or demanding. It explained his feelings and his desire to reestablish a relationship.

We had discussed in advance the different ways in which his father might react, such as writing a hostile letter in return or not responding at all. We did not expect what occurred: Mr. Larsen's father ripped his son's letter into small pieces, placed the pieces in an envelope, and mailed them back.

Mr. Larsen was not upset as he recited this news. He smiled and stated, "You've often said that you have to focus on what you have control over. I had control over communicating with my father but not his response. I did what I had to do, and now that I know my father's reaction, I can get on with my life and concentrate on making certain I have the best possible relationship with my family." He added with profound insight, "From the time I was born, he couldn't accept me, couldn't love me. He wanted me to be something I could not. I used to think it was my fault, but now I realize it wasn't. I can give up the fantasy of being accepted by my father and concentrate on accepting *my* sons."

Given other life events, including a loving wife who represented the "charismatic adult" in his life and success in work, Mr. Larsen could find acceptance from others, which eventually led him to accept himself. This experience teaches an important lesson: we must accept ourselves before we can begin to accept others. While this book surveys the guideposts for raising resilient children, the examples of Mr. Larsen and others tell us that developing a resilient mindset and acceptance of self is a lifelong endeavor.

Acceptance in the Development of Appropriate Expectations and Goals

Acceptance is the link between parents' love and the process of defining realistic, attainable goals and expectations for their children. We are frequently asked what we consider to be realistic goals and expectations for a four-year-old, for an eight-year-old, or for a thirteen-year-old. Although certain guidelines apply based on developmental principles, goals and expectations should not be determined by a child's chronological age.

For example, most parents would feel comfortable permitting their nine-year-old to cross a busy street, knowing that their child possesses and uses the skills important in crossing streets successfully. However, parents of a nine-year-old who has poor self-control and who is prone to impulsive behavior would be less inclined to allow their child to cross busy intersections without the presence of an older, responsible person. Likewise, we know parents who have no hesitation taking their six-year-old into a store filled with fancy glassware because they are sure the child will not touch anything. However, these same parents would not take their inquisitive, impulsive ten-year-old into the same store, knowing that within a few moments there might be hundreds of dollars of damage, not as the result of their child's purposeful misbehavior but as the result of the child's impulsivity and poor self-control.

The best way we can respond to the question of how to determine realistic expectations is by saying, "First tell us about your child, and then we can provide an intelligent view of appropriate goals and expectations." If parents do not match their expectations with acceptance and appreciation of the unique qualities of their children, then as we have seen, the stage is set for family stress, friction, and the disintegration, rather than the building, of a resilient mindset.

Mr. and Mrs. Cerano sought a consultation about their six-year-old daughter, Larissa. "We can't take Larissa out in public," said Mrs. Cerano. "Trips to supermarkets or department stores are a nightmare. The first thing that happens is she wants us to buy things. If we refuse, she gets upset and eventually has a tantrum."

Mr. Cerano attested, "At first I thought my wife was spending too much time trying to reason with Larissa and making her tantrums worse. Then my wife would become more upset, and she would yell or spank Larissa. I learned my lesson, though. When I took Larissa to the store, even when I threatened a spanking before we even entered the building, she still was excessively demanding and eventually began crying after a few moments."

Based on the recommendation of a friend, "we went out and bought a book on preventing tantrums," said Mrs. Cerano. "The book suggested that we prepare Larissa in advance by telling her that we are going into the store but we are not going to buy anything and please don't ask. Even when she agreed, we still had problems."

It was clear that Larissa's limited capacity for self-control was quickly overwhelmed when enticing materials were placed within sight. The lure of seeing many things that she desired soon eclipsed her promise not to make requests. What ensued, despite the advice of the parenting text, were lengthy arguments in the store that again led to the playing out of the expected negative script, including escalation on Larissa's part, a spanking, and everyone's leaving the store in distress.

A neighbor then proffered another technique that had worked with her child. "She suggested we tell Larissa in advance that if she asks to buy something, we will immediately leave the store," said Mrs. Cerano.

On the surface this approach sounded good. It appeared to promise the avoidance of a screaming match, spanking, and frustration. To the Ceranos' dismay, however, after leaving the store, Larissa quickly began to cry and scream.

"We were so frustrated that we told Larissa we would buy her one item of her choice as long as it wasn't too expensive. Well, this didn't work," said Mr. Cerano. "Larissa's idea of inexpensive just didn't match ours. Once again she ended up demanding and crying."

As we have done with many families, we began by noting to Larissa's parents that the strategies they attempted were good ones for some children but by themselves would likely not work well for Larissa. We introduced the concept of temperament and the importance of beginning by accepting Larissa's temperament. We provided the Ceranos with reading material about the impact of poor impulse control and an insatiable style on children's behavior and relationships with their parents.

At the next session, we began by making certain the Ceranos understood the material they had read. We then explained that given Larissa's temperament and impulsivity, she was not ready to enter a supermarket or department store with them. In those situations, it was more likely than not that she would experience problems. We made the case that their expectations for Larissa were not congruent with her temperament and style.

"I have read the material," said Mr. Cerano, "but I still believe that a six-year-old should be able to control herself. She has friends of the same age who do not have these problems."

We told him, "You raise a very good point, but it's likely that any child with this pattern of temperament would experience difficulty at this age in this type of setting."

Mrs. Cerano responded, "Like my husband, I believed Larissa could control herself if she wanted to but that because she was so demanding, we had spoiled her, given in to her, and she wasn't going to behave. But after reading the material you provided, I am beginning to think I was wrong."

We reinforced Mrs. Cerano's statement by asserting that many six-year-olds can show more restraint than Larissa, but Larissa's inability to do so was part of her temperament and not the result of their spoiling her. It was important for the Ceranos to understand that their difficulty in accepting their daughter's temperament had prompted expectations that Larissa could not meet, even though other children of her age could.

Not being able to take Larissa out with them, they said, would create complications. "It is not always convenient for one of us to stay home or to arrange for a baby-sitter."

"You're absolutely right," we answered. "But consider how frequently your outings, particularly shopping, are disrupted by Larissa's behavior. The disruptions in your relationship with Larissa because of these outbursts are far more inconvenient and disabling than having one of you stay home or arranging for a baby-sitter." We helped the Ceranos comprehend that this pattern of negative behavior between them and their daughter reflected more than just an immediate problem; it was setting up many future conflicts in other family areas.

"But how will Larissa ever learn self-control if she doesn't have experiences in which we set limits?" asked Mr. Cerano.

Again we concurred but qualified. "You're absolutely correct. It's a great question, but think of it this way: When you're just learning to swim, you would swim in the shallow end. If you were just learning to bowl, we could put bumpers in the gutters. The goal of these activities is not only for you to learn but also, in the process, for you to feel safe, successful, and happy."

Taking Larissa into a large supermarket or store at this time was not the best way to teach her limits. It was more likely than not to lead to conflict. We explained that it appeared to be too overwhelming an experience for Larissa, one that would not result in her learning new skills. Instead, we advised them to incorporate several principles that would ease the situation and reinforce a resilient mindset in Larissa.

We suggested that they start small. One way would be to take Larissa into a convenience store, a place from which they can depart rapidly. We encouraged the Ceranos to continue to incorporate choice but to be more specific and less open-ended—for example, "You can have ice cream or a chocolate bar" rather than "You can have something that is not expensive." We also reinforced the importance of reminding Larissa before entering the store of these conditions as well as the consequences should a problem arise—for example, after informing Larissa of the choice, reminding her that if it was difficult for her to do what they said, they would leave the store, and that her crying or screaming would not be of any help. We suggested a number of activities within the home as well, including a process to help Larissa develop self-control.

Mr. and Mrs. Cerano agreed to assume a more proactive, empathic, problem-solving approach in which they accepted Larissa's basic style and temperament and then worked to accommodate themselves, within reason, to that style. Though Larissa's response was not always optimal, the Ceranos' willingness to accept Larissa gave them strength to maintain their chosen course of intervention when push came to shove. At the outset Larissa had some tantrums and fell back on her negative script, but these outbursts were handled calmly. Within several months, Larissa successfully made what her parents termed the "big jump" into larger stores.

Four Steps to Developing an Accepting Mindset with Your Children

Parents can take four helpful steps to nurture the process of acceptance of their children. This course will lead to clearer guidelines for setting appropriate goals and expectations. These four steps are:

1. Become educated.
2. Measure your mindset.
3. Make necessary adjustments.
4. Begin the process of collaboration.

Step One: Become Educated

The key to your effort is to become familiar with the differences in children's temperament, development, and behavior and to use this information proactively in your parenting practices. Many parents concede and demonstrate that they are unaware of these differences, and even those who are superficially aware can fall into the trap of "I accept you but. . . ." In a range of the foregoing examples, well-meaning parents reacted to their son or daughter as if all children were the same: the Ceranos with Larissa, the Thomases with Carl, the Whites with George, the Holts with Mimi, and Ms. Peterson with Cindy, to whom she ascribed a "personal vendetta." If we are unable to understand and subsequently accept children's innate differences, we are likely to expect behaviors and skills of which they are incapable. In such circumstances, a child's inability to accomplish certain tasks (e.g., remain seated) will often be interpreted as willful or manipulative.

Mr. and Mrs. Sargent offer another striking example of what occurs when parents fail to recognize, understand, and accept children's inborn differences. The Sargents had three sons. They characterized their first two, ages sixteen and thirteen, as a "pleasure to raise." The two older boys were outgoing, had "infectious" smiles, had many friends, were excellent athletes, and were solid students.

"If we had stopped having children after the first two, we would have thought we were the most wonderful parents in the world," said Mrs. Sargent.

In contrast, the Sargents described their youngest son, Damon, as "having been born with a frown on his face."

"It is almost impossible to satisfy Damon unless he gets his own way," Mr. Sargent remarked.

On an intellectual basis, the Sargents recognized—and even verbalized—that Damon had taught them how different children could be. However, their weariness and disappointment led to the *but* and interfered with their ability to appreciate the impact of these differences on Damon's behavior and development.

"I felt terrible," said Mr. Sargent. "We were looking at pictures from a family outing. There wasn't one picture in which Damon was smiling. He always seems to have this scowl on his face. I just turned to him in front of his brothers and asked, 'Why can't you ever put on a smile?' He stuck out his tongue and walked away."

Damon's coping strategy was to act as if he didn't care.

In an individual therapy session, Damon, who typically presented a tough exterior accentuated by an "I don't care" attitude, uncharacteristically communicated his feelings. He had recently overheard his two brothers complaining that the family would be much better off if he hadn't been born.

Damon teared up as he confided with much emotion and insight, "I think my parents wish they'd never had me. They said that I don't smile, but they never smile when they're with me. I see them smiling when they're with my brothers. I don't think they love me."

Damon's revelation is a powerful summary of what occurs when we fail to accept our children for who they are. Lack of acceptance is a breeding ground for defeatist patterns of behavior. To begin to break that cycle, we asked Damon to spend the next two weeks in a "secret experiment." We asked him not only to observe whether his parents smiled when they were with his siblings but also to notice whether there were times they smiled in his presence as well. Damon returned two weeks later and reported that a number of times his parents had smiled in his presence.

"I told my mom a joke. She laughed and told me it was funny."

We then set up a second secret experiment. Damon agreed, this time, that he would make an effort to smile and to get his parents to smile. We made a list of behaviors in which he could engage, including telling jokes, that might result in smiles on everyone's part. We also explained to Damon's parents that we were conducting a secret experiment and that in the next session, before we revealed the details and the results, we would ask them to report on anything they had noticed different in the past two weeks.

Two weeks later as Damon and his parents entered our office, Damon actually had a smile on his face.

We asked if the Sargents had noticed anything different in the past two weeks.

His mother said, "Damon seems happier. I have noticed him smiling."

Damon piped up, "Well, Mom, I'm smiling because you're smiling! That was the secret experiment: to see if I could make you smile."

As parents, we must educate ourselves to the unique qualities that our children bring from birth. By doing so, we foster acceptance. We can use this knowledge to foster a resilient mindset.

Step Two: Measure Your Mindset

Can you remember a time before your first child was born? In the professional field we refer to this period as B.C., not "before children" but "before chaos"! Certainly we were all concerned about having a healthy baby. Most of us envisioned our children as bright, happy, and successful. We also all thought about what wonderful parents we would be. We would be fair, nurturing, democratic, and loving. We would meet our children's needs and, even in trying situations, never give in to anger. These descriptions are rooted in our history and reflect the dreams and expectations for children that all parents hold. When children don't meet those dreams and expectations, parents are put to the test.

In our clinical work, when we ask parents about the images and dreams they had held for their unborn children, it is not unusual for them to eventually recognize that some of the tension they are experiencing with their youngsters is based on their view that these expectations were unfulfilled.

To take a measure of your own mindset, try the following exercise. Divide a sheet of paper in half. On one side, write down the behaviors and feelings that you had *hoped* to view in your child (e.g., kind, caring, respectful, outgoing, happy, content). On the other side, write the behaviors and feelings that have *emerged*. In some instances what you had hoped for and what you observe will be very similar. In other cases you may discover large differences. For example, although you might have expected an outgoing, spirited child, you perceive that your child is shy and unhappy.

Next, on a sheet of paper divided into thirds, first write down how you *thought* you would respond and react to your child (e.g., patient, kind, loving, never angry). Then, write down how you *actually* respond. In the third section, note the instances in which a mismatch between your expectations and your child's behavior leads to actions and feelings on your part that you had not considered. This exercise will help you see more clearly what role your dreams and wishes have played in determining your feelings of acceptance or disappointment toward your children.

When Ms. Langston, a single parent with two teenage daughters, did this exercise, she wrote that when she had dreamed about having children, she pictured them as outgoing and socially at ease. While this dream was realized with Lena, her fifteen-year-old, it was not with Wendy, her twelve-year-old. Wendy tended to be somewhat aloof, less affectionate and more difficult to satisfy. On paper, she described her reactions to the behavior of Lena as "proud, happy, made me feel like a good mother, I liked to be with her." In stark contrast, when describing her feelings about Wendy, she wrote: "disappointed, did I do something wrong?, she doesn't try hard enough to say hello, I don't enjoy taking her places, embarrassing."

Like many other parents who have engaged in this activity, Ms. Langston was surprised by the intense feelings that emerged and how different they were for each daughter. The realization of these contrasting feelings versus expectations helped Ms. Langston begin to appreciate how her early dreams of her daughters influenced the ways in which she responded to them and her ability to help them develop a resilient mindset.

As you consider your reaction to your children's behaviors and feelings, it may help to refer back to the empathy exercise in Chapter 2 in which you described your children's view of you. Ms. Langston wrote that she thought Lena saw her as "supportive, available, loving." For Wendy she wrote: "critical, angry, disappointed." Ms. Langston began to cry as she read these words and truly recognized for the first time that her dreams and expectations for her daughters were powerful forces determining not only her interactions with them but also her misguided belief that it was her younger daughter who had to change, not herself.

Step Three: Make Necessary Adjustments

If there is a good match between your expectations and what your children can "deliver," then you are one of the few parents who do not need to proceed any further. When our children behave in ways that match our expectations, it is easy for us to accept them. If, on the other hand, there is a mismatch, then you must be the one to initiate change.

There is nothing wrong with holding wonderful dreams and wishes for our children. However, dreams can quickly become unrealistic, leading to parental perceptions of failed hopes and, in some cases, "broken promises." We must be able to step back and modify our expectations and dreams in keeping with our knowledge of the inborn temperament and style of our children. If we do not, our relationship with our children will be marked by ongoing anger and disappointment, feelings that compromise the emergence of a resilient mindset.

Making adjustments is similar to Principle One in Chapter 4 concerning changing negative scripts. That is, if our children are to change their behavior, in most instances we as parents must first have the courage to change our own mindsets and behaviors. Once we understand the different temperaments in children and how our expectations may conflict with our child's style, the next step is to explore what we can do differently so that our children will feel more accepted and our expectations for them will become more realistic.

Carl, the ten-year-old who could not sit still at the dinner table, and his father illustrate this point. When Carl's father learned to accept that his son could not remain seated for the entire meal and permitted him to get up from the table when necessary, Carl's behavior and his relationship with his father took a sharp turn for the better. Related to that development, Carl found it easier to get to school on time when he was appointed "assistant to the principal."

Carl's case and many others in this book show that the various components of the mindset of parents who foster a resilient mindset in their children are interwoven. The threads of this fabric, which include empathy, feeling loved, changing negative scripts, and feeling accepted, gain their strength from being joined together.

Ms. Langston sought ways to change her attitude and behavior when she recognized the disappointment she felt about Wendy and her problems accepting her daughter. One of the first attitudinal changes was simply Ms. Langston's acceptance that Wendy was not Lena and probably would never be as outgoing or as easy to please as her older sister. This accommodation did not result in Ms. Langston's "giving up" on Wendy or assuming that Wendy would "never change," but rather it led her to be more realistic about what to expect. At our suggestion, she instituted "special times" with both girls. She stopped telling Wendy to "cheer up" or to "greet people with a smile." She modeled empathy and told Wendy that she knew she did not always feel comfortable with some people. She reassured her that as she grew up, she was likely to find people with whom she would feel more at ease.

Ms. Langston also began to notice and reinforce Wendy's strengths. Although Wendy tended to be aloof with people, she loved animals. Her mother made a point to comment to Wendy how responsible she was with the family pets. A few years later when Wendy looked for a part-time job, she encouraged her to apply at a local pet shop. Wendy followed through, was hired, and received positive feedback from the store owner. The job also involved interaction with customers, but since this occurred in Wendy's "territory," she found it easier to speak with others and began to develop a more outgoing, interpersonal style.

Ms. Langston reported one further modification in her view. In the past, Wendy's moodiness or her desire to be alone angered her mother and was interpreted as Wendy's way of "getting even." As she put it, "One day Wendy can be so sweet, and the next day it's as if you don't even exist. She just goes to her room and wants to be all by herself."

Ms. Langston learned to accept that Wendy's moodiness and her change in behavior from one day to the next were not signs of willfulness or manipulativeness but rather were part of Wendy. This recognition led to a reduction not only in anger but also in feelings of guilt that she had done something wrong as a mother. The falloff in anger and frustration made it easier for Wendy and her mother to find positive common ground; however, it was Ms. Langston who made the change happen.

The importance of parents' making adjustments is also illustrated by the Wilson family and their nine-year-old son, Jimmy. Mr. Wilson loved sports, particularly football and basketball.

He was able to articulate clearly the dreams he had held for his yet-to-be-born son: "I can remember accompanying my wife for an ultrasound when she was pregnant with Jimmy. When the doctor told us we were going to have a boy, I envisioned him playing all of the major sports."

Jimmy was a good athlete and, similar to his father, his favorite sport was football. During one game, Jimmy caught two touchdown passes. He also dropped a pass.

When the game ended, Mr. Wilson's first comment was, "How come you dropped that pass?"

He recalled during our session, "Jimmy looked devasted and walked away. I thought that by focusing on his mistakes, I was helping. Obviously, I wasn't."

This tack seems to be favored by many parents: Let's focus on what you are doing wrong so it can be fixed. In essence, Mr. Wilson approached his son with a chisel in hand, always ready to chip away.

Mr. Wilson's inability to see and reinforce Jimmy's strengths was crippling. His negativity was so strong and his relationship with his son was suffering so greatly that he and his wife eventually came in for consultation.

What emerged was the picture of a father who had been, by his own description, a "mediocre" player, one who was often selected next to last when captains chose up teams. With our assistance, he came to realize that he wanted Jimmy to be the star athlete he had never been. In many ways his dreams and expectations for Jimmy were his efforts to rewrite the frustrating childhood he had experienced. Unfortunately, this rewriting was done at the expense of accepting Jimmy for who he was, a solid athlete but not a superstar.

Given the unmet needs for recognition from his own childhood, Mr. Wilson's expectations for Jimmy were unrealistic, placed strain on their relationship, and caused difficulty in the critical link of acceptance. Our counseling sessions helped him better understand the dynamics of his relationship with Jimmy, and he began to alter his discourse. He vowed to say more positive things and, in some situations, not to say anything negative unless his son brought up a particular issue himself. In a relatively brief time, the number of positive comments he offered Jimmy far exceeded any negative statements. Even the latter were increasingly experienced by Jimmy as "constructive advice."

During our final session, Mr. Wilson noted, "I was almost brought to tears when Jimmy told me how much he enjoyed the fact that, unlike a lot of other dads, I came to all of his sporting events."

As these families illustrate, we must separate our dreams for our children from who they are as individuals. We must be careful not to impose expectations on them based on our own needs, interests, or goals. If we are stuck in a pattern in which our dreams and wishes blind us from appreciating and accepting our children for who they are, we must find the insight and courage to change.

Step Four: Begin the Process of Collaboration

Though the responsibility of closing the gap between your dreams and reality falls on your shoulders, it is also important that you work collaboratively with your children to develop appropriate goals and expectations. So, while the previous step emphasized the need for you to initiate changes, we don't want you to form the impression that your children are bystanders. Once you learn to accept your children for who they are, gain a clearer picture of each child's unique temperament and style, and begin to make changes in your relationship, it is easier for you to engage with them in problem-solving discussions of appropriate goals and expectations. A sense of control over one's life, the development of self-discipline, and engagement in problem solving are core components of a resilient mindset, and all three are advanced by the reasonable involvement and input of your children in formulating goals and solutions.

This book has offered numerous examples of children assisting parents in formulating expectations and goals. This partnership is best achieved when you can accept your children for who they are and not be sidetracked by what you want them to be. For example, once Barry and Len's parents gave up unrealistic dreams of how brothers should behave, they were able to engage their sons in deciding which television programs to watch and how to take turns sitting in the front seat of the car. When Mr. and Mrs. Smith appreciated that Gregory's poor showing with organization and neatness was very much a part of his temperament and style, they were able to abandon their stream of complaints and engage their son in developing solutions to the problem.

The aforementioned story of Mr. and Mrs. Castle and their son, Joel, also fits the bill. Joel was the boy who quit almost every activity he started. His parents used his eagerness to take saxophone lessons as an opportunity to discuss their concerns about his lack of follow-through and tendency to give up as soon as the going got tough. In the course of their conversations, they were able to encourage Joel to develop a plan of action. In essence, the ability of Joel's parents to moderate their anger toward him permitted Joel to articulate reasonable goals and consequences for his behavior. This reinforced in him a feeling of responsibility and accountability.

Finally, remember four-year-old Robert, who had tantrums before going to bed each night because he was afraid of nightmares? Robert's parents held that four-year-olds no longer required a night-light and incorrectly interpreted his tantrums as an attempt to agitate them. However, when Robert was asked what he thought would help him to be less fearful at bedtime, he proposed a night-light and a photo of his parents by his bed. His solution proved very successful.

You'll find, as we have, that children working in concert with their parents have an impressive ability to formulate goals and expectations for themselves that are not just realistic but also creative and challenging. The fear harbored by some parents that their children will want to establish objectives that are "too easy" is often unfounded. In fact, when parents convey expectations in an accepting, loving, supportive manner, children are often motivated to exceed those expectations.

7

Experiencing Success

Nurturing Islands of Competence

While waiting to board a flight in a crowded airport, a young child, followed by his mother, walked through the waiting area. The unsteadiness of his gait told that he had just learned to take his first steps. He happily toddled from place to place with his mother close behind. His steps, cautious and wobbly, were accompanied by frequent squeals of glee. Often he fell backward on his bottom; without hesitating he grabbed whatever was nearby—a suitcase, even passengers' legs—and pulled himself up. The joy on his face as well as that of his mother telegraphed that in their minds this young boy had accomplished the equivalent of climbing Mount Everest.

The instinct to walk, accompanied by perseverance, was leading this child to new mastery. But even more important, he experienced the success of walking as an island of competence, a key ingredient in developing a resilient mindset. Through this and other early experiences, this child was developing a sense of accomplishment, a reservoir of emotional strength that he would tap to help him face and master routine as well as stressful life events. Islands of competence are activities that children do well, enjoy doing, receive positive regard for doing, and, most important, recognize as personal strengths.

Even passengers were caught up in this young child's adventuresome jaunt through the airport, patting him on the back and smiling. One elderly man gave him a thumbs-up, which prompted the boy to look at his own hand and then attempt to imitate the gesture. Most likely the child did not understand the meaning of "thumbs up," but from the man's facial expression he appeared to glean that the thumb in the air was positive, and in response his own smile broadened. For a few moments this child's energy, enthusiasm, and mastery brought pleasure to everyone in his view.

All of us can recall the satisfaction we and our children experienced as they encountered and mastered developmental challenges. Most of us can remember our children taking their first steps, pulling themselves up for the first time in the crib, or scooting around the room in a walker, like an explorer hungry for new discoveries. Most of us can recall our children, like the little boy in the airport, persevering despite repeated falls as they learned to walk; hitting the ball with a baseball bat, even if the ball traveled no more than a few feet; building a tower of blocks; skating across an ice rink; learning to ride a bicycle—all moments of great pride.

At every age, children face countless daily situations that can and do bring them a sense of accomplishment and pride. For many, their literal and figurative falls are met with continued perseverance until they master the chosen activity. This experience of success is another powerful component of a resilient mindset. Resilient children relish their successes. Each accomplishment reinforces future efforts and ultimately achievement, as a positive cycle is set in motion. We readily join our children in this process, encouraging them with our words and affection.

What begins as instinct, with perseverance leads to mastery, success, and, in the developmental process just discussed, an island of competence. For the child in the airport, until walking becomes routine, the pleasure derived from the activity and the success experienced in moving from place to place foster a resilient mindset. This experience promotes a general sense of pride and fills a well of perseverance the child can draw from as each new challenge is faced. In this way, success builds upon success; each new accomplishment reinforces self-esteem.

In the best of all worlds, the celebratory process observed in the airport would continue day after day, marking the child's developmental milestones as well as life accomplishments, and nurturing a strong, resilient mindset. Although it may happen in some cases, this ideal is not the pattern for many children. Children, their parents, and their teachers provide personal meaning to accomplishments. We must remember that while success is important, equally important are parents' and children's perceptions of their successes.

This chapter exposes five common obstacles that children confront in experiencing success and nurturing islands of competence. Then you'll learn five principles that you can use to guide your interactions with your children to reinforce their islands of competence. Keep in mind that the ways in which you and your children view success are directly related to a resilient mindset. For success to engender an island of competence and a general sense of accomplishment requires more than simply a "successful experience." When you are able to understand your perceptions and those of your children, you will be in a better position to support their islands of competence.

One framework that has been most helpful to parents and professionals in articulating the different processes by which parents and children view success is *attribution theory*. This theory places the spotlight on the factors to which we attribute our successes and mistakes. Not only is the accuracy of our attributions important, so too are the words and ideas we use to shape those attributions. The importance of the former is obvious and is explored in a number of obstacles covered in this chapter. The latter, however—the semantics—is somewhat more difficult to understand.

Semantics refers to the difference in meaning inferred as the words used to describe an experience vary. For example, a supervisor may describe your work as "careful" and appreciate the time and patience you put into the job, while another reviewer may define the same pace of work as "slow" and request that you "speed up." The pace of your work is no different, but the interpretations of the beholders vary considerably, as do the messages provided by the observers to you.

The attributions that we make regarding ourselves and those around us are shaped by our life experiences, knowledge, understanding, mindset, and even physical factors. For example, most of us interpret daily life events more negatively when we are feeling under the weather. The lessons of attribution theory in dealing with mistakes are probed in Chapter 8. This chapter takes on the implications for success—nurturing islands of competence and developing a resilient mindset.

As we have documented, children with resilient mindsets possess high self-esteem. They feel a sense of control over their lives and believe within reason that they are masters of their destiny. They share a belief that what transpires in their lives is based in great part on the choices and decisions they make. They perceive success as rooted in their efforts and ability. Research about attribution theory supports this dynamic. For example, when children with high self-esteem learn to ride a bicycle, obtain a good grade in school, score a goal, or perform impressively in a concert, they typically acknowledge the help of the adults in their lives but believe that they are the influential architects in determining positive outcomes. They assume realistic credit for what they have accomplished.

Obstacles to Nurturing Islands of Competence

The portrait just described is noticeably different for many children because of either their temperament, negative feedback they have received, poor choices, or parental influence. For them the road to success is filled with twists, turns, and bumps, as delineated here. As you review each of these obstacles, keep an open mind about the role they may play in your family.

Obstacle One: The Inability to Experience the Joy of Success

Previous chapters discussed the concept of temperament particularly as it relates to insatiability, impulsivity, or shyness. However, there is also a quality of temperament that influences feelings of success. For reasons that are not well understood, from a young age some children simply don't experience the joy of success. Often this is true of children with severe depression. Yet, many children who are not depressed simply view the world through mud-colored glasses.

Imagine how you would feel if your accomplishments, though praised and reinforced by others, did not give you joy or pleasure. The process by which mastery fosters success, an island of competence, and ultimately a resilient mindset is derailed for these children because of their inability to experience the joy of success. These children are quick to discount any accomplishments or abilities.

The great mystery that these children pose for us is the lack of an observable explanation for their mindset. The best explanation we can offer is temperament, a biological quality that impedes but does not necessarily prevent children from experiencing success as successful. The case of Andrew, a nine-year-old with whom we worked, exemplifies this problem and one path toward a solution.

Andrew, a fourth-grader, was quite bright but had mild learning problems. His daily school experiences, however, were not significantly negative. He managed to succeed in a regular classroom with tutorial support. He had a number of friends and was an accomplished athlete sought out as a teammate on the playground and in group sports. Yet, from a very young age it was clear that Andrew experienced difficulty with the joy of success. The "bigger the deal" his parents made about his successes, the more bland and negative was Andrew's response. During counseling, Andrew described taking very little pleasure in life's accomplishments and everyday activities.

The following memorable exchange took place during one of our sessions. The previous week, we had discussed islands of competence and asked Andrew to think about something that he was successful at doing and felt good about. Andrew opened this session by saying, "I thought about what you said last week and decided that I am not good at anything." He then crossed his arms and stared straight ahead.

"You are absolutely not good at anything?" we asked.

"Yes, there is nothing I am good at!"

It was clear that Andrew was digging in his heels and perhaps expecting us to try once again to talk him into "feeling good." Instead we took a different approach: we decided to change our script so that perhaps Andrew could change his.

"Well, if you're sure you're not good at anything, then we believe we've found something you *are* good at."

"Nope, I'm not good at anything."

"Well, we think you're the first child we have met who is good at being good at absolutely nothing."

Andrew had to think about that for a moment. Seizing the opportunity, we continued, "To see if that's the case, we better make a list of everything anyone could be good at and make sure it doesn't contain something you're good at."

Andrew quickly joined in, asserting "I'm not good at soccer, school, baseball . . ."

Pulling out a pad and pencil, we interrupted Andrew.

"We'll have to make a list. In fact, there are so many things people could be good at that we probably should explain this to your mother and have you take the list home. With your parents' help, write down everything you can think of that someone could be good at to make certain you're not."

Andrew agreed, and we had his mother join us. She looked quizzical as we explained Andrew's assignment for the week, but she agreed to help him make a list of everything anyone could be good at to make certain he wasn't. Andrew left the session smiling.

A week later, instead of returning with pages of items, Andrew produced a single sheet, listing about a dozen things. As he entered the room, he held up the list and proclaimed, "We found some things that I am good at!"

"Are you sure?"

He repeated that he had discovered a number of things, including a few school and athletic activities, that he had decided he was "good at." He then proudly told us about the number one thing on his list: "We also decided that I am the very best in our family at making my mother angry quickly!"

Andrew had begun the process of examining and changing his seemingly hollow experience of success.

Another nine-year-old, Jack, also ran up against this obstacle. Jack played on the same Little League team as the first author's son. Jack struck out all eight times he was at bat during his first four Little League games. Almost any child would find this performance discouraging, but like Andrew, Jack was temperamentally blinded to experiencing success.

In his first at bat in the fifth game, he hit a single and ran to first base. His coach, standing by the bag, patted Jack on the shoulder and said, "Nice hit." Although this should have been Jack's moment of glory, instead of acknowledging his coach's words with a smile or a thank-you, he looked sad and said, "I think the pitcher threw the ball soft to me."

In contrast to the child in the airport who appeared to experience joy and excitement with each step he took, Jack experienced success in the absence of joy. He had come to view success as something over which he had little if any control. It wasn't that he hit a single based on his skills; for some reason, he attributed his hit to the pitcher's throwing the ball softly. Jack's inability to experience the joy of success had negatively shaped his mindset. In Jack's mind, success was not truly his.

Obstacle Two: Reinforcing Low Self-Esteem

Some children truly struggle to master challenges or activities at home, in school, or on the playground. Often, their general lack of success leads them to attribute whatever success they do attain to luck, chance, or fate, all factors outside of their control. This reduces their confidence that they will be capable of succeeding in the future. This obstacle is often encountered when children have a temperamental basis for their pessimism, and the problem is exacerbated by the struggles these children experience to feel competent or capable.

For example, when Jack said that "the pitcher threw the ball soft" to him, not only was he minimizing his specific achievement owing to his lack of a joyful experience, but also he was perpetuating his belief that success would elude him in the future. In essence, he assumed that since he was lucky to get a hit, he would be even less likely to hit the ball again. Laboring under such doubt and pessimism limits the opportunity for success, the building of an island of competence, and the development of a resilient mindset.

Mr. and Mrs. Stern came to see us about their eight-year-old daughter, Samantha, who had a number of learning disabilities and was doing poorly at school. Her parents, however, were especially concerned about Samantha's increasing tendency to "downplay" her achievements.

"Even when Samantha does well on a spelling test, she tells us she was lucky and it probably won't happen again. She certainly isn't viewing her world through rose-colored glasses. She is becoming so pessimistic about herself," said Mrs. Stern.

Mr. Stern remarked, "At first I thought we were placing too much pressure on Samantha, so that when she did well, she made excuses for it so we wouldn't expect her to be successful all the time. However, now I wonder if she really believes that she isn't a very capable learner and that when she does earn a good grade, it was simply luck."

Mrs. Stern pointed out, "It's not just at school." She then relayed an exchange she had with Samantha at home.

"I got upset the other day when Samantha had a friend over and they were playing checkers. Samantha won the first game and told her friend that she was just lucky."

"How did her friend respond?" we asked.

"I don't know," said Mrs. Stern. "But she didn't stay very long. I asked Samantha, 'Why can't you realize that you weren't lucky when you won, that you may be a very good player?' It only made her angry. She shouted, 'I was lucky! I'm *not* a good player.'"

Mr. Stern added, "We know that Samantha often feels insecure, but you would think that earning a good grade on a test or winning a game would help her to feel better. Instead, she can't seem to accept these good things. Why would a child do that?"

We explained to the Sterns that children may minimize their successes for a variety of reasons. Alluding to what Mr. Stern had said, we noted that some children in fact downplay their accomplishments out of concern that more and more will be expected of them. (This obstacle is discussed next.) We also emphasized that parents may not be pressuring or expecting more of their children, but children interpret things in their own way, based in part on their temperament and experience.

In Samantha's case it appeared that she actually believed that success was a fluke. This often occurs when children struggle at school and don't experience as many successes as those around them. Despite teachers' best efforts to help each child succeed, most children are well aware when they don't perform at the level of others.

To help the Sterns understand the mindset of children with low self-esteem, we explained attribution theory and emphasized that many children with school struggles dismiss a good test score with such comments as "I was lucky" or "The teacher made the test easy." Conspicuously absent is the belief that the child contributed in some fashion to his or her success.

Children facing this obstacle come by this proclivity naturally. Since they have had so few successful experiences, it is difficult for them to accept success as a predictor of future outcome. Given their limited confidence, they often lack a sense of ownership for their experiences and lives and thus do not believe that they have the inner resources to make things better.

In our interview with Samantha, we witnessed firsthand what her parents had described. As we talked, Samantha successfully completed a jigsaw puzzle in a relatively brief amount of time. When we complimented her, she answered with the negative script often heard by her parents: "I was lucky."

"Why do you say that?" we asked.

She answered, "I don't know if I will be able to do it again."

Samantha reiterated her belief that her achievements were luck, and despite our efforts to offer a logical explanation, she steadfastly maintained this position.

A lucky experience is just that; although luck may lead to success, the attribution of that success as random will not foster an island of competence or a resilient mindset. We knew that in our work with Samantha and her parents, we would have to devise strategies for changing this self-defeating attitude.

We reviewed with the Sterns the principles of empathy, effective communication, and changing negative scripts as a means of beginning to change Samantha's mindset. We suggested that from now on, when Samantha attributes her success to luck, instead of attempting to convince her otherwise, they first empathize and validate her expressed belief.

We recommended that they tell Samantha, "We know that you feel you were lucky when you do well on a test or when you win a game, but we wonder if you really were lucky. Maybe other things helped you to do well." We stressed that validating what a child says is not the same as agreeing with the child. When you begin with validation, children are more likely to listen to an alternative perspective.

In our next session with the Sterns, they happily reported a small shift in Samantha's perception of success. They noted that after they validated her feeling of being lucky, she again said that she felt she was just lucky when she won a game. However, the following conversation ensued:

"We know that you feel that way, but we wonder if there may be other reasons you did well. Do you know what we think?" asked Mr. Stern.

"What?"

"Well, you may not agree, and that's OK," said Mr. Stern. Giving permission in advance for a child to disagree is a strategy that often diminishes defensiveness and opens the child to new ideas. Mr. Stern continued, "We think that when you earn a good grade or win a game, you might not just have been lucky, but rather you did a good job studying or playing the game."

Samantha answered, "I don't know."

Mrs. Stern then asked, "Do you know why we would like you to think about this?"

"No, why?"

"We think that if you feel that anything good that happens was just luck, then you won't enjoy yourself as much or you won't be as confident about doing OK on the next test or game. It takes a lot of the fun away from doing well."

"But I do think I was lucky."

"We know," said Mr. Stern, "but we still wonder if it's more than luck. It's just something to think about."

Samantha responded, "I'm not sure, but maybe I'll think about it."

Mr. and Mrs. Stern were pleasantly surprised by Samantha's willingness to entertain an alternative view. We encouraged them to explain this process to Samantha's teacher in the hope that she too could help Samantha begin to reattribute her success. The Sterns' initial conversation with Samantha laid the foundation for continued discussion. Samantha slowly accepted that not all of her success was outside of her control. By helping Samantha attribute success as internal, the Sterns facilitated her ability to experience the joy of success and to form a resilient mindset.

The importance and lifelong impact of our attributions were highlighted by a mother who attended one of our parenting workshops. She declared that our description of attribution theory "really hit home." She had recently returned to college after dropping out eighteen years earlier. She was candid in stating that she had left because she thought she was not capable of doing the work. Then, as her children grew up, she felt an urge to return to college part-time.

She revealed, "I was scared, but I said that I would begin by taking one course and see what happens. I took my first test last week and got it back today. I couldn't believe it, but I earned an A−."

"How did you feel about this grade?" we asked.

"The first thing I did was check to see if this was *my* test. Then I looked to see if the professor had added my score correctly. Then I actually said to myself that the professor must feel sorry for me and gave me a better grade. Finally, I said that if this *was* my test, I was lucky to earn an A−; I probably won't be able to do it again."

"How has the information we've been discussing about attribution changed your mindset?" we asked.

She said simply, "I guess the people who wrote about attribution theory knew all about me. Now I have to work on accepting my successes."

Obstacle Three: Misattributing Success

In a desperate effort to deflect feelings of low self-esteem, some children choose negative activities as their goals for experiencing success. For example, a child with weak academic performance may become the class clown to deflect the teacher's attention away from his abilities. Children and teens engaging in antisocial activities, joining gangs, or committing status offenses are other examples. These are all activities at which some children can be "very successful," yet at a very high price. This type of success creates a false sense of security in the child or adolescent and does not ultimately foster a resilient mindset. Although some children who engage in these behaviors may be rated as having "very good self-esteem," their so-called esteem is likely to be hollow and incompatible with a resilient mindset.

Brett, an eighth-grader, exemplifies this problem. Brett was referred to us because of his poor performance in school. His teachers suspected attention deficit hyperactivity disorder (ADHD) owing to the disruptive nature of his behavior in class. However, as we reviewed Brett's history with his parents, the early signs of ADHD were not apparent.

Brett had performed well in school up through third grade. From that point forward, he began to falter, and his behavior in class became progressively more disruptive. Elementary teachers frequently referred to him as the class clown. Fortunately, Brett possessed a good sense of humor, and often his antics were entertaining not only to his classmates but also to the faculty.

Brett nevertheless continued to struggle academically. Upon entering middle school, he became overwhelmed. In reaction, his humor became increasingly sarcastic and his behavior more noncompliant. He began violating curfew, staying out late, and experimenting with drugs and alcohol.

Though he tried to mask his academic weaknesses with his "pseudo island of competence," disruptiveness, he couldn't disguise the fact that he was lagging behind his classmates. Based on Brett's history, we suggested a neuropsychological evaluation to better understand the causes of his struggles. The evaluation revealed a conceptual-based learning disability, a problem that often manifests itself by middle elementary school and causes children to have difficulty with reasoning, judgment, and comprehension as the demands of school increase.

Though he was resistant at first, by the close of the assessment we were able to engage Brett in a discussion about his behavior and feelings. We told him "The testing suggests that although you are quite intelligent, Brett, you require more time to form and understand ideas. As school became more difficult, your teachers didn't understand this problem, but you knew the work was getting much harder."

He responded, "So, you're saying it's my teachers' fault."

"We are not suggesting anyone is at fault," we said, "just explaining why school became more difficult. What we don't understand is why your behavior became more disruptive."

With that Brett responded insightfully, "I'd rather misbehave than be dumb."

Brett's misbehavior was his strategy for coping with the frustration of being unable to perform well at school. We met with Brett's parents and teachers and formed a plan to provide Brett with support at school. We also jointly tried to identify socially acceptable activities at which Brett could succeed so that he could begin to rebuild his self-esteem.

Obstacle Four: Setting the Bar Too High

Some parents view B grades as success, while others respond negatively. We should of course encourage our children to perform their very best, but we also must remember that success is often an experience that is independent of the level of performance. If we want our children to achieve higher grades, we must help them feel successful first with the grades that they are earning.

It is not always easy to understand why children minimize or excuse their successes. We often begin our search, as in the first two obstacles, by examining the child's life and mindset, yet we know that other factors contribute to children's attribution of success and to their sabotaging the achievement. For instance, let's look back to Mary, the thirteen-year-old first described in Chapter 2. Here the root problem wasn't temperament or negative experience but rather that her parents set the academic bar too high. They found her less-than-perfect grades hard to accept and offered their love contingent upon her raising her scores. Things eventually improved as the Brewsters became more empathic and supportive.

Before that, however, Mary had demanded "Why should I get good grades? They're never good enough for my parents, and then my parents just put more pressure on me."

"Why do you think they feel this way?" we asked.

With much perceptiveness, she observed, "I think when I get good grades, it makes my parents feel like good parents. I wish they would just love me for who I am."

The negative response of Mary's parents to her suboptimum grades resulted in Mary's experiencing little joy or satisfaction in her school success. For her, success was a means of buying her parents' acceptance, but at a price of her becoming increasingly angry or having to perform beyond her capabilities. It was only after Mary's parents lowered the bar that she could find genuine happiness in her achievements.

Obstacle Five: Parents Alone Defining a Successful Experience

George, another thirteen-year-old, who was introduced in the last chapter, likewise found the experience of success tainted by well-meaning parents. George had difficulty in school but enjoyed gardening and taking care of plants. This was one of the few areas that brought him feelings of pleasure and success. But it was not one that was admired or reinforced by his parents. They heaped praise on his older sister for her scholastic and athletic accomplishments but tended to demean George's interest in gardening. Thus, any feelings of success he might have experienced in the activities he enjoyed were diminished by the negative posture of his parents. In stripping away the pleasure of success, their actions were counter to their goal of helping George develop a resilient mindset. In this situation, the excitement of being successful was tarnished, and George's frustration and anger were increased. It is difficult for a resilient mindset to develop in the shadow of this obstacle.

Principles for Experiencing Acceptance and Success

What Andrew, Jack, Samantha, Brett, Mary, and George have in common is the derailment of success en route to developing islands of competence and a resilient mindset. The experience of success not only is a building block of a resilient mindset but also helps children overcome daily stresses and challenges. However, for these six children, achieving success is not associated with inner peace and true satisfaction. When children experience the obstacles just outlined, positive results don't lead to heightened self-esteem but to negative feelings likely to reduce the probability of future success.

Andrew, Jack, and Samantha had succumbed to the belief that positive outcomes were not based on their own resources but rather on external forces. For Mary, success was intertwined with conditional love and acceptance, while George's success in areas not deemed important by his parents was met with derision. Finally, Brett's choice of successful activities provided him with only fleeting experiences of "pseudo success." If success does not build on success, if success is not experienced joyfully, if it does not build confidence and a feeling of control of one's life, then it will not serve to reinforce a resilient mindset.

How many of these obstacles apply to you and your children? Unfortunately, numerous children face more than one of them. In many cases they appear to feed on each other. It is important for you to understand these obstacles as you clear the path to fostering true success. Sometimes you must begin by accepting and understanding your child's temperament and daily life experience. Sometimes you must start with self-evaluation of your opinions and biases about what defines your children's success. Sometimes you must lead with empathy and a search for the reasons why some children, like Brett, resort to "hollow successes."

Parents often ask what they can do beyond understanding and addressing these roadblocks to help their kids experience success. What can parents do to facilitate the process by which success leads to islands of competence and a resilient mindset? The simplest answer is that we must provide opportunities for our children to be successful and also convey the message that their accomplishments are based in great part on their own inner resources. The way to begin is by examining the obstacles cited, accepting and understanding attribution theory, and setting in place the following five principles.

Principle One: Openly Enjoy and Celebrate Your Children's Accomplishments

As our children grow, they will encounter countless challenges. Many of these seem like small steps to adults, but to children they represent major advances. Each mastery brings with it a sense of success and accomplishment: the first steps taken, the first solo ride on a two-wheeler, the first time being left alone with a baby-sitter, the picture we tape to the refrigerator, the hit in baseball or the kick in soccer, the made bed, the clean dishes, a sleep-over at a friend's home, or the first date. Each represents a small but important step in the journey. We must learn to celebrate these achievements not by telling our children that they are the next coming of Picasso, Michael Jordan, Mia Hamm, or Mark McGwire but by conveying appropriate messages of support and enthusiasm.

Our children are proud when we display their drawings on the refrigerator, shout "Nice kick!" or "Good hustle!" at a game, or hug them after they have done a thorough job of cleaning off the table. Such words and gestures convey to our children not only that they are loved but also that we recognize and appreciate their achievements and successes. Even when obstacles obstruct the course, such as with Andrew's temperament or Samantha's attitude about her schoolwork, we must be resolved and persistent in providing support.

Take a tip from Mr. Spillane, a parent who eagerly awaited the first snowfall each winter. When enough snow had accumulated, he herded his three children outside to help build the "family's snowman." It was a delight to watch the children work with their father. He skillfully engaged them in creating the different parts of the snowman and asked them what they might use as eyes or a nose. His enjoyment was evident, especially when they posted a sign in front of the snowman that read "Our snowman welcomes you to the Spillanes'." When neighbors passed, he would say in front of his children, "Look at the wonderful work my kids did." In spring he would plant seeds with them, and as the plants bloomed, he would compliment the children on the nice job they did.

These seemingly small gestures established the foundation for the Spillane children to feel successful, especially in the eyes of their parents and other adults in the neighborhood. Remember that children will feel more successful when their achievements are acknowledged and appreciated by significant people in their lives.

Principle Two: Emphasize Your Children's Input in Creating Success

According to attribution theory, children capable of accepting ownership for their successes will have higher self-esteem than those who believe their achievements are based on external forces or on circumstances beyond their control. Your guiding principle here must be to provide experiences and offer comments that convey to your children that they are active participants in what transpires in their lives. An obvious example is the snowman and sign in front of the Spillanes' home offering vivid testimony of the contribution that the children make. With the advent of warmer weather, plants replace the snowman as a mark of the children's accomplishments.

Robert, the four-year-old whose tantrums at bedtime were traced to nightmares, was eventually recognized for his success. In Robert's case success was expressed by his arriving at a creative solution to his problems: a night-light and a photo of his parents next to his bed. As his parents became more empathic and recognized that Robert's tantrums were not efforts to agitate them, they complimented him on the strategies he had suggested for quelling his fear of going to bed. They told him that he had a "really smart mind" for solving problems. Robert loved the idea. The description boosted his self-esteem in two ways: as a positive comment on his contribution and as an assessment that he was capable of solving problems.

This second point is the clincher. The more we can communicate to our children that they have within themselves the capability to find ways to be successful and to solve problems, the more likely they will incorporate and put to use this important feature of a resilient mindset.

The story of Casey, an impulsive ten-year-old, is another lesson in the ways in which we can communicate to our children a sense of ownership for accomplishments. Casey was referred to us because of problems with impulsivity, which influenced all aspects of his life, particularly school. His physician had made a diagnosis of attention deficit hyperactivity disorder. Casey's teacher noted that he often blurted out answers, yelled at his classmates when he thought they had taken advantage of him, constantly came up to ask her questions about instructions, and left his seat to sharpen his pencil at least four or five times a day.

To improve Casey's prospects for controlling his actions, his parents and teacher made a number of behavioral accommodations. Casey's teacher provided additional prompts and instructions for him. Activities were arranged in a pattern that allowed him to move, talk, and ask questions in the classroom without being disruptive. A behavior management system was implemented at home to avert the negative parent-child interactions that often occur in families with impulsive children. Casey's physician also started a trial of medication, which led to a marked improvement in Casey's behavior.

When we interviewed Casey about his progress, he said, "I can control myself now because I'm taking a pill." While there is truth to this statement, we were concerned that Casey viewed the source of his improvement as the pill rather than something within himself. We explained that pills don't control people, but rather people control pills. Taking a pill is not a substitute for working hard, making a friend, or listening to parents. In other words, "pills will not substitute for skills." We helped Casey understand that the medication offered him the ability to make choices but did not make those choices for him.

We suggested to his parents that they reinforce this message by telling him, "The pill has helped you be calmer (a word Casey had used), and now that you're calmer, it will be easier for you to decide how to behave." While that may seem pretty similar to Casey's explanation, there is a significant difference: Casey viewed success primarily in terms of something external, namely the pill, whereas the explanation we offered placed more responsibility for success on Casey's shoulders.

We always emphasize in our work with children who are taking medication that the main function of the medication is to allow them to gain more control of their lives through the choices and decisions they make. The medicine acts as a tool, increasing their ability to think about choices and make decisions. Casey's parents reported that when they emphasized Casey's contribution to the positive changes in his life, he not only liked what they had to say but also began taking the medication without having to be reminded.

A final point that must be stressed about ownership is that when we help our children with tasks or projects such as homework or cooking a meal, we must be careful not to "do" the activity for them. If they feel that the final project is more ours than theirs, they will not attribute their success to their resources. We would not enjoy being relegated to watching someone else engage in an activity in which we want to participate, nor would our children. Observation alone detracts from the feeling of control and ownership and in some cases deprives children of the true joy of their accomplishments. We must perform a balancing act, being available to assist our children but not doing everything for them. We must be guided by the knowledge that children with a resilient mindset assume realistic credit for their successes.

Principle Three: Identify and Reinforce Your Child's Islands of Competence by Engaging in Environmental Engineering

Chapter 5 advocated that in raising and teaching our children, we "build them up" rather than "chip them down." We accomplish the "building up" by concentrating on their strengths and successes.

While not ignoring the false steps, parents must find ways to highlight the attributes that help children to shine and feel a sense of accomplishment. In counseling, we often tell children that we are not so much interested in what is wrong with them as what is right with them. "When you leave school, an employer doesn't ask about your worst academic subject and most annoying behavior and then create a job involving those two features! In fact, it is just the opposite. It is through our strengths and abilities that we find joy, pleasure, and success in life."

The educational plans developed for children with problems at school reflect the dilemma of achieving this goal. The plans often list a child's strengths and weaknesses but then list goals only for the weaknesses! In an informal survey, we asked parents and teachers why they thought strengths are listed on the educational plan. The most common responses were: "It allows us to start with something positive in the planning meeting" and "So we know what we don't have to work on." The latter is completely contradictory to the strength-based model that this book advocates.

We advise parents attending educational planning meetings to insist that goals be written for strengths. Though the weaknesses reported on these educational plans must be targeted for remediation, engagement in strength-based activities is equally important, if not more relevant, to nurture self-esteem and motivation. We should not expect that when children who require help with reading spend an hour after school completing additional reading, they will feel a dramatic sense of accomplishment and pride and will thank us for the time invested. We recommend that for every hour of additional work that children in need spend, they spend an hour engaging in activities that are strengths. These activities help them feel good, experience success, and develop a resilient mindset.

We had a specific reason for introducing the metaphor islands of competence in describing a child's strengths. Many youngsters with whom we have worked exhibit low self-esteem and a defeatist mindset. They contend with many of the obstacles listed in this chapter. These children appear to be swimming in a self-perceived "ocean of inadequacy" characterized by feelings of low self-worth and a lack of confidence. Within this ocean of inadequacy, we believe that each child possesses at least one small island of competence, an area that is or has the potential to be a source of pride and achievement. As these islands are located and reinforced, a "ripple effect" may take place in which youngsters are more willing to venture forth and confront areas that have been difficult for them and from which they have retreated in the past. We have seen this occur time and time again.

Parents must learn to identify and reinforce these islands so that they will soon become more prominent than the ocean of self-doubt. We must appreciate that these islands of competence differ from one child to the next. We must avoid engaging in such obstacles as not sharing our children's interests or setting the bar too high. We can all think of some children who are much more confident playing basketball than taking a math test, while other youngsters are comfortable in the classroom but self-conscious on the playground. Some children may display unusual artistic talents but have difficulty speaking with their peers, while the reverse may be true for many other children.

Try the following exercise: On a sheet of paper write down what you consider to be your child's islands of competence. Ask yourself if your child would also view these as areas of competence. Next to each item on the list, beginning with the areas your child would likely also perceive as islands of competence, describe briefly how you reinforce this area and display it for others to see.

Far too often, as in the educational planning process, we train our attention and energy on our children's mistakes and vulnerabilities rather than on their strengths. In addition, as witnessed with George's parents, we may view a child's main area of interest and expertise as an embarrassing weakness.

Rather than complimenting George on his knowledge of plants and gardening, his parents diminished an activity that brought him a sense of pride. It was not surprising that George's anger became increasingly intense.

Mr. and Mrs. Lemrow consulted us about nine-year-old Amelia, who experienced a number of developmental delays. Her expressive and receptive language skills as well as her fine and large motor abilities were several years below her chronological age. Given these problems, she struggled in school and her social skills were poor. She had very few friends. In her attempts to be accepted she often resorted to clownlike behaviors that set her apart from her peer group. As with Brett, Amelia attempted to find success even in inappropriate ways.

After discussing Amelia's shortcomings, we asked the Lemrows to list her islands of competence. At first they were at a loss.

Finally, Mr. Lemrow said, "Amelia has a nice sense of humor."

"But she often uses it in silly ways," Mrs. Lemrow pointed out.

We said, "We can see that it is difficult for you to articulate Amelia's strengths. We recognize how frustrated you must feel in helping your daughter." We then rephrased the question and asked, "What characteristic of Amelia's brings you joy?"

Mrs. Lemrow responded, "She really likes to help others, but because of her problems we are not sure how she can help. A few times, she has wanted to set the dinner table, but twice she broke a plate. She said she would like to help cook, but I'm afraid to let her get close to the oven. She might burn herself."

We then prompted, "We appreciate your concern about Amelia's safety and the dishes, but can you think of some helping activities that Amelia could handle, activities that might bring her a sense of pride and might display her islands of competence?"

The Lemrows agreed to discuss this prospect at home and observe Amelia before the next session. When they arrived the following week, they had already initiated several activities that they said they wished they had thought of previously.

"We've put Amelia in charge of setting the silverware on the table," said Mrs. Lemrow. "Silverware doesn't break when it's dropped."

"We also contacted a close friend who is the director of a local nursing home and asked if there was something Amelia might do there. He said there was a woman with few visitors who enjoyed playing card games. He wondered if Amelia would like to come and play with her," said Mr. Lemrow.

"We told Amelia about this nursing home resident and asked her if she would be interested in meeting her," Mrs. Lemrow said. "We were surprised when Amelia's face lit up. She told me she would love to play cards with this woman."

Similar to many other children with developmental lags, Amelia found it easier to relate to younger children and adults than children of her age. Two sisters, five and seven, lived next door to the Lemrows. Amelia enjoyed playing games with them, and from the observations of Mr. and Mrs. Lemrow, the sisters enjoyed playing with her. They also observed that Amelia assumed a teaching role with these girls.

Mr. Lemrow wondered, "Should we set limits on the amount of time Amelia spends with these girls? She always plays with younger children. How will she ever learn to relate to children of her age?"

We agreed that Amelia shouldn't become isolated from her classmates but asked the Lemrows to consider whether there were other benefits in the time Amelia spent with these sisters.

"Amelia does see these girls as her friends. It is important to have friends," said Mrs. Lemrow.

Mr. Lemrow acknowledged, "It also allows Amelia to help others. That is one of her islands of competence."

We suggested that they let Amelia continue to play with these children as a way to enhance her self-esteem and interpersonal skills as well as become more resilient.

We also troubleshooted ways to increase Amelia's interactions with children of her age. One of Amelia's problems was that when she played with classmates after school, she had difficulty maintaining conversation or knowing what to say. We discussed with the Lemrows a concept we call "environmental engineering." We first heard these words as a job title at a summer camp: Environmental Engineers were the campers who were in charge of cleaning the grounds. We borrowed from this nomenclature to describe the "behind-the-scenes" work that parents might do to maximize a child's opportunities for success. We suggested that the Lemrows conduct environmental engineering to help Amelia be successful in her play experiences.

In Amelia's case we suggested that the Lemrows help her choose peers who were more accepting of her. They could then structure activities at home with one of these children at a time that would not place Amelia at a disadvantage in her interactions with this child. The Lemrows proved to be most skillful in planning such activities, and Amelia began to enjoy satisfying play sessions with classmates.

Amelia's contact with the nursing home resident, her teaching role with younger neighbors, and the planned, structured contact with her peers slowly yielded positive results. Mr. and Mrs. Lemrow increasingly accentuated Amelia's islands of competence, especially her genuine love of helping others.

Some parents try to use participation in an enjoyable, self-esteem-building activity, as a reward for a child to achieve other, more problematic objectives. Sixteen-year-old Brendan and his parents, Mr. and Mrs. Fischer, exemplify the risks involved when parents take this gamble.

Brendan was completing his sophomore year in high school. His school performance was characterized by missed assignments and numerous warning slips. Although he carried near failing grades into several of his final exams, with additional effort he was always able to perform well and secure a C average for the semester.

Brendan did not have a history of learning or attentional problems, although at times he appeared somewhat disorganized. When questioned about his inconsistency in school, Brendan simply responded that school was "boring." He cited a host of other activities, such as being with friends, that he placed in priority above schoolwork. Yet, on one occasion Brendan conjectured that perhaps he made school more difficult because he would lose track of school-related requirements when he was thinking about other things.

The Fischers summarized the fruits of their recent dealings with Brendan.

Mr. Fischer began, "We know that Brendan is quite bright but not performing up to his capabilities. We saw him as an underachiever. We read an article that showed that underachievers could be motivated by restricting them from participating in activities they enjoy."

Mrs. Fischer then explained, "Brendan was active in the church youth group and spent hours helping plan the group's activities. The youth group adviser was very impressed with Brendan's contributions and asked him to serve as youth group president. Since this position was important to Brendan, we decided to use it as a reward for his being more conscientious with schoolwork. We told him that his grades were especially important in his junior year, particularly if he decided to attend college. Therefore, before we would let him accept the position of youth group president, we wanted him to prove that he could become more organized at school and earn good grades. We told

Brendan that if he obtained a B average in the last semester of his sophomore year, he could become youth group president."

"How did it turn out?" we asked.

Mr. Fischer responded, "We were convinced that this incentive would prompt Brendan to take his schoolwork seriously. We never expected what happened. He became increasingly angry with us. Even given his poor schoolwork in the past few years, he had maintained a loving, respectful relationship with us. However, with the establishment of a B average as his passport into the presidency, his relationship with us suffered, and his grades didn't get any better!"

According to the Fischers, their household became increasingly tense. Each day, they would ask Brendan if he was keeping up with his schoolwork, and each day, he responded that they should leave him alone. Mr. and Mrs. Fischer were confused: a seemingly reasonable plan of action was turning into a bigger disaster. They weren't certain what to do.

Although our work with the Fischers and ultimately Brendan covered a number of areas, including helping him learn how to organize, one of the most important questions we asked the Fischers was what they saw as Brendan's strengths, or islands of competence.

Without hesitation, Mr. Fischer proudly said, "Brendan is a real people person. Kids and adults like to be with him. He has especially demonstrated this in youth group activities: he knows how to bring people together, motivate them, and plan programs. The youth group is one place that all of his skills are put to use, and he uses them well."

"Brendan is quite talented," we commented.

"Yes, he is," said Mrs. Fischer, "except for his school performance."

Mr. Fischer added, "We figured that since youth group is so important to him, he would buckle down to his grades so he could participate and be their next president. But what we thought would happen hasn't happened at all. Not only have his grades remained low, but he's even more tense and angry. Our relationship with him is the pits."

Inadvertently, the Fischers, like a high-stakes gambler, had placed all of their chips on a single bet. We explained that sometimes, using an activity that is highly valued as an incentive or reinforcer to change behavior can produce positive results. However, access to a youngster's island of competence as the reinforcer earned for modifying behavior stands an equal chance of backfiring, for several possible reasons.

First, some children may not be capable of meeting the expectations set by their parents. Remember, this occurred for Mary: in response she too became angry and hopeless. In this instance, while Brendan was obviously bright and did not display any apparent learning or attentional problems, by his own admission he was at times disorganized and lost track of school requirements. Holding out the presidency of the youth group as a reinforcer would not be effective if Brendan was not *capable* of consistently completing all of his work.

We explained to the Fischers that Brendan likely experienced problems with organizational skills. They acknowledged that even in youth group Brendan at times was disorganized. Although the Fischers had withheld the youth group presidency, they had not offered Brendan any additional assistance or discussion of what he thought might be helpful. They assumed that Brendan was capable of handling the work since, as his mother said, "He is able to do it when he wants to."

We explained that inconsistency is common among adolescents with organizational problems. Being able to meet the requirements on some days did not mean they could meet them every day.

"But when Brendan is motivated and involved in the planning of youth group activities, he can stay up until midnight, and his work is finished," said Mr. Fischer.

We said that this kind of pattern is not unusual since it was obvious that the youth group activities were very motivating and relevant to Brendan. He overcame his problems with organization during youth group by investing more time and effort, something he could not or perhaps would not do with school.

The second problem with using an island of competence as a reinforcer, in this case youth group presidency, is that when the gamble doesn't work, the results are often greater anxiety, anger, and deterioration, not only in family relationships, but also in the very behavior that parents wish to change.

A subtle but equally powerful third problem relates to the other two. It centers on the loss of the island of competence when behavior is not changed.

We asked the Fischers, "What do you believe Brendan gains from his participation in youth group activities?"

"Youth group provides many important experiences. Brendan has made close friendships there with some really nice kids," said Mr. Fischer.

Mrs. Fischer stated, "It has also taught him to be more responsible and to be a better problem solver. Some of the activities involve helping others. In doing so, Brendan has become a more understanding and compassionate person. We believe that Brendan would learn even more responsibility as president of the group."

As Mr. Fischer tallied the many benefits that Brendan accrued from his association with the youth group, he reached an insight: "Not to minimize the importance of school, but as we're talking about this, I'm realizing that what Brendan learns in the youth group may be more important in life than the information he gets in some of his classes. By restricting the youth group, I may be depriving him of showing his islands of competence, which may actually be more important than the grades he attains. And, if anything, the approach we took isn't working. But what else can we do?"

It was rewarding to work with the Fischers since they were responsive and open to examining and changing their negative scripts with their son. They had the courage to alter their approach. They were forthright in concluding that requiring Brendan to obtain a B average as a condition to becoming president of the youth group was not a good idea, and they decided to remove it.

"We told Brendan that we still expected him to obtain passing grades," said Mr. Fischer. "But we also began a problem-solving dialogue of what he thought would help. The tension in our household decreased markedly."

Brendan ended his sophomore year with a C average. During the following year, while he was president of the youth group, his average increased slightly and the number of warning slips for incomplete work dropped significantly. As youth group president, Brendan engaged in the many important activities that the Fischers had outlined in our meeting: relating with his peers and adults, planning programs that involved problem solving and perseverance, and helping others in the community. Since he had to represent the group at various meetings, he also became more at ease speaking in public. Many opportunities arose for him to display his islands of competence that he and others judged to be important.

In his senior year, Brendan's grades jumped from C to A−. He went on to graduate Phi Beta Kappa from college.

Numerous factors contributed to Brendan's developing a resilient mindset. From the Fischers' perspective, however, it was their change in attitude over Brendan's grades that made the most significant contribution, not only to their relationship with Brendan, but also to his ability to create balance in his life.

Although not every youngster will demonstrate such a marked improvement in grades, and the optimum approach varies based on the situation, we learned a valuable lesson from working with Brendan and his parents: If parents are to help their children experience success, they must learn to define their children's islands of competence, provide opportunities for these islands to be reinforced and displayed, and not use these islands as enticements for other behaviors. In most instances, when parents allow children to engage in and demonstrate their strengths, their self-esteem and sense of ownership increase, as does their resilience. The strengthening of their self-esteem and resilience typically results in positive changes in other aspects of their lives—in Brendan's case, an increased investment in school and an improvement in grades.

Of course, parents must still hold their children accountable, but in that quest they must be careful not to remove the very activities that will foster a resilient mindset. It is through these activities that an internal sense of accountability is best developed. Once Brendan's parents changed their script, engaged Brendan in examining what might help his grades (it still took him more than a year to demonstrate improvement in school), and allowed him to be involved in an activity that fostered many important life skills, Brendan became less tense and more directed, and most important, his relationship with his parents benefited.

We must be creative in reinforcing areas of competence in our children, and at times we must engage in "environmental engineering," as Amelia's parents discovered. This type of reinforcement is most effective when it becomes a routine part of the family system.

A final example of helping children use successful experiences to build a resilient mindset features fifteen-year-old Pattie and her mother, Ms. Blanchard. Ms. Blanchard brought Pattie to see us because of her verbal and, at times, physically abusive behavior at home and school. Pattie was an only child. Her parents divorced when she was six. Her father moved a long distance away, remarried, and had two children in his second marriage. Although Pattie visited her father during holidays and summer vacation, she reported never feeling very comfortable or welcome with her father's new family.

Ms. Blanchard relayed that Pattie sometimes was extremely resistant when limits were set. In school she was viewed by others as a bully. Her behavior was often belligerent toward teachers.

Pattie refused at first to come to see us. We met with Ms. Blanchard, who was ready to "ship Pattie to her father." We wrote a note to Pattie explaining that since we would be working with and making recommendations to her mother and school team, it would be helpful if we had an opportunity to meet her. She came once, proclaiming that the idea of seeing a counselor was "stupid" and that she would not return. She spent the session blaming others for her problems and was resistant to exploring any strategies for change. Pattie was true to her word and did not return. We continued to meet with her mother and also to communicate with her guidance counselor.

We asked Ms. Blanchard what she saw as Pattie's islands of competence.

"That's easy," Ms. Blanchard responded. "Pattie is an all-star soccer player."

"Are you saying that she is a good player or that she plays well?" we asked.

Ms. Blanchard looked confused and responded, "I don't understand the difference."

"Pattie may be a good soccer player," we responded, "but does she play well? Is she a good team member?" The latter is important for soccer to truly be an island of competence.

Ms. Blanchard responded quickly, "Absolutely not! Although Pattie has great skills, she doesn't listen to the coach and has been close to being dismissed from the team because of angry outbursts directed at team members."

The next week an incident occurred that turned out to be a blessing in disguise. Pattie was suspended from school and the soccer team. A player on another team had made an obscene remark to Pattie, whereupon Pattie punched the girl. The girl fell backward and appeared to lose consciousness for a few seconds. She was taken to the hospital but fortunately was not injured. Pattie was more shaken and scared than she would admit and was told that as a condition for returning to school and possibly the team, she had to see a counselor. Pattie called us and said, "So, when's my next appointment?"

The Pattie who came in this time seemed much less resistant than the one we had met several months before.

"Let's examine what's happening on the team. Maybe we can help things be better," we offered.

Pattie preempted, "If she hadn't called me an obscene word, I wouldn't have hit her."

"No one likes to be called a name," we responded, "but if you want to avoid getting into trouble and want to play on the team, you are going to have to learn more effective ways of responding to such provocative comments." Using several real-life examples, we discussed with Pattie the importance of avoiding provocation and keeping one's "goals in mind." Not wanting this session to dwell on negative events, we asked, "What is it you enjoy doing or feel successful at doing?" This is a question that we ask essentially all of the children and teens we counsel.

In a flash, Pattie responded, "I love to play soccer." She added, "The thing I hated most about my school suspension was not being able to play with the team."

"Sounds as if soccer gives you a great deal of pleasure."

"It sure does."

Pattie then launched into a lengthy monologue. We listened with few interruptions as she recounted her accomplishments on the team. We learned that she was the leading scorer yet also one of the youngest players. Then seemingly out of the blue, she asked, "Would you like to come to one of my games and see me play?"

Although the request might have been a "test" to see how sincere our interest was, we sensed another reason for Pattie's invitation: that she wanted us to observe her while she was displaying her island of competence.

After she met with her coach to work out alternative ways of handling confrontation and promised to act more responsibly during games, Pattie was invited to return to school and rejoin the team. Her coach also knew that she had started counseling. We accepted her invitation to attend a game and discovered that she was in fact a superb player. During the game an incident occurred that could have been scripted in Hollywood. A player from the opposing team accidentally tripped Pattie and drew a penalty card. Pattie started to walk toward the girl, and it appeared for a moment that she might say or do something hostile. Instead, Pattie smiled, said nothing, and walked away. A few minutes later, Pattie "got even" by scoring what turned out to be the winning goal.

In the next session, we were greeted by a more personable Pattie.

"Thanks for coming out to watch me play. It meant a lot," she said.

We said in return, "You're every bit as good as your mom told us. We also noticed the restraint you demonstrated when that other girl tripped you."

Pattie responded in a half-kidding, half-serious tone, "I wouldn't hit her. There are strict rules about that. I could have been kicked out of the game."

"Good for you."

We spent the session discussing how "excellent thinking skills and restraint" could be used in other parts of Pattie's life, such as at home or school.

As she left, Pattie's last words were, "You shrinks really know how to make your point."

Pattie started coming to counseling on a regular basis, dealing with many concerns including her anger toward her father, which she often directed at her mother. We believe that her willingness to open up was enhanced in great part by our witnessing her island of competence on the soccer field. By

Pattie's junior year she was the assistant coach for a young girl's soccer league. That same year, she was named an all-state soccer player. She proudly sent us a copy of a newspaper clipping. Alongside the clipping she wrote, "Thanks for being there."

Having now read about Amelia, Brendan, and Pattie, you may wish to review the exercise you completed earlier in this chapter in which you listed your children's islands of competence to make certain you are reinforcing and displaying these islands. In the daily hassles of life, we often lose sight of the strengths and successes of our children. An unmade bed or a missed homework assignment may loom larger than it should. In the course of events, we fail to appreciate our children's strengths. Keep in mind that strengths can assume many forms, such as repairing a motor, visiting with residents in a nursing home, or creating artwork. Also remember that children will feel greater ownership for their success when they experience it as meaningful to their lives.

Principle Four: Give Strengths Time to Develop

Over the years we have had the great pleasure of coaching our children and others in youth basketball. In doing so, we have learned much about the development of skills and strengths. When the first author coached a fifth-grade team, he met Monty, who was physically awkward and seemingly uncoordinated. This was the first time Monty had played league basketball. Although lacking in basketball skills, Monty was a delight to have on the team. He displayed an unbridled and contagious enthusiasm, together with a strong motivation to improve his game. He worked hard at practice. Monty's father said that Monty faithfully spent time each day trying to improve his dribbling and shooting.

Despite his efforts, Monty demonstrated little outward improvement in skills during the season. Anyone observing Monty's play and demeanor would comment on what a great kid he was, but no one would list basketball as one of his islands of competence.

Then something happened between Monty's first and second years of league play. By the start of the second season, he had grown about three inches, and his growth in height was accompanied by a significant improvement in his coordination and skills. It was difficult to believe that this was the same player who had scored two baskets in the entire previous season. In his first game he scored fifteen points. As the season progressed, Monty would easily have been voted one of the top three players in the league. His basketball prowess, along with his enthusiasm, comprised two valuable islands of competence. They were displayed for the entire community to witness and admire.

Parents must recognize that there are many Montys in the world. Many children require time to develop and mature. Not long ago, a ten-year-old with learning and emotional problems commented during a session that the greatest problem he faced while growing up was that it "takes too long." Whether this child's views were formed by cultural or experiential factors, in his mind if you couldn't do it well the first time, "why bother doing it at all?"

Although this child may represent an extreme, the same interventions described in this chapter apply. If a youngster shows an interest in a particular activity, even if his or her skills are below average compared with peers, we must, within reason, support and nurture the development of these skills. We can never be certain which skills will someday become a child's islands of competence, reinforcing a sense of success and, most important, a resilient mindset. Many great scientists, educators, and athletes developed slowly. Remember that one of Thomas Edison's teachers labeled him "addled," prompting his mother to remove him from that school, and that Michael Jordan, perhaps the greatest basketball player of all time, was cut from his high school team.

Principle Five: Accept the Unique Strengths and Successes of Each Child

This final principle is closely related to the other four and also incorporated within the main theme of the previous chapter, accepting our children for who they are and not what we may wish them to be. This was the problem in the cases of Mary, whose grades weren't as good as her parents expected, and George, whose parents viewed his interest in plants as unacceptable. This principle stands alone here to emphasize its importance.

Let's return once again to the exercise in which you listed your child's islands of competence. This time, make a separate list of what you *wish* were your child's islands of competence and compare it with the first list—what you currently view as your child's strengths. How close is what you perceive are your child's strengths to what you wish they were?

In most cases there is some discrepancy between the two lists. For example, many parents naturally hope that social relations, academic ability, and even arts or athletics become islands of competence for their children. Reflect on the ways in which any existing discrepancies impact the quality and tone of your interactions with your child. Do these discrepancies interfere with your ability to notice and accept the unique strengths and successes of your child?

Children are aware of our disappointments when they don't meet our expectations and are particularly sensitive when their successes are not viewed as important or relevant by us. The consequences were demonstrated when George's parents could not accept his success in caring for plants. Disappointed that he was not successful in school or athletic arenas, Mr. and Mrs. White dismissed any other activities that might have been used to develop islands of competence, including an activity that brought him a sense of contentment and achievement.

In contrast to the reactions of George's parents were those of Mr. and Mrs. Breem. The Breems had two sons. Similar to George's parents, the Breems grew up as star athletes and students. They expected that their sons would follow in their footsteps, demonstrating successes in the same areas as they had. Their fourteen-year-old, Phillip, displayed the same islands of competence as his parents. The Breems' wishes for him were in accord with his accomplishments. However, Wade, their twelve-year-old, took a much different path. His grades were average at best, and he showed little interest in sports, although he was willing to participate in youth leagues in the town in which they lived. At first, Mr. and Mrs. Breem were puzzled and even disappointed since Wade's journey was leading down a different road from the one they had taken or that his brother was currently traveling.

However, unlike with the negative script into which the Whites fell, the Breems were able to adjust their perspective. They probed for Wade's interests, which turned out to be in the fields of acting and singing. They obtained information about classes that Wade could take to learn more about acting and improve his skills. They also encouraged him to take singing lessons, which he was happy to do. They did not harp on his less-than-exemplary grades, although they did set clear expectations for him to complete his homework and be prepared for school. They exhibited delight in his singing skills and recorded several of his songs to send to each set of grandparents. They attended his plays, and just as they conveyed to Phillip how proud they were of his achievements in sports and academics, they let Wade know how proud they were of his accomplishments. They acknowledged his many hours of practice and rehearsal. Through their words, they reinforced his feeling of ownership of success.

Wade truly enjoyed and felt responsible for his success. This success may not have been in the areas that the Breems originally anticipated, but they were able to recognize early in their sons' lives that each was different and each could achieve success with parental support in his own areas of interest and expertise.

Success Is Worth Repeating

It is virtually impossible to conceive of children developing a resilient mindset if they do not experience the joy and excitement of success in areas that they and significant others in their lives deem to be important. Unfortunately, most children run up against some obstacles along this path. For some, the problem results from a quality of temperament, making it difficult for them to experience the joy of success. Others may set the bar of success too high, even when support is provided. Still other children, simply based on their daily encounters with failure, may write off success as fleeting and transient. Parents too may play a part in creating obstacles, either by unfairly placing their agenda of successful experiences on their children or by setting the measure of success too high.

Success will be exciting and satisfying only when it is free of conditional love and unrealistic expectations, when it is linked to the child's interest, and when the child feels a sense of ownership and responsibility for the success. When these conditions are met, a wonderful process is set in place and is repeated time and again throughout the individual's lifetime. A task is undertaken, perseverance leads to mastery, an island of competence is reinforced, and the experience of success fosters self-esteem and a resilient mindset. In this scenario a resilient mindset blossoms as each new success brings further nourishment.

8

Learning from Mistakes

As the previous chapter underscored, not all children experience apparent success in the same way. For some, the excitement and satisfaction are missing and, consequently, resiliency is compromised. Likewise, the response to mistakes also varies from one child or parent to the next. The ways in which a child understands and responds to mistakes are an integral feature of a resilient mindset.

As part of a child evaluation, we typically ask parents, "When your child makes a mistake or when something doesn't go right, how does he or she react and handle the situation?" Think about your response to this question. We have found that one of the most effective ways of assessing self-esteem and confidence as well as the presence of a resilient mindset is to examine how children perceive and cope with the mistakes and setbacks that are a natural part of growing up.

Let's visit two nine-year-old boys, Bryant and James, and chart their reactions during a Little League game and during a test at school. Bryant and James each struck out the two times they were at bat in the Little League game. After the game, Bryant approached the coach and said, "Coach, I keep striking out. Am I holding the bat wrong? What can I do differently to hit the ball?" In contrast, after James struck out the second time, he flung the bat and screamed at the umpire, "You are blind, really blind. Has anyone ever told you that you need glasses?" James then ran off the field in tears, much to the chagrin of his parents.

At school, Bryant and James failed a spelling test. Bryant went over to his teacher after receiving the test score and said, "I think I need extra help with spelling. Can I talk with you later about what I can do to improve?" James took a different route. Upon arriving home, he shouted, "My teacher stinks. She never told us that these words would be on this test. You should get her fired. She deserves to be fired!"

Understanding Our Mistakes and Setbacks

Bryant and James encountered the same strikeouts in a baseball game and the same failing grade on a spelling test, yet each perceived these situations differently. Why? Just as attribution theory helps us to understand the different ways in which children experience success, it provides a framework for understanding a child's perception of mistakes and setbacks. Knowledge of this framework can guide parents in helping their children to manage setbacks and mistakes.

Children such as Bryant possess high self-esteem. For them, mistakes are experiences from which to learn. They attribute mistakes, especially if the task is realistically achievable, to factors that can be changed, such as applying more effort in a particular situation or using more productive strategies. They look on parents and other adults such as teachers and coaches as available to help them and don't hesitate to seek assistance when needed. These children possess one of the most important features of a resilient mindset: the belief that adversity can lead to growth, that difficult situations can be viewed as challenges rather than as stresses to avoid. In this regard, it is relevant that in the Chinese language, "crisis" and "opportunity" are represented by the same word.

When Bryant struck out during the baseball game, he believed that with the help of his coach, he could improve his skills and become a more proficient batter. Similar feelings prevailed when he received a failing grade on a spelling test: by improving his study habits, he told himself, he could improve his test scores. In addition, while resilient children persevere with difficult tasks, they have the insight and courage to recognize when a task may present demands that are beyond their current ability. However, at such times, rather than feeling dejected, they remain upbeat and direct their energies toward other tasks that are within their capacity. They also recognize that what appear to be insurmountable challenges at one time may not be so in the future. Thus, an air of hope, optimism, and realism characterizes their lives.

In striking contrast to Bryant's outlook are children like James. These children perceive mistakes as resulting from conditions that cannot be easily changed or modified, such as a lack of ability or low intelligence. Their mindset is not one of optimism but rather is dominated by what psychologist Martin Seligman referred to as "learned helplessness," that is, the feeling that "regardless of what I do, nothing good will come of it anyway." In their sense of helplessness and hopelessness, they act to avoid what they perceive to be further humiliation. They are likely to resort to blaming others, offering excuses, or assuming the role of the class clown or bully. They are often accused of not trying. A more accurate description of their actions, however, is that they don't try because they feel that their efforts will not lead to positive results. The very strategies they use to avoid mistakes serve only to exacerbate their plight as they move further and further away from possible success, as was true of Brett, who said that he "would rather misbehave than be dumb."

Joel, the boy in Chapter 3 who did not stick with activities such as his saxophone lessons, was another victim of this negative cycle. Fortunately, his parents were able to engage him in a problem-solving mode and help him to persevere with tasks that had proved difficult at first.

The devastating impact of a negative view of mistakes and the often desperate but counterproductive quest for relief were vividly captured in the case of ten-year-old Ron. His parents, Mr. and Mrs. Rollins, sought a consultation for their son because of his angry outbursts at school and his oppositional, sullen behavior at home. Each morning when Ron entered the school building, he hit the first child he saw. There was no other pattern to whom he hit, just the first student who crossed his path. He was immediately sent to the principal's office, which led to several in-school suspensions. When we spoke with the principal, he said that he didn't know if there was anything else the school could do. He wondered about suspending Ron from school and trying to find an alternative placement in a class for children with behavioral problems.

Our meeting with Ron's parents established that he was a boy with learning and attentional problems for whom school had always been a challenge but was even more so now in the fifth grade, given increased writing requirements. School was not a place from which Ron gathered strength. The very act of entering the building was stressful for him. In response he sought to escape. The Rollinses reported that Ron underwent treatments and surgeries for several medical problems during his first five years of life, beginning with pyloric stenosis, or projectile vomiting, when he was only four weeks old, followed by tubes being placed in his ears, and then by a hernia operation. They noted that while Ron's medical care was excellent, he frequently voiced concerns about his body, which he felt had defects from birth.

The first few minutes of our initial session with Ron were among the most powerful moments we had ever spent with a child. Ron came in with an angry, yet sad, expression. We mentioned that we were there to help.

He responded angrily, "Why are you trying to help me?"

We asked, "Why wouldn't we want to help?"

Whereupon, Ron said in a serious, intense voice, "I was born to quit, and God made me that way."

If we interpret Ron's statement in terms of attribution theory, we can appreciate how entrenched his views of mistakes were and how difficult the therapeutic task would be to modify his perception.

Ron attributed his mistakes and quitting to God. One of the most difficult tasks in developing a resilient mindset is to modify the negative self-image and loss of hope experienced by many youngsters. When youngsters attribute their perceived failure to God, the task takes on special challenges.

Because the ways in which children understand and respond to mistakes and setbacks are integral to a resilient mindset, it is incumbent on parents to understand the factors that contribute to more optimistic perceptions such as Bryant's, compared with pessimistic views as held by James and Ron. This understanding can aid you in saying and doing things that will reinforce in your children the belief that mistakes are not only accepted but also expected.

In this regard Willie Stargell, a Hall-of-Fame baseball player for the Pittsburgh Pirates, was asked after his retirement what he thought baseball had taught him. His answer resonates with the chords of a resilient mindset:

> *Baseball taught me what I need to survive in the world. The game has given me the patience to learn and succeed. As much as I was known for my homers, I also was known for my strikeouts. The strikeout is the ultimate failure. I struck out 1,936 times. But I'm proud of my strikeouts, for I feel that to succeed, one must first fail; the more you fail, the more you learn about succeeding. The person who has never tried and failed will never succeed. Each time I walked away from the plate after a strikeout, I learned something, whether it was about my swing, not seeing the ball, the pitcher, or the weather conditions, I learned something. My success is the product of the knowledge extracted from my failures.* (Stargell 1983, 11)

Obstacles to a Positive Outlook About Mistakes

Chapter 7 described obstacles that prevent some children from acknowledging or taking satisfaction in their successes. Similar obstacles block some children from appreciating that mistakes are not indictments of their skills or capabilities. As Willie Stargell testified, mistakes and setbacks can provide crucial information for future success. However, many well-intentioned parents are stymied in communicating this message. As you read through the following descriptions of these roadblocks, you may relate one or more to your family and recognize the need to institute change. The second half of the chapter offers a set of principles to help you in this mission.

Obstacle One: *The Power of Temperament and Biological Factors*

Children come into this world with a unique makeup. This makeup influences how parents respond to their children and how their children perceive the world. It follows that, as with conflicts regarding success, some children are born with a predisposition to react more strongly and negatively to mistakes than other children and therefore are more likely to experience frustration and engage in self-defeating coping strategies.

Mr. and Mrs. Fargo sought our help with their nine-year-old son, Anthony. The Fargos as well as Anthony's teacher were concerned about his low frustration threshold, difficulty sticking with any activity that proved problematic, tendency to blame others for any mistakes he made, and level of perfectionism, which contributed to his problem accepting and learning from mistakes.

Recently, Anthony had wanted a model airplane kit, which his parents bought for him. He insisted that he could assemble the model by himself, but his attempts led to broken pieces as well as parts not adhering. When Mr. Fargo explained to Anthony that he had to let the glue dry or the pieces would not stick, Anthony angrily retorted, "The glue is bad. It's not like superglue. This glue is really stupid."

The next day the Fargos found the airplane pieces in Anthony's wastepaper basket. Mr. Fargo told us that when he saw what Anthony had done, he became so annoyed with his son that he said something he regretted:

"You're a real quitter. If something doesn't go right, you don't take any responsibility. You just blame it on something else instead of learning from mistakes. When are you going to grow up?"

That led Anthony to yell, "It's your fault! Why didn't you buy me the right kind of glue? If you did, the plane would have been OK."

Another example the Fargos provided of Anthony wrestling with mistakes and perfectionism occurred in school. Anthony obtained a score of 85 percent on a math test, certainly a respectable grade. However, he had expected his score to be 95 percent or 100 percent. He became angry and told his teacher that his three incorrect answers were the teacher's fault because she had not written the questions in a way that could be easily understood. He proceeded to argue about the wording of each of the three questions.

Anthony's teacher told the Fargos, "I felt I was up against a prosecuting attorney who wouldn't listen to anything I had to say."

The Fargos could not understand why Anthony was like this, especially since they had never pressured him or his younger sister to be straight A students or to be perfect in what they did. From the details of Anthony's developmental history, it was evident that at least part of his perfectionism and difficulty in dealing with mistakes was rooted in his temperamental style. Mrs. Fargo remembered that when Anthony was a baby and would build a tower out of blocks, he would become very upset if the blocks were not lined up perfectly or if they fell.

"One time after the blocks fell, he picked one up and threw it at me. He was twenty months old, and it was frightening to see how upset he was getting. I wondered, 'Why is he getting so upset?'"

That account prompted Mr. Fargo to recall that when Anthony was learning to ride a tricycle, he initially had difficulty, as many children do, coordinating his leg movements. Anthony proceeded to get off the tricycle and began to kick the wheels while screaming repeatedly, "Bad bike!"

Mr. Fargo continued, "Anthony is a child who does not like to display mistakes. Even when he was learning to ride a two-wheel bike, he did it on his own and didn't ride in the street for other kids to see until he was able to ride without falling down. It's as if he doesn't want anyone to see when he makes a mistake."

As the Fargos traced Anthony's developmental history, we informed them about the influence that temperament can have on a child's frustration level and response to making mistakes. We noted that even Anthony's perfectionistic qualities could be largely inborn. Hearing this, the Fargos seemed both incredulous and relieved.

Mrs. Fargo asked with a smile, "Are you actually saying that some children from birth are already little perfectionists and have more problems dealing with mistakes and that it isn't caused by bad parenting?"

"Yes," we answered, "but we're not saying that parents aren't important or that they cannot play a major role in helping children feel more comfortable with mistakes. What we are saying is that because of different temperamental characteristics, children have predispositions toward certain behaviors."

Mr. Fargo wondered, "But if these behaviors are inborn even to some extent, what can we do to help Anthony feel less pressure about making mistakes?"

We reviewed with the Fargos some possible strategies, but we cautioned that whatever course of action they decided on would take time since Anthony's "negative script" about mistakes was entrenched and related to his inborn temperament. Similar to what we recommended to the Sterns about helping Samantha accept ownership for her successes, we told the Fargos that a beginning step was to be empathic and to validate what Anthony was experiencing rather than becoming angry and accusative. We emphasized that validating what your child is expressing does not mean you agree with your child; rather it communicates the message that you are empathic and are attempting to understand the child's point of view.

As an example, we reviewed the incident with the model plane. We suggested that when Anthony said he could assemble the plane by himself, their response might be, "We're glad you want to try it on your own. However, it doesn't look too easy. Many kids might need some help, so if you need any, we're here."

The intent is to acknowledge in advance that the task may be difficult, perhaps reducing Anthony's defensiveness if he should encounter problems. In addition, by stressing their availability to help, they make it easier for Anthony to approach them for assistance.

We continued, "When Anthony blamed the glue for the failure of the parts to stick together, it was probably a face-saving technique, although it was a rather poor one. Instead of yelling at Anthony, you could change the script and actually concede that it may be the glue or that maybe the directions about how much to apply weren't clear. Then offer, 'Let's see what happens if we clean the parts off and begin again. Maybe you have some ideas about what would work better.'"

The Fargos were intrigued by this line of reasoning. In a heartfelt manner Mr. Fargo said, "I guess it's much better than telling your son that he's a quitter."

We agreed but reiterated that given Anthony's intensity and perfectionism, it would take time for him to change course. As the Fargos engaged in this new script, they found Anthony more willing to listen and to accept their help. To their delight, he also became less of a perfectionist and less defensive. As an illustration of Anthony's change in mindset, they noted a recent situation in which a test score was not as high as he had expected, and instead of blaming the teacher, he approached the teacher to say he was having trouble understanding the concept involved. The teacher responded by helping Anthony.

"When Anthony told us what had occurred," said Mr. Fargo, "I couldn't believe that this was the same young man who months before would not own up to his responsibility and would blame anyone in sight. What a pleasure to see."

Let's return to Ron for another expression of the influence of temperament and biology on a child's experience of mistakes, especially his sense that he was "born to quit." As noted earlier, when Ron was only four weeks old, he was rushed to the hospital because of pyloric stenosis and required immediate surgery. Subsequently, he underwent surgery for a hernia and had tubes placed in his ears on several occasions.

Children will draw their own interpretations and conclusions about what they have experienced. These may be very different from what the adults in their lives perceived. In our therapy with Ron, he created stories that were extremely revealing, featuring individuals with physical deformities: one involved an individual who had been shot and as a consequence had a hole in his stomach, and another concerned a person who was in a fire and badly burned. These stories provided a glimpse into Ron's world and helped us to realize that from birth he felt "deformed." He attributed his condition to God since it began at birth, and consequently, he felt that he was not able to change the situation because, in essence, he was a "quitter."

When we asked him why he thought God would want him to be born this way and to become a "quitter," he said he didn't know but just felt that way. In our interactions with Mr. and Mrs. Rollins, we suggested that they tell Ron that they could understand why he would feel that way, especially given all of the surgeries he had faced, but that perhaps his conclusion that he was born to quit was not accurate. Such a statement empathized with his viewpoint but also introduced the possibility of a different explanation.

Mr. and Mrs. Rollins also encouraged Ron to think about activities at which he did not quit. One of Ron's islands of competence was his ability to build things out of wood and to fix things. He was a person who did not seem to require a manual to assemble many toys or other objects. Ron's parents reminded him of the hours he spent building a birdhouse that was now "displayed" on a tree in their backyard.

In one session, Mr. Rollins said, "I mentioned to Ron that the things he quit were things that were not only difficult for him but also things he felt he could not improve on, especially schoolwork. But I pointed out that when something that he liked to do was difficult, he would spend hours working on it."

Mr. Rollins continued, "It was like a revelation to Ron. At first he almost wanted to discount what happens when he is doing woodworking, but then he said that when he had problems with woodworking, he felt he could figure things out, and that's why he stuck with it, but he didn't feel that way about school. I told Ron that I knew figuring out schoolwork was much tougher for him than figuring out how to work with wood, but one of the things that made school so tough was that right away he sort of told himself he couldn't do it, and when he felt that way, he just quit. Ron seemed to be listening closely to what I was saying, so I told him something I learned from our sessions: I said that maybe we could figure what else he could do instead of quitting when he had trouble with his schoolwork."

We complimented Mr. Rollins on how skillfully he had used empathy to begin to present to Ron an alternative view. Mr. and Mrs. Rollins also initiated another intervention that proved very successful. They recognized that to Ron, his surgeries were a sign that he was "deformed" and that there were things that were wrong with his body. They talked with Ron's pediatrician, who was able to obtain x-rays of Ron's body when he underwent surgery. The doctor reviewed with Ron the many operations he had undergone and showed him the x-rays. He also noted that Ron's body was fine now and that he should be proud of all that he was able to do in spite of his earlier problems. This last statement especially served to reinforce a resilient mindset.

Ron continued to have learning problems in school, but with the support and input of his parents and pediatrician, his confidence and self-esteem improved, and he began to appreciate that mistakes are experiences from which to learn. In a revealing story that he wrote in therapy about an animal that thought it was born to quit (obviously, a representation of himself), the animal eventually realized that this was not so, and by the end of the story Ron had the animal's name changed from "Quitter" to "Try."

Obstacle Two: The Negative Comments of Parents

We routinely ask parents how their children would respond to the following question: "When you make a mistake, if you fail at something, what do your parents say or do?" Some parents have answered half-kidding, "Please don't ask my kids that. I wouldn't want you to hear what I say to them when they make a mistake." For a child to understand that mistakes are part of learning, parents have to respond to the child's mistakes in ways that teach rather than humiliate, that rely on problem solving rather than on blame.

Even well-intentioned parents react to their children's mistakes in manners that are counterproductive. This may occur because of baggage from their past that takes the form of negative scripts characterized by frustration and anger. Examples previously described include Jimmy, Michael, and Billy.

Jimmy was the nine-year-old who caught two touchdown passes in a game but also dropped one. When he came off the field, his father didn't praise him for the two touchdowns he scored but instead wondered why Jimmy had dropped a pass. When parents primarily call attention to mistakes rather than to accomplishments, the message the child often hears is that mistakes are unacceptable. While Jimmy's father may not have intended his communication to be so negative, it can be experienced in that way by a child, who is then likely to develop the feeling that mistakes are shameful.

Michael became so frustrated while attempting to build a radio from a kit that he quit. In response his father yelled, "I told you it wouldn't work. You don't have enough patience to read the directions carefully."

The father's own frustration drove him to convey a message to Michael that only weakened his son's resolve and resiliency. Rather than helping Michael to make the best of his mistakes, the comment reinforced his urge to retreat from the task, especially the prophetic "I told you it wouldn't work."

Similarly, when Billy spilled milk and his father reproved, "Why can't you be less clumsy! You just don't seem to think about what you're doing," Billy was not helped to develop a resilient mindset. From the perspective of attribution theory, his father's words contained the implicit message that Billy was a clumsy child, a characteristic that is not easily modified; thus, Billy could easily assume that his mistakes were the result of a condition that could not be corrected.

Obstacle Three: Parents Setting the Bar Too High

When the expectations of parents are unrealistically high, they influence how children experience successes and mistakes. If parents do not consider the temperament and skills of their children, they may expect more of them than they can possibly deliver. When children do not meet these expectations, parents may communicate a very negative message about making mistakes, as we saw with Jimmy, Michael, and Billy.

Chapter 6 made the case that one of your most important tasks is to accept your children for who they are and not what you want them to be. When parental expectations are inflated, such as in Mary's case when her parents got upset that her grades weren't high enough, the deck is stacked for children to experience ongoing failure. If children hear the subtle or not so subtle message from an early age that their physical, interpersonal, or learning skills are not as advanced as parents think they should be, they are likely to become more anxious when confronting other challenges. They are prone to become upset when they do not meet the standards set by their parents. This kind of situation does not nurture a sense that one can learn from mistakes; rather, children begin to believe that their mistakes are testimony to their incompetence and must be avoided at all costs. A resilient mindset is not likely to arise under these conditions.

Mr. and Mrs. Charney turned to us for aid with their eight-year-old, Sarah. Sarah had a thirteen-year-old brother and a ten-year-old sister. The Charneys' anger toward Sarah was apparent. They talked about the joy they experienced with their two older children but only the difficulties they had with Sarah.

Mr. Charney said, "Sarah is scared of her own shadow. The moment something goes wrong, she says it's stupid and she quits."

"Can you give us an example?" we asked.

"One of the final straws that led us to call for an appointment was what happened a couple of weeks ago," said Mr. Charney. "We finally convinced Sarah to try ice-skating. Everyone else in the family ice-skates, and we thought it would be a nice family activity. Sarah had always said no before, but for some reason she said OK. What a mistake! She fell two or three times, told us she hated skating, and left the rink. We should have expected it since she seems to quit at everything."

Mrs. Charney said, "When we left the rink, I was so angry with her. I felt she was ruining a fun family time."

"How did you respond?" we asked.

Mrs. Charney continued, "I felt like yelling to her to get back to the rink, but I didn't want to make a scene, so we just let her go into the stands to sit. I could see that she was crying. I almost felt bad for her, but I was also very angry. After we all finished skating, I went up to her and told her that she would never succeed at anything if she kept quitting at everything she did."

"What did Sarah say?"

Mrs. Charney responded, "Sarah did what she always does when we tell her she shouldn't quit: she got angry and said it was too hard for her. Then she tried to use a guilt trip, saying she knows that we love her brother and sister more. This time she also told me that she knew we hated her. I told her that we didn't hate her, that we were disappointed with her behavior, but she just repeated that she knew we hated her."

As we continued the discussion, a pattern emerged that was similar to that of other families described in this book, that of parental disappointment with one child in comparison with other children in the family who were meeting expectations. This was true of the Sargents with their youngest son, Damon; the Whites with their son, George; and Ms. Langston with her daughter, Wendy. Here the concern is the impact of what Mr. and Mrs. Charney said to Sarah on her reaction to mistakes.

We told Mr. and Mrs. Charney that we could understand how they felt, but similar to our interventions with other parents, we tried to instill a more empathic perspective by asking them how they thought Sarah felt at the ice-skating rink and how Sarah would describe what had occurred. The Charneys pondered for several moments.

Finally, Mr. Charney said, "Sarah would probably say that we think she's a quitter but that she really isn't, that some things are very hard for her. She might say that we always nag her about quitting."

Mrs. Charney observed, "She does feel we nag her, but the only reason we keep talking to her about quitting is that she always quits."

"Always? Are there some things she sticks with?"

Mrs. Charney said, "Not many. As soon as something becomes difficult, she just quits."

"Why do you think she quits so quickly?" we asked.

"I'm not sure," said Mrs. Charney. "No one else in the family quits. Both her brother and sister could skate by the time they were four. What a pleasure they were. They could both read by the time they entered kindergarten. Sarah wouldn't even pick up a book. We told her that she could read if she just tried, that she was as smart as her brother and sister. Even at five, she began to say she wasn't as smart as her brother and sister and begin to cry."

It became evident as the session progressed that Mr. and Mrs. Charney held the same expectations for Sarah that they had for their two older children. They expected her to ice-skate and learn to read at the same age as her siblings. While intellectually Mr. and Mrs. Charney could acknowledge that all children are different, their parenting practices did not take those differences into consideration. Given these unattainable expectations, Sarah began to believe that there was something wrong with her, that she lacked, as she told us in one of our sessions, the "smarts" to succeed. She believed that her mistakes and failures were beyond her control to change since she lacked the intelligence and skills. Sarah's mindset is a prime illustration of the principles of attribution theory and how mistakes are perceived, just as Jack's earlier comment at the baseball game that "the pitcher threw the ball soft" to him exemplified the perspective on success that attribution theory offers.

Our work with the Charneys involved an ongoing discussion about the differences in temperament, intellectual interests, and learning styles in children from birth. We discussed their expectations for Sarah and how comparing Sarah with their two older children not only was causing Sarah distress, sadness, and anger but also was contributing to the development of a negative mindset that would become a major obstacle to future success. Using the framework of attribution theory, we explained that Sarah was beginning to feel less and less empowered to change things and that when youngsters feel helpless, they are likely to quit at tasks that prove problematic for them. A sense of "learned helplessness" could dominate her mindset with its insidious view to the effect of "why try? Nothing good will come of it anyway."

Once the Charneys gained a more empathic and accurate understanding of Sarah's concept of herself and the world, we were able to implement several strategies that succeeded with other families whose stories have appeared in this book. We asked the Charneys to make a list of what they perceived as Sarah's islands of competence so that we could begin to promote a more positive self-image and to analyze the expectations they had for her and how these expectations related to her siblings' accomplishments at a similar age. Most important, we requested that they notice what they said and did when they were disappointed with Sarah and whether their well-intentioned comments to motivate her were actually causing her to retreat further from situations.

During our sessions with the Charneys, they began to recognize the negative script that had been established in their interactions with Sarah. Instead of thinking about what Sarah's siblings had been able to do, they began to zero in on Sarah's areas of interest and competence. Although Sarah had appeared to be frightened about ice-skating, when her parents asked what activities she might be interested in, Sarah answered to their surprise, "Gymnastics." Not only was one of her closest friends involved with gymnastics, but also, and perhaps more important, neither her brother nor her sister had ever taken gymnastics. Thus, gymnastics would not invite comparisons with her siblings.

Sarah showed unusual perseverance with this activity, even when she fell. Her parents were supportive, providing positive comments when she was successful and encouragement when she had difficulty. Instead of imploring her to try harder, they told her that learning gymnastics or any new activity involved falling and making mistakes and that these mistakes could serve as opportunities for growth.

As Sarah found her own way and her own islands of competence, as her parents decreased their comparison of her with her siblings and developed more realistic expectations for her (i.e., lowering the bar), and as they continued to offer her encouraging comments, she became more comfortable in persevering with challenging tasks. Sarah's shining moment arrived when she placed third in a regional gymnastics competition. The third-place finish was wonderful, but the Charneys asserted that of even greater significance was the fact that during the first trial of one of the events, Sarah slipped off the bar. As Mr. Charney noted, "The 'old' Sarah might have found a reason not to continue, but the 'new' Sarah got up and prepared herself for the next jump, which she executed flawlessly."

Obstacle Four: Dealing with the Fear of Making Mistakes in Ways That Worsen the Situation

This particular obstacle is connected to the others but places the spotlight on the coping strategies that children use to deal with mistakes. If children believe that mistakes cannot be corrected, if they develop a feeling of "learned helplessness," they are likely to become desperate and to resort to self-defeating ways of coping.

During his therapy sessions, Ron attempted to understand why he had hit his classmates at the beginning of each school day. He demonstrated impressive insight when he said, "I think I would rather hit another kid and be sent to the principal's office than have to be in the classroom where I felt like a dummy."

This is very similar in nature to Brett's comment that he would "rather misbehave than be dumb." While it could be said that Ron (and Brett) went from the frying pan into the fire in the attempt to improve the situation, we must remember that some children are so desperate not to look stupid that they would rather be punished or quit at a task than suffer further humiliation.

We are not suggesting that parents and other adults should accept Ron's hitting his classmates, Sarah's quitting at skating, or Michael's quitting at building a radio. The point is that when our children resort to such counterproductive behaviors as lashing out, giving up, or playing the part of class clown, we must recognize the behaviors as ineffective ways of coping with perceived failure and humiliation. These behaviors are often signs that our children are experiencing a great deal of stress and pressure. The more they engage in these kinds of behaviors, the more likely they are to push others away and to flee from challenges. Rather than possessing a resilient mindset, they are rife with feelings of inadequacy and hopelessness.

In these situations, we must step back and reflect on our expectations of and responses to our children. We must ask if we are appreciating their strengths, and we must help them learn to develop better ways of coping. When Mr. and Mrs. Rollins helped Ron to appreciate his strengths in woodworking and to deal with his feelings of deformity and helplessness by arranging for him to review his medical history with his doctor, they created an atmosphere in which he felt more self-assured and hopeful. Ineffective ways of coping were replaced by productive behaviors as Ron began to recognize that mistakes could be understood as challenges to confront (with the help of others) rather than as stresses to avoid.

Guiding Principles to Help Children with Mistakes

Four principles can guide you in helping your children become comfortable with the role that mistakes play in one's life. These principles are founded on the notion that when youngsters view mistakes as temporary setbacks and as opportunities for learning rather than as indictments of their abilities, we as parents will have helped them to develop a resilient mindset filled with hope and problem-solving skills.

Principle One: Serve as a Model for Dealing with Mistakes and Setbacks

Whether we like it or not, we serve as primary models for our children. Our words and actions in response to life's daily challenges cannot help but affect our children. If our children witness us backing away from challenges and quitting at tasks, we should not be surprised when they follow the same course of action. Children may not do what we say, but they often do what we do.

When asked to describe their parents' reaction to mistakes, children have contributed a wide array of answers, including:

"When my father has trouble fixing something in the house, he screams and then blames my mother or my sister or me for causing the problem. He actually once blamed us for a leaky faucet because we ran the water for a bath. I don't know how else he thought the water was going to get into the bathtub."

"My mom's great. She just doesn't seem to get frazzled by things. One time, we were having relatives over for dinner and she left a roast in the oven too long. I thought she would be so upset, but she said, 'I really goofed this time. I'll have to be more careful next time. It's too late to cook another roast. We'll just have to bring in food from a restaurant.' She told her relatives what happened, and we brought in food, and everything turned out fine."

"They yell and scream a lot and accuse each other of being dumb."

One of our favorite responses to the question was that of an innocent young boy who said, "What's a double martini?"

We asked, "What?"

He answered, "Every time they make a mistake or get upset, they say, 'Let's have a double martini.' I know it's some kind of drink. Is it supposed to help you with mistakes?"

Parents are often surprised by what children notice and the behaviors they model, which are often ones the parents wish they did not. Children in fact notice not only what we say to them but also how we lead our lives. A case in point is the Seligs.

Mr. and Mrs. Selig had two children, Rebecca, age eleven, and Donny, age nine. They came to see us primarily because of Rebecca, who they felt was quick to avoid situations that she experienced as too challenging. However, they also noticed some of the same characteristics appearing in Donny. They were concerned that as their kids reached their teenage years, a pattern was being established in which they would back away from many things.

Mrs. Selig said, "We'd like to see Rebecca take more risks and not worry if something doesn't work out."

They had told Rebecca and Donny of their plans to come to see us and even asked if they wanted to come along to meet us. Both of the kids said no but left the door open for future sessions. Prior to the second session, the Seligs talked with Rebecca and Donny about some of their concerns and said they thought it would be helpful if the children would attend the next session to provide their input. Rebecca and Donny said OK. What occurred was not what the Seligs expected.

Mr. and Mrs. Selig were very open in describing how much they loved their children, and their children acknowledged feeling loved. Then the parents expressed their concern that Rebecca and Donny often found excuses to avoid certain activities, and we asked them to provide us with a specific example.

Mrs. Selig said, "Rebecca was invited to try out for a class play. We think she would do a wonderful job, but she told her teacher she was too busy with other responsibilities. We love Rebecca, but we think if she wanted, she could have found the time."

We asked Rebecca what she thought, and she answered, "Maybe, but I really didn't want to be in the play."

We wondered why not.

Rebecca was impressively honest. "I don't think I'd be very good at remembering the lines and would look pretty foolish on stage if I forgot what I was supposed to do."

Her father was empathic and said, "Almost everyone worries about that, but if you focus on the mistakes you might make, it will keep you from doing things that you might find enjoyable, even exciting. So many people look back and regret that they ran away from doing things."

Rebecca then surprised everyone by saying, "Well, what about Mom?"

"What about me?" wondered Mrs. Selig.

Rebecca said, "Last year I overheard you on the phone. You turned down a request to speak at the Rotary Club, saying you were busy, but you really weren't. Isn't that the same as my not wanting to try out for the play?"

Mrs. Selig demonstrated impressive openness. "Rebecca, you're right. I did make up an excuse not to speak at the Rotary Club."

Rebecca asked, "But why?"

"I'm not very used to public speaking. I know most of the people in the Rotary Club. You would think that would make it easier for me to speak, but all I could think about was that if I did a poor job, these would be people I would be meeting all the time, and I would feel embarrassed."

"Well, that's how I would feel seeing other kids at the school if I forgot my lines," Rebecca answered.

We reinforced the value of honesty that was being expressed, noting that most people experienced the same worries that the Seligs were describing, and asked for suggestions on a solution.

Mrs. Selig said, "I guess I shouldn't be telling Rebecca to try out for the play and not to worry about what might go wrong if I'm not doing the same thing."

This was a remarkable session. Mr. Selig was equally understanding, sharing some of his own anxieties when he had to present a report at business meetings. Although Donny didn't say much, he listened intently. All four said that they wanted to return for a follow-up session but that in the meantime they planned to discuss what might help the situation.

We wish we could report that all of our therapeutic endeavors produce such quick and favorable results. When the Selig family returned the following week, they had already undertaken steps that they believed would work. Mrs. Selig called the head of the Rotary Club and scheduled a time to speak with the group. Rebecca went to the tryouts for the play and won a speaking role. Both of them asked Mr. Selig to tape-record their "practices" at home so that they could critique their performance and make appropriate changes. The fear of mistakes had greatly diminished as this family implemented strategies for dealing more effectively with anxieties about speaking and performing in public.

Principle Two: Set and Evaluate Realistic Expectations

Many of the families profiled in this book are living proof that if we set the bar too high, if we expect more from our children than they are capable of giving, if we expect them to engage in activities we like but for which they show little interest or inclination, we will create a climate in which our children will retreat from challenges. A "What's the use?" attitude will prevail. Mistakes and failure will be perceived as indictments of their talent rather than experiences from which to learn. George, Wendy, Mary, Damon, Sally, and Sarah readily come to mind as youngsters who faced expectations for accomplishment that, for a variety of reasons, they could not achieve.

Melissa, the nine-year-old only child of Mr. and Mrs. Porter, is another youngster who became increasingly anxious about making mistakes in response to unrealistic expectations on the part of her parents. Much of her anxiety stemmed from school, although anxiety was present in other areas of her life as well. Melissa was experiencing headaches on a daily basis. A medical workup was negative. Her pediatrician thought that the headaches were in response to the stress she was experiencing and recommended that her parents seek a psychological consultation.

Mr. and Mrs. Porter described Melissa as a child who "does the minimum amount to get by in school." A year ago, she was evaluated by an educational psychologist because of her underachievement. The psychologist found that Melissa tested in the "superior" range of intellectual abilities, with no indication of any learning problems. However, his report also noted that Melissa was very anxious throughout the testing, often inquiring if her answers were correct and wondering if other children her age knew "the right answer." While the Porters acknowledged Melissa's anxiety, they felt that if she applied herself and did well, she would be more proud of herself and not as anxious.

Mrs. Porter said, "Since she was a little child she's been anxious. We feel we've been supportive parents and have told her that if she didn't worry as much, she could perform at a higher level."

The Porters understood Melissa's anxiety as something that she could control if she had the will to do so. We introduced the notion that many children are born with a predisposition toward anxiety and that just telling such a child to be less fearful would be ineffective and typically would only add to the child's worries.

When we met with Melissa, her extreme anxiety was immediately apparent. She rarely looked at us, and many of her answers were brief and spoken in a near whisper. It took her several meetings to feel more comfortable. Finally, she acknowledged her anxiety to us and said sadly, "I don't think I will ever change. I'll always be this way."

We asked her, "Has anyone ever told you that things could not improve?"

Melissa then responded, "My mom and dad keep saying that if I don't try harder in school, I won't do well. But I feel I am trying as hard as I can. When I'm taking a test, I tell myself to do well, but then when I get a bad grade, I feel I'm not very smart and will never learn. I know that the man who tested me last year said I was smart, but I keep making mistakes, so I don't know if I'm really smart."

We were moved by Melissa's comment and the pain she was experiencing. We told her that it might be helpful if she could share these thoughts with her parents at one of our meetings. We pointed out that sometimes adults, even parents, don't understand how kids feel and may say things without intending to that make kids feel even more worried that things will not get better.

Melissa was willing to have a family meeting. At first it was difficult for the Porters to rewrite their script. Their attempts at empathy were short-lived, as they quickly added to almost any comment, "If you would be less worried, then you would do better, probably get As on your tests, and see how smart you really are." At one point, they couldn't resist ending with, "Then you wouldn't say you couldn't do something."

We had several parent counseling meetings to help the Porters understand that although Melissa possessed the intellectual capabilities to achieve better-than-average grades, other factors were contributing to a very negative self-image and impacting adversely on her performance. We noted that these factors included her temperament as well as the pressures she felt from them to be an A student. We led them to see that simply telling Melissa to be less anxious likely served only to increase her anxiety and sense of failure. Instead, it was important to indicate to Melissa that they knew she felt anxious and that perhaps they could figure out what would help her to be less anxious. We also raised the prospect of their letting Melissa know that they might have been placing too much pressure on her to earn top grades.

Mr. Porter wondered if doing so would be "lowering our expectations of what she is capable of doing."

We responded that it need not and that if we helped Melissa learn ways to be less anxious, her grades might improve.

Mr. Porter said, "But isn't that what we have been saying to her? We've said, 'If you were less anxious, your grades would be better.'"

We responded, "But Melissa has been hearing what you've been saying to mean a matter of 'will,' that she could change if she wanted to. The distinction we're making is that it is not a matter of 'will'; it's having more realistic expectations and everyone working together to figure out how Melissa might become less anxious and less afraid of making mistakes."

We also asked the Porters to put thought and effort into activities that bring Melissa success and satisfaction, such as her artwork.

Melissa's anxiety about failure and not living up to her parents' expectations was very strong, but as Mr. and Mrs. Porter followed through on our recommendations and removed the pressure for her to obtain primarily A grades, while doing more fun things as a family so that the spotlight was not continually on academic achievement, Melissa became less anxious. Although she did not obtain A grades, she became a solid B student, but most important, when something did not turn out as she had hoped, she no longer demonstrated a defeatist attitude. A more resilient mindset was emerging.

Principle Three: In Different Ways, Emphasize That Mistakes Are Not Only Accepted but Also Expected

If we are to nurture resilient mindsets in our children, we must communicate to them that mistakes are a natural part of life. Opportunities are present almost every day to convey this ideology. One way is to follow Principle One and model a more positive, less defeatist attitude toward mistakes. If you spill something, if you forget someone's name, if you trip while walking outside, attempt to remain calm, verbalize what you could do to lessen the probability of your making the same mistake again, and, when possible, use humor. Humor is very effective at minimizing the negative power of mistakes.

Many youngsters have shared wonderful stories with us about their parents' reactions to an event that didn't go as planned. One boy told us about his father, who was not handy with tools. Whenever his father had to fix something, he immediately talked about all of the things that could go wrong, which certainly was not a good model for this boy on how to handle mistakes and frustration. However, his mother produced a solution one day when she joked to her husband as he picked up a tool, "Curse now and get it out of your system." Much to the delight of his son, his father did curse (nothing too obscene), and it helped him relax and adopt a better frame of mind to tackle the job successfully.

If applicable, parents may wish to share with their children their own report cards and the comments that teachers made about them. At one of our parenting workshops, a father, who was a successful lawyer, told of a discussion he had had with his teenage son and daughter.

"They were putting a lot of pressure on themselves to earn good grades. It was as if they felt their entire future was being established by their grades in high school. I didn't think this attitude was based on anything my wife or I had said but was just a result of the pressure so many kids feel. I began to talk with them about enjoying themselves more, when my daughter said, 'It's easy for you to say. You probably always got As with little effort.' I realized when she made this comment that I had never really discussed my school performance with them. My parents had saved and given me all of my report cards. We all got a kick out of looking at my grades and reading some of the comments, including one from my tenth-grade social studies teacher that said, 'The level of his work is not what he is capable of doing, but his arguments about why he deserves higher grades than I gave him suggest that law may be a good field for him to enter.' I don't think this teacher wrote this in a humorous way, but when my kids and I read it, we all laughed. They also discovered I was not the straight A student they thought I had been."

As important as how you model dealing with mistakes is your reaction to your children when they make mistakes. Are your comments free of the anger and sarcasm displayed by Michael's father when Michael had difficulty building a radio? Do you avoid statements that reinforce a negative mindset, such as "You'll never be successful if you rush through things!" or "Why don't you use your brains!" or "How often do I have to remind you that what you're doing won't work!"

It is easy for parents to lose composure when children make mistakes that we think could have been avoided, but if our outrage prompts us to insinuate that our children are not capable of learning, they will begin to believe that mistakes are a sign of their incompetence. Be guided by the question introduced in the chapter on empathy—"Would I want anyone to say to me what I am saying to my child?"

You can also prepare your children for mistakes. For example, when teaching a child to ride a two-wheel bike, you can say in advance that it takes time to learn to balance a two-wheeler and that most kids will have difficulty at first.

One father told his daughter, "But don't worry, I'm here to catch you and help you get on again, and after a short time you'll be able to ride on your own."

A simple but powerful message such as this teaches children that they can all expect to fall at different times, but we are there to help them get up.

In addition, when your children make mistakes, assume a problem-solving stance that will reinforce the notion that mistakes and failure are accepted and expected. When your children are having difficulty with a task, you can engage them in a discussion of what they think might help; this conveys the belief that situations can improve, that there are ways to remedy mistakes. When a plan of action is agreed on, parents can ask, "What if it doesn't work? What's our backup plan?" Raising the possibility that a plan will not work should not be interpreted as a self-fulfilling prophecy for failure. It is simply an acknowledgment that not every plan will be successful. In fact, facing the reality that a plan may not work actually helps youngsters learn to better deal with mistakes, as long as they know that there are other possible strategies to try.

When Mr. and Mrs. Porter gained a better understanding of the temperamental basis of Melissa's anxiety, they asked her what she thought might help to ease her anxiety while taking tests. At first she said she didn't know. Her parents reassured her that was OK and allowed that she might be able to think of something at a future time. A few days later Melissa told them that she had thought of something that might be helpful: she wondered if her teacher would allow her to take the test in an office outside the classroom. The Porters asked Melissa why she thought this would help.

She told them, "I keep looking at the other kids, and they seem to be working much faster than I am, and I start to feel that they know the answers and I don't. Then I get more anxious."

While some children would feel singled out and self-conscious taking a test outside the classroom, Melissa did not harbor this reservation. The Porters discussed her proposal with the teacher, who was willing to give it a try. We also recommended to Mr. and Mrs. Porter that they tell Melissa that this is a good plan but in case it doesn't work, she should have another possibility in mind.

Melissa responded, "Maybe I can try to sit near the teacher's desk at the front of the room so I wouldn't see the other kids and wouldn't get as worried."

In fact, Melissa decided that she liked this second plan better than the first. However, when she implemented it, she found herself turning around and looking at her classmates as the test was being taken. After two tests, Melissa asked that her original plan be used. It worked very well. Melissa took four tests outside the classroom and found that she was much less anxious.

As her anxiety abated, she said, "I think I can return to the classroom to take tests," which she did with satisfying results. From this experience Melissa learned the valuable lessons that she had within herself the ability to arrive at solutions to problems and that if one solution did not work, there were other solutions that would.

Principle Four: Loving Our Children Should Not Be Contingent on Whether or Not They Make Mistakes

Many children believe that they are accepted and loved only when they do not make mistakes and fail. Often, this belief is intensified when parents hold expectations for their children that the children cannot meet. When Mr. and Mrs. Charney compared Sarah with her older brother and sister, expecting her to be as successful as they had been, they communicated the message that you will be more loved if you do not make mistakes. This becomes an untenable situation for a child, and in Sarah's case she responded by quitting at various tasks. Obviously, quitting did not help to gain her parents' love and approval, but it was the only way she felt she could assuage her sense of anxiety and failure.

Unconditional love remains an underlying principle for helping our children learn to deal with mistakes and perceived failure. It is when our children make mistakes and experience setbacks that our ability to be empathic is really tested, but these are also the times that provide an opportunity to educate our children about the positive results that can follow from mistakes.

Doing What Comes Naturally

The very nature of resiliency requires that we help our children learn that mistakes and setbacks are natural occurrences in any child's development. A resilient mindset is one that holds the following belief: "At times I will make mistakes and suffer setbacks. I can learn from these mistakes and become a stronger person, better able to handle future challenges." One of our most important duties as parents is to help our children to develop this belief so that the fear of failure is minimized. In that way, our children will be more willing to take appropriate risks in life and truly "taste" all of the good things that life has to offer.

In this regard, it's helpful to remember the following observation about the role of mistakes, which appeared in a report issued by the California Task Force to Promote Self-Esteem and Personal and Social Responsibility.

> *Mistakes are a natural part of life. We learn by experimenting; mistakes and failure can be important parts of our learning process. Einstein flunked grade-school mathematics. Edison tried over 9,000 kinds of filaments before he found one that would work in a lightbulb. Walt Disney went bankrupt five times before he built Disneyland. If we accept our setbacks, we can continue to risk, learn, and move on with excitement and satisfaction.* (California State Department of Education 1990, 31)

Einstein, Edison, and Disney were very successful, talented, resilient people. None of us knows what our own children can accomplish. We do know that our children's accomplishments will be greater if they are not burdened by the fear of mistakes and failure.

9

Developing Responsibility, Compassion, and a Social Conscience

Young children are strongly motivated to be helpful. They take great pleasure in helping us and beam bright smiles when their contribution is complimented and appreciated. Children appear to come into the world with a need to be helpful and valued. Perhaps someday a gene or group of genes will be identified that promotes this pattern of behavior. It appears to be a universal common denominator. Three-year-olds will eagerly approach their parents while watching them mow the lawn and ask if they can help. They want to help us cook, take care of younger siblings, rake leaves, build things with our tools, sweep the kitchen, and set the table. One four-year-old listened as his father mentioned to an acquaintance in the grocery store that he was quite tired from many activities. Afterward the boy excitedly said, "Don't worry, Daddy, I'll drive if you want me to. I know how to drive my bike. I'm a good driver."

In observing our children through this perspective, we can marvel at how helpful and responsible they wish to be. Some of this behavior is rooted in the excitement that most children experience when they undertake new activities and challenges; this appears to reflect children's drive toward mastery and a sense of accomplishment. However, that explanation alone doesn't explain this pattern of behavior. We believe that children possess an inborn need or drive to help and to make a positive difference in the lives of others. While most children can be very self-centered at times, placing their own needs first, this trait is often accompanied simultaneously by a pattern in which they achieve pleasure in reaching out and being helpful. As a matter of fact, children generally welcome invitations to be of assistance.

Many parents tell us that their children have lost this drive by the middle childhood years. They appear to resist many opportunities to be of assistance unless "there is something in it for them." In order for this pattern of helpful behavior to emerge and be maintained, parents must nurture this quality, shaping what appears to be an inborn trait into a sense of responsibility, compassion, and social conscience.

Many years ago we set out to test our theory that children not only are excited about but also embrace the opportunity to contribute to the well-being of others. We asked a large group of adults to tell us the most positive and negative memories they held from their school years. We asked specifically about positive incidents that included something a teacher said or did that enhanced self-esteem and motivation and that was recalled fondly through the years. Before reading further, pause for a moment, and think of a former teacher, coach, or other nonparental figure of whom you have a very positive memory. What was it about that individual or specific experience that in one way or another positively impacted your life? You will likely discover that your answer reflects the most common theme among the responses from the survey group. These are representative of many we received:

> "As a first-grade student, I had the responsibility of raising and lowering the coat closet doors because I was one of the taller boys in the class. This made me feel so good because I was so self-conscious about my height."
> "In a one-room school, the teacher had me sit and do spelling with the second-graders, once I had shown some ability in this subject."
> "My English teacher asked me to tutor a senior who was not about to graduate because she was failing English grammar. I was in tenth grade."
> "In the third grade, I was chosen to help get the milk and straws."
> "In the eleventh grade, my art teacher asked me to paint a mural in the school. I still correspond with her."

Is your memory similar to the theme of the ones just listed? All of these experiences embody a child's opportunity to contribute in some positive manner to the school environment. These responses validate psychologist Urie Bronfenbrenner's observation that part of every student's curriculum at school should be a "curriculum for caring" in which youngsters are taught ways to take care of others. These accounts also convey that the act of caring, learning to be compassionate, and teaching responsibility go hand in glove.

Responsibility, Caring, and Resilience

This chapter explores the close relationship between reinforcing a responsible attitude in our children and the development of a resilient mindset. One of the most effective ways of nurturing responsibility is providing children with opportunities to help others. Thus, the spotlight here is on the ways in which reinforcing responsibility can be paired with teaching compassion and a social conscience.

Although the ties between responsibility and resilience may seem obvious, it is helpful to examine the nature of these bonds. When children are enlisted in helping others and engaging in responsible behaviors, we communicate our trust in them and faith in their ability to handle a variety of tasks. In turn, involvement in these tasks reinforces several key characteristics of a resilient mindset in our children, including:

- The ability to be empathic and understand the needs of others
- The willingness to demonstrate compassion
- The capacity to see oneself as a contributing member of the family and of society
- The capability to solve problems that may arise in the helping role
- The feeling of ownership for one's behaviors
- A sense of satisfaction in the positive impact of one's behaviors
- A more confident outlook as islands of competence are displayed

As children develop this foundation of a resilient mindset and develop responsibility, a commitment to be accountable for one's life emerges. Responsible children are more likely not only to acknowledge credit for their own success but also to perceive mistakes as experiences from which to learn rather than blame others. As shown in the previous two chapters, this perception of success and failure is integral to resilience.

Chapter 1 included the difficulty experienced by Laurie in getting along with her peers. The fifteen-year-old was described by her parents as the "pied piper" of her neighborhood. Her enthusiasm and ease in the presence of younger children were obvious, and these children loved to be with her. In this regard, she was similar to Amelia in Chapter 7, the nine-year-old child who had developmental problems but found strength in helping out at a nursing home and serving as a "mentor" for two younger sisters who lived next door.

Laurie's parents, Mr. and Mrs. Laramie, consulted us because of Laurie's difficulty in making friends with children her age and the "lack of responsibility" she displayed in various areas of her life. Her parents' description of her development indicated that she was socially immature and felt ill at ease with her classmates. As Laurie's difficulties were disclosed, we also asked the Laramies to describe their daughter's strengths, or islands of competence.

Mrs. Laramie immediately said, "It's a pleasure to watch Laurie with younger children. She has such a gentle style and is very patient with them, so that they love to be with her. The other day, three eight-year-old neighbors came by to see if Laurie was available to teach them a game. Her entire face brightened when she saw them. She's so much more talkative with them than she is with kids her own age." It was then that Mrs. Laramie referred to her as the "pied piper" of the neighborhood.

Mr. Laramie remarked, "What my wife just said is so true. But in contrast, the other day when I drove Laurie and several other girls to an evening youth group meeting at our church, I noticed that she barely said one word to the other kids, and they hardly said anything to her. When they all got out of the car, Laurie walked into the church by herself. The other girls weren't really being mean to her; it was as if they didn't even realize she was there. It was painful for me to watch. It's amazing to see the difference between her behavior with kids her age and how she acts when she's with younger kids. She's like two different people."

We asked if they could cite examples of Laurie's lack of responsibility, which they had mentioned earlier.

Mrs. Laramie responded without hesitation, "She often forgets to make her bed or put her clean clothes away, so that they are stacked on the floor. Sometimes we're not sure what's clean and what's been worn. We also feel she should take more responsibility for getting ready in the morning. She sets her alarm, but sometimes she falls back to sleep, and we have to come in and wake her up."

"My wife and I have discussed our concern whether Laurie will become a responsible person or will have to rely on others to get things done," added Mr. Laramie.

Our suggested interventions for the Laramie family involved several strategies for increasing Laurie's sense of responsibility, all of which were based on reinforcing Laurie's islands of competence, her sense of ownership, and her feeling of control of her life. We suggested that the Laramies take advantage of Laurie's obvious strength in relating with younger children. Fortuitously, she had recently been asked by a neighbor to baby-sit for her five- and seven-year-old sons two afternoons a week. Her parents encouraged her to accept the job, which she did. Laurie's mother was available should Laurie experience any problems. In addition, we recommended that the Laramies and Laurie jointly decide on other ways in which Laurie could take more responsibility in her life. We suggested that they ask Laurie to think about what would help her to remember to fulfill these responsibilities, as well.

The baby-sitting job provided experiences that boosted Laurie's self-esteem and sense of responsibility in several ways. First, the very act of taking care of the two brothers conveyed to Laurie that she was a capable person. Also, her ability to solve problems was strengthened as she talked with the parents about what kinds of things she could do with the boys while baby-sitting. Mr. and Mrs. Laramie frequently spoke with Laurie about her baby-sitting and found many opportunities to praise her for the wonderful work she was doing and her responsible behavior. Laurie also received positive feedback from the parents of the boys. For her, meeting the cognitive and social challenges of baby-sitting served as a nutrient in the establishment of a more resilient mindset.

This mindset was further reinforced by her concentrating on becoming more responsible in other areas of her life, one of which was getting ready for school in the morning without constant reminders. To facilitate this process, Mr. and Mrs. Laramie consulted with Laurie's guidance counselor at school. We had raised the point that it might be easier for Laurie to be at school on time if there were an appealing activity waiting for her. Laurie's high school was located next door to a nursery school, where several high school students earned credits by assisting in the early morning. Laurie was asked if she would be interested in helping at the nursery school. She readily accepted, as this activity involved one of her islands of competence. Since Laurie knew that the children at the nursery school were depending on her, she made sure to be ready on time, which was earlier than she would usually awaken for school. Her parents were very willing to drive her a half-hour earlier, especially since this new responsibility created a calmer atmosphere at home.

There was an additional benefit to this activity. With the assistance of her guidance counselor, Laurie wrote an article for the school newspaper about her experiences working in the nursery school. As Mrs. Laramie said, "When Laurie saw her name in print, it was worth several years of therapy."

Once children are engaged in these "contributory activities," that is, activities in which they contribute to others, they are more likely to develop responsibility and compassion. In addition, as this sense of responsibility is reinforced, they are more willing to accept ownership for their behavior and less likely to resort to self-defeating coping strategies.

The Myths of Irresponsibility

If children do possess an inborn need to help, then why do so many parents complain that their children are irresponsible, self-centered, or selfish? At parenting workshops, we are constantly asked about how to motivate children to be more caring, considerate, and responsible.

A father recently said, "I drive my fourteen-year-old son to his games, to buy things, to the movies, and to meet friends. I go out of my way to do so, but the other day when I asked him to take out the trash, he had a million and one reasons why he couldn't do it right away."

Similarly, a mother lamented, "It's a battle every time I ask my eleven-year-old daughter to do her chores. We don't expect unreasonable things from her—she is supposed to clear the dishes and put them in the dishwasher—but she always seems to have an excuse. The other night, she said she had a lot of homework, but the first thing she did when she got to her room was call one of her friends. I was very angry. My daughter said that her friend was upset and she was just trying to cheer her up. Maybe she should have first thought of cheering her mother up by meeting her responsibilities at home."

Do most children want to help, or are most basically self-centered? Are most children responsible or irresponsible? We may sound like Solomon, dividing the baby in half, in asserting that depending on the perspective, the day, the activity, and who the players are, the same child may appear to be responsible or irresponsible. Basically, we believe that most children are born with a wish to help and to make a positive difference. However, at times, this wish is not nurtured as strongly as it might be, even by well-intentioned parents. Also, the ways in which youngsters think that they can make a difference may be at odds with parental perceptions. Thus, when parents contend that their children are irresponsible or inconsiderate, the children may have a very different opinion of the situation.

But why the divergence in perspective? And why are some children seemingly less helpful than others? Let's examine a few reasons for this difference in viewpoint.

1. Equating Chores with Responsibilities

The label we choose to describe responsibilities we want our children to fulfill is one that unfortunately takes on negative connotations. That label is "chores." We often tell our children, "Remember to do your chores." Many parents refer to the first responsibilities they expect their children to meet as chores. In addition, chores often become synonymous with homework, another unwelcome activity. We have yet to interview a child who says, "I am so fortunate to have chores and homework to do." In fact, we would probably be suspicious if a child ever said those words. When we ask groups of parents, "How many of you love to do chores?," nary a hand is raised. However, when we next ask, "How many of you like to help others?," almost all hands go up in unison.

Can a label such as "chores" make a difference in a child's perception of what is being requested? We believe it can. Of course, removing the word or similar ones from the English language wouldn't suddenly make children more responsible. However, when parents maintain that their children are not very responsible, they often offer as their examples failure to complete household chores. When we are preoccupied with day-to-day chores, we often lose sight of the many areas in which our children can be and are responsible. In addition, while it may seem obvious to us why certain chores have to be done, it is not necessarily so to our children. One nine-year-old boy asked his parents, "Why do I have to put the games away in the playroom? I'm just going to take them out again tomorrow." Another child asked, "Why do I have to wash my hands? They're going to get dirty right away."

2. Taking a Narrow View

Closely related to parents' failure to distinguish between chores and other responsibilities, a second contributing factor to viewing children as irresponsible is the difficulty in assuming a broader perspective of children's lives. When you have reminded your children for five consecutive days to clean their rooms, put their toys away, or put their dirty clothes in the hamper and they neglect to do so, it is easy to jump to the conclusion that you're raising irresponsible children. As we place the spotlight on what our children are not doing, it is easy to miss the many responsibilities that they are meeting.

Ms. Malone consulted us about her only child, eleven-year-old Marty. It was obvious that this mother felt hassled and harried.

"I'm a single parent, and I never get any help from Marty. He doesn't make his bed, he never empties his wastepaper basket, he leaves his dirty dishes out, and just yesterday I tripped over his shoes, which he left near the door. I was ready to scream!"

We empathized with her and asked if she had spoken with Marty about his seeming lack of responsibility.

"I speak with him all the time. It's as if it goes in one ear and out the other. He should be more helpful. He knows that I have no one else to help. He also lives in the apartment. All he thinks about is himself."

"Does he *ever* help out with things?" we asked.

She quickly answered, "Very seldom."

We then rephrased the question. "We can see that you would like him to be more helpful, but if you can tell us about those times when he *is* helpful, perhaps we can build on those experiences." When we worded the question in this way, she listed several ways in which Marty contributed to the functioning of the household.

"He will often help with grocery shopping, and he actually likes to cook, so sometimes he has cooked dinner." She quickly adjoined, "But there are so many small things he could be doing to help out."

We suggested that she make a list of responsibilities that she felt Marty was not meeting and a list of ways in which he helped. As she created this second list, she was surprised to see the many ways that Marty did help. While not minimizing her concerns for the areas he neglected, we asked about the kind of feedback she gave Marty when he assisted her.

She replied, "I'm a little embarrassed to say that when Marty has done things to be helpful, I don't think I thank him enough, and sometimes I've even told him if he could remember to do the cooking, why can't he remember to do other things. It's funny looking at this list and realizing that Marty helps out in more ways than I realized."

Unintentionally, this mother, perhaps because she was feeling so hassled, habitually emphasized things that her son did not do rather than the many ways in which he contributed to the household. She had fallen into a negative script characterized by a "praise deficit." This particular pattern is discernible to a greater or lesser extent in many families. In our intervention, we suggested that she acknowledge Marty's helpfulness. We also recommended that she select one or two responsibilities that she considered most important for Marty to accomplish and discuss them with him, clarifying their importance and how he might remember to do them.

When Ms. Malone assumed a broader view of her son's contributions to the home, it was easier for her to become more positive and "less of a nag." Marty reacted well to his mother's praise, which permitted him to be less defensive and more open to listening to what she had to say about other responsibilities that he had neglected.

Another example of a "narrow view" is a rather common one. Celia's parents, Mr. and Mrs. Saunders, complained about the self-centeredness of their fourteen-year-old daughter.

Mrs. Saunders said, "She never helps out. Everything is a battle. If you remind her to do something, she gives you that 'look' that says, 'Why are you bothering me?' Once when I asked her to clean her room, she shouted, 'Do you think I'm your slave? It's my room.'"

"Has she always been this way?"

Mr. Saunders replied, "She used to help out more, but in the last year or two, she has been less cooperative. I'm concerned that she is becoming a selfish person."

At that point, Mrs. Saunders interjected, "She doesn't hesitate to help her friends if they ask her, but she won't help us around the house."

We asked her, "Do you think that when Celia helps her friends, it might be an indication that she is not a selfish person?"

"Maybe toward her friends, but she only seems concerned about herself at home," Mrs. Saunders responded.

We told Mr. and Mrs. Saunders that we agreed that it would make things easier if Celia were more helpful at home but that her behavior at home did not necessarily indicate that she was an irresponsible child. We emphasized that it was important to examine what she did in all parts of her life. We noted that most adolescents increasingly devote their attention to their friends and expend less energy to help at home.

We commented, "We're pleased that Celia is at least spending time helping her friends. We would be more concerned if she were not helping anyone."

Similar to our recommendations with Ms. Malone about Marty, we suggested that the Saunders change their script and tell Celia that they believe it is important for her to help her friends, that it indicates that she is a caring person and a good friend. Highlighting the *positive* aspects of the attention that Celia gave her friends would make her less defensive when they then brought up required responsibilities in the house.

While Mrs. Saunders thought this might be a good approach to take, Mr. Saunders voiced reservations. He stated, "We are the ones who do so much for Celia. She should first be helpful in the house, and then she can help her friends."

To better understand Mr. Saunders's reluctance to accept our recommendations, we asked him how he *felt* when Celia turned to her friends.

At first he answered, "It gets me angry. I feel as if she has turned her back on us." Then he became misty-eyed and conceded, "I miss the little Celia we used to have. I miss throwing her up and catching her, and I miss the hugs she always gave me."

Mrs. Saunders took her husband's hand and said, "I miss some of that also, but we have to realize that Celia's no longer that little girl."

This was a remarkable session. Mr. Saunders became aware of the distress he was having in "giving up" his "little daughter" and of how these feelings intensified his view that Celia was self-centered. Both Mr. and Mrs. Saunders came to recognize that their view of Celia was narrow and that by adhering to it they failed to appreciate that when Celia spent time on the phone consoling a friend or assisting a classmate with a homework assignment, she was demonstrating that she was a caring and responsible young lady. This change of perspective permitted them to become more positive in their interactions with Celia, and as we have seen with many youngsters, Celia responded by becoming more responsible about several activities at home.

3. A Mismatch of Expectations and Abilities

Chapter 6 discussed the importance of developing expectations for our children that are in accord with their temperament, cognitive skills, and learning style. Throughout this book, numerous scenes have unfolded of parents expecting behavior that their children had difficulty delivering, such as Carl getting ready for school, John completing his homework, or Mary achieving higher grades. In many of these kinds of situations, parents refer to their children as irresponsible. However, the issue is not one of responsibility but rather, as referenced in the previous two chapters, of setting the bar too high.

When youngsters are asked to do things that they feel lie beyond their control, they will often back away from the task. This is why you must ensure that as you teach your children to be responsible, you choose tasks that they are capable of achieving.

We all fall victim to unrealistic expectations with our children at times. By not allowing these "myths" to guide your behavior, you enhance the role of responsibility for your child.

Guiding Principles to Help Children Develop Responsibility, Compassion, and a Social Conscience

This section offers five principles to help shape your mindset and guide your behavior toward your children. The goal of these principles is not necessarily to create certain skills but to foster and strengthen qualities that are inherent in all children.

Principle One: Serve as a Model of Responsibility

Keeping in mind that children are very observant not only of what parents say but, more important, of what parents do, how would you answer the following questions?

- If we asked your children the ways in which you are responsible, what would they answer?
- If we asked your children what behaviors they have observed in which they felt you were not responsible, what would they say?
- If we asked your children what charitable activities they have observed you involved with in the past few months, what would they say?
- If we asked your children what charitable activities they and you have been involved with together in the past few months, what would they say?

We pose these questions to stimulate parents to examine the ways in which they serve as models of responsibility and caring.

Mr. and Mrs. Palmer came in to see us about their sons, fourteen-year-old Roy and twelve-year-old Duane. They described the constant bickering between the boys.

"Things can be calm at the dinner table, but you can almost predict that before long one of them will say something provocative to the other, and soon they are screaming and shouting at each other. When they are watching television, there are always battles about what show to watch, who will control the remote, what chair to sit in. Quite honestly, it's draining," said Mr. Palmer.

"And they always have to be reminded to do things," said Mrs. Palmer, "They will throw their clothes on the floor, forget to put their games away, forget to shut off the lights when they leave a room, forget to do their homework, forget to empty their wastepaper baskets. I can keep going on using the word *forget* to describe them. My husband is right when he says it's draining."

We asked what they did about all of this forgetting.

Mr. Palmer responded, "We usually end up screaming and yelling. That usually gets them to do what they're supposed to do, but as we said, it's draining, and it's no way for a family to live. We feel that everything is a battle."

We asked him then if there were any consequences for the forgetting *other* than the yelling.

He wavered, "We usually take TV away or send them to their rooms, but it seems to do little good. We must have done something wrong to have two sons who are so irresponsible."

Hearing their frustration, we told the Palmers that it can be helpful to think about how children perceive us and our actions. We commented that they had used the word *irresponsible* to describe Roy and Duane, and we invited them to consider their sons' assessment: "If we asked Roy and Duane in what ways they observed their parents being responsible or irresponsible, what might they say?"

Both Mr. and Mrs. Palmer responded that they were not certain.

We added, "It's something you may wish to think about. It may be helpful to have your sons come in with you for the next session so we can figure out ways that the situation at home can improve."

Mr. Palmer said, "I'm sure they won't yell in front of you, and I'm sure they'll tell you that they do meet their responsibilities but we still nag them."

We reassured the Palmers that if their sons said these things in the session, it would not be unusual, since most children have a different perspective from their parents, and most behave more respectfully in our office. We said that if Roy and Duane conveyed very different views from their own, they could examine these different perceptions as a family as a first step in resolving some of their difficulties.

The next session with Mr. and Mrs. Palmer and their sons was revealing. The Palmers began by reiterating the problems they had told us about in the previous session. We asked Roy and Duane what they thought. At first each was somewhat defensive, with Roy saying, "We don't fight as much as they say. They're always on our backs."

Mr. Palmer said, "What you call 'being on your back' is Mom and me reminding you to meet your responsibilities and to help the household be less tense. However, whatever we're doing doesn't seem to be working, since we keep having to remind you. We just want you to be more responsible."

We asked Roy and Duane about their father's comment, especially if they thought it was important for them to help out at home. We routinely ask this kind of question to assess if children understand their roles in the household.

Duane answered, "Some of the things are dumb. What if toys *are* left out or we don't make our beds? Is that such a big deal?"

"It is to us," said Mrs. Palmer. "What if none of us helped out? What if Dad and I didn't cook? What if no one did the dishes? What if your clothes weren't cleaned? How would our house be then? Everyone has to pitch in. If the two of you don't chip in, then you will keep thinking we're nagging you."

Her comment prompted us to ask, "Do all of you feel that you are responsible? Do you follow through on what you say you will do?"

What transpired was fascinating to observe and underlined the important role that parents play as models.

Pointing to his parents, Duane said, "They tell us we don't do things, but there are plenty of times they don't keep their promises. Also, they say we don't clean up, but you should see *their* room. They have their clothes on their dresser. They just leave their clean clothes there, but then they yell at us if we haven't put our clothes in the drawer." Roy nodded in support of his brother's rendition.

Mr. and Mrs. Palmer looked a tad embarrassed. Mrs. Palmer turned to her husband and scolded, "I've told you that you shouldn't leave your clothes out."

Duane added, "And they tell us we don't keep our promises, but they don't always keep theirs. Just the other night, we were supposed to go out to eat, but Dad was late coming home from work, and we never went. He apologized, but this has happened a lot."

Roy chimed in, "They tell us to clean up, but sometimes they leave their mail and newspapers on the table or kitchen chairs. Also, Mom has been reminding Dad to fix the front door that keeps getting stuck for at least a month, and Dad says he will get to it."

The parents' defensiveness soon gave way to the father's admission, "I guess we all have to be a little more responsible."

This elicited a discussion of the most important responsibilities that had to be met in the household, who would be in charge of each, and what the consequences would be if they were not done (one was no television until your responsibilities were completed, and that applied to the parents as well). In addition, Mr. Palmer made certain that if he said he would be home by a certain hour or would take his sons out, he followed through. Clothes were also put away in the parents' room, and they cleaned up the mail and newspapers. Mr. Palmer even repaired the door.

We found working with the Palmers to be a delightful experience. After their initial defensiveness, the parents displayed unusual openness to changing their script and reflecting on what they could do differently. They were able to convey to their sons, and to themselves, the importance of family members' accepting the responsibilities each had in the family. They replaced nagging by joining with Roy and Duane in a problem-solving approach to difficulties that arose.

This change process took shape when the Palmers made changes in their own script that served as a model for their sons.

Principle Two: Provide Opportunities for Children to Feel They Are Helping Others

Children's inborn need to help is an obvious fit with reinforcing a sense of responsibility and compassion. Engaging in the task of helping others strengthens children's self-esteem and feeling of ownership and instills the message that what they do contributes to the well-being of other people— all elementary to a resilient mindset.

For this reason we advocate that when children reach age three, perhaps even earlier, parents should designate one activity to become the child's responsibility. Rather than calling this assignment a chore, they should say, "We need your help." This is not semantics for its own sake but rather places the accent on communicating to children from an early age: "You are a valuable person with something to offer others." This message reinforces responsibility and a resilient mindset.

When each of the first author's sons turned three, the child was asked to put his dirty clothes in the hamper; the clear message was that by doing so, he was helping out. They responded very well.

When our children assist in this way, we should remember to offer praise such as saying, "You make such a big difference in this house. You are so helpful." Children's faces light up with smiles when they believe their actions help others. Even adults want to feel that they make a positive difference. If we do not provide our children with opportunities to make a difference in a positive way, they are more likely to make a difference in a negative way.

The belief that our actions have an impact on others is a powerful incentive to meet one's responsibilities. If possible, parents should attempt to use their children's islands of competence in this task. For instance, Wendy became more responsible and felt more competent when she was taking care of pets, an area of interest to her. Similarly, nine-year-old Amelia's desire to help others was used in the nursing home setting, in interacting with two younger neighbors, and in helping to set the silverware at home. When Pattie, the fifteen-year-old soccer star, began to channel and control her anger, she took on the role of assistant coach in a young girls' soccer league. Pattie never missed a practice. It was obvious that her sense of responsibility and caring deepened from this experience.

To help put this principle into practice, monitor your diction with your children: Does the word *chore* occur more than such constructions as "We can really use your help." We are suggesting not that *chore* be banned from your vocabulary but that you should rely on the motivating force of a child's wish to help. If that force can be emphasized and harnessed, the likely outcome is children who are compassionate, caring, and responsible in following through on activities that they believe will help others.

Seven-year-old Ryan had difficulty getting to school on time. Part of the reason lay in his temperament, another part in his learning problems, so that school was not the place in which he most wanted to be. When we consulted with his parents, Mr. and Mrs. Warner, they characterized Ryan as an "irresponsible child" and interpreted his struggles in getting to school as manipulative.

Initially we worked on increasing their empathy by helping them understand the role of temperament in Ryan's problems and in defining the impediments that he faced related to learning. We reframed his problems in getting to school as a coping strategy to avoid what he perceived to be a failure situation. Our interventions centered on Ryan's receiving additional help for his learning difficulties. We also recommended that he be given a task to do at school when he first arrived that would involve assisting others.

Ryan's parents and teacher agreed, noting that Ryan liked the principal and the principal liked him. The teacher and principal worked out a plan, which they then presented to Ryan. The principal said that each morning before class began, he needed someone to help him to see if any of the floors were scuffed or if any of the lights were out. He offered Ryan the position of "Assistant Custodian," which Ryan accepted with delight. Given this responsibility, Ryan had a highly motivating purpose to be at school before class began. The principal even printed him a certificate that read "Assistant Custodian," which Ryan proudly displayed at home. The responsibility that Ryan demonstrated in this role had a ripple effect in his efforts in class and in other parts of his life. The moral is to never underestimate the power of feeling that you are making a positive difference.

Principle Three: Develop Traditions to Become a "Charitable Family"

Principle One enlisted children's responses to four questions regarding responsibility. Two of those questions dealt with charitable activities: Have your children observed you involved in those activities, and have you and your children been involved in such activities together? These questions are founded on the belief that it is easier to teach responsibility and compassion when we serve as models of responsibility and compassion and when we actively engage our children in contributory activities.

Obviously, we would not want children to answer that their parents are out every evening in performance of different community activities, since that would indicate that parents are sacrificing valuable time with their children. However, we are reassured when children tell us about a town committee on which their parents serve, or that one of their parents is a coach on a youth team, or that their parents help to raise money or give time for at least one charity.

We don't always receive that reassurance. On one memorable occasion, an adolescent who had a strained relationship with what he considered to be "overbearing, critical parents" responded to our question about how his parents helped in the community with the sarcastic rejoinder, "I've never seen them help out in any way, but they can tell some of the best racial and ethnic jokes you'd ever want to hear."

Not only should children observe parents engaged in bettering the lives of others, but also, from an early age they should be involved in these kinds of activities themselves. Even preschool children may accompany their parents to a soup kitchen to serve meals, help their parents deliver food to elderly people at holiday times (or other times), or participate in walks for hunger or AIDS.

In our clinical practice, we too have had opportunities to play a supporting role. We have purchased candy, cookies, wrapping paper, and magazines as part of a school or scouting group's fund-raising. We have sponsored scouts in their quest for the highest scouting honor, the Eagle. Youngsters have pledged us to give money to their chosen charity based on how many miles they walked; as these children collect their money, it's wonderful to observe the joy on their faces and to realize their sense of accomplishment.

A "charitable family" develops a tradition of involving the entire family in helping others. In so doing, parents reinforce in their children the belief that they are important, that they have the capability of helping others, that they are appreciated, and that they make a difference. A child who develops this belief is also acquiring a sense of responsibility and caring, and a mindset that is filled with the characteristics of resilience.

Principle Four: We Can't Get Away from "Chores," So Distribute Them Fairly

Even if we are careful to express to our children that we need their assistance for the household to run more smoothly, it remains that many jobs are rather boring and tedious. How many of us like to clean our room, clear the dishes, take out the garbage, or vacuum? These are the kinds of activities about which we procrastinate or "forget." If they are left unfinished, the results are typically a home that does not run as smoothly and comfortably as it might and children who are not engaged in contributing to the household. What can help to facilitate the completion of so-called chores?

First, discuss with children why certain activities are important and what would happen if they were not completed. One set of parents made this point by telling their three children that if their dirty clothes were not placed in the hamper, they would not be washed. When the older son in the family, a fourteen-year-old, discovered one morning that he did not have a clean pair of pants or a shirt to wear, he quickly learned the consequences of his noncompliance. At first, he tried to blame his parents, saying he didn't know they had done a wash the day before. They calmly told him that he had a choice: he could remember to place his dirty clothes in the hamper or he could do his own wash. To their surprise, he selected the latter and from that point did his own wash and his own ironing. Not many youngsters make that particular choice!

Second, it is helpful for a family to sit down and make a list of the responsibilities that are necessary to be done in the household. While differences of opinion may arise about what responsibilities are important, these differences can serve as the basis for further discussion during family meetings. Some chores that at one point are deemed important may later be discarded. Once a list of responsibilities has been created, your family can review which items can be done only by certain members of the household and which ones can be done by anyone. This decision is typically determined in great part by children's ages and physical and cognitive skills. Obviously, a family would not expect a four-year-old to clean leaves out of the gutters, but that child could help rake.

Third, when a list of responsibilities and responsible parties has been generated and prioritized, your family can then develop a system for how these responsibilities should be delegated and for how long. Some responsibilities are more tedious than others. Many families create a rotating schedule so that chores among family members change every week or every month. The Palmer family used monthly rotation very successfully.

Fourth, recognize that even with the aid of a list and rotating chores, children may forget to meet their responsibilities. Thus, the final step in a family discussion of the distribution of responsibilities is to raise the question of what the family should do if anyone, including parents, forgets to meet a responsibility. Many families build in simple reminders in the form of brief verbal comments such as, "You forgot to clear the dishes" or "You left the family room without putting the games away." Others place a chart of the specific responsibilities at key places around the house, and when a responsibility is not met, family members point to the chart.

Whatever the strategy, a guidepost for parents is to involve their children in understanding why it is important for everyone in the family to help and how the work can be distributed equitably. While parents can reserve the final say, children will appreciate their role in family life if they believe that their views are being heard. When this occurs, they are more likely to develop a sense of responsibility and ownership.

Principle Five: Take a "Helicopter View" of Your Child's Life

A helicopter view helps to offset the "narrow view" defined earlier in this chapter. As observed with Ms. Malone and Marty and with Mr. and Mrs. Saunders and Celia, it is easy for parents to place too much weight on an area in which the child is seemingly not very responsible and in the process undervalue other areas in which the child is being very responsible.

Assuming a helicopter view challenges you to observe your child's life from a broader perspective. We often ask parents to write down in what ways their child is not meeting responsibilities; we then ask them to write down examples in which their child is fulfilling responsibilities and being helpful. For many, this exercise is a revelation of all of the responsible things that their children do.

Some parents at first are unable to come up with any responsible activities in which their children are involved, but we request that they be close observers for a week. If they notice any responsible behaviors, we ask them to begin to acknowledge and reinforce them. This positive approach will then make it easier for them to discuss with their children the areas that need improvement. If they are still unable to notice any behavior of merit, we suggest that in a calm moment they initiate a problem-solving dialogue with their children about the importance of everyone's contributing to the household, following the steps outlined under Principle Four. This approach paid rewards with both Ms. Malone and the Saunders family and has proved successful with many other families.

Instinct and Opportunity

The act of learning to accept responsibilities implies that children have developed many characteristics associated with a resilient mindset, including empathy, a sense of ownership for their lives, an appreciation of how their behaviors impact on others, and a feeling of genuine success. Based on the belief that children have an inborn need to help and that they receive much satisfaction when they do, one of the best ways to encourage responsibility is to provide them with opportunities to engage in contributory activities in which they assist others. Not only will this nurture responsibility but also it will promote compassion and a social conscience. Thus, parents play a pivotal role in shaping and developing the human instinct of helpfulness, which otherwise, for many children, can become lost in the demands of everyday life.

This point is captured by *Boston Globe* writer Linda Weltner in a column titled "Ever So Humble: Kids Need to Give as Well as Get." Weltner notes:

> *In her book* Raising Compassionate, Courageous Children in a Violent World, *Dr. Janice Cohn suggests that kids need genuine accomplishments in order to develop a healthy sense of self-esteem. Empty praise, she says, has a destructive effect upon children's character. In contrast, when kids help others, they come to feel truly competent, powerful, and proud of themselves. Cohn cites studies which show that those with a commitment to caring for others not only have higher levels of self-esteem, but perform better academically and socially, and are at lower risk of suffering from depression or anxiety disorders. It turns out that those who are involved with something beyond themselves are most likely to report high levels of well-being and life satisfaction.* (Weltner 1997, E2)

Weltner's and Cohn's description of the benefits of helping others parallels our description of the mindset of resilient children, including the key roles of responsibility, compassion, and a social conscience.

10

Teaching Our Children to Make Decisions and Solve Problems

Problem-solving and decision-making skills are basic components of a resilient mindset. Regardless of the particular situation, parents have countless opportunities to engage their children in activities that involve problem solving and decision making, activities that reinforce a sense of control and mastery.

It is difficult to imagine a day passing that does not involve children making even small choices and decisions. Earlier chapters described how Mrs. Jones might have handled things differently to help Jane tackle the problem of being excluded by classmates at the lunch table. A rewritten script for Mr. and Mrs. Smith involved Gregory in meeting his responsibilities, including cleaning his room. The approach taken by Mr. and Mrs. Castle involved their son, Joel, in a solution for his propensity to quit at different activities. Four-year-old Robert suggested a strategy to confront his difficulty going to sleep because of nightmares: a night-light and a portrait of his parents by his bedside. Melissa arrived at two possible plans to help her be less anxious while taking tests; when one plan fizzled, she moved on to the second one.

Problem Solving and the Resilient Mindset

The ability to solve problems is linked to all features of a resilient mindset. It enables children to meet challenges by relying on what they can control. They explore various options. They modify any negative scripts in which they are mired in order to improve decision making. They are less likely to engage in power struggles since they feel a sense of empowerment. Finally, they anticipate possible obstacles to the choices they make and treat any setbacks or mistakes as experiences from which to learn.

In contrast, when children struggle to problem solve, they often lack the ability to articulate and define problems, to think of options, to plan, or to navigate adversity. In many ways, they are adrift, like captains lost at sea without a compass, following one course or another but without any sound judgment to guide their actions. In such a situation some children may become "paralyzed," not knowing what to do, while others act impulsively without considering the consequences of their actions. One of the reasons some clinicians have used the label "difficult" to describe certain youngsters is that these children have a difficult time reflecting on what to do. Their behavior is characterized by actions seemingly in the absence of thought.

The lives of two eleven-year-old girls, Ashley and Anna, are a study in contrasts of how children react to everyday problems. Both had conflicts with learning to read, being accepted by their peers, and meeting responsibilities at home, including completing school assignments.

Mr. and Mrs. Satin characterized Ashley as a child who "does not stop to plan, who lets things slide, who can act impulsively without thinking ahead of the consequences; and when things don't work out, she tends to blame others for the problem." They offered several anecdotes in illustration.

Mr. Satin said, "We saw that Ashley was not being called by certain friends who we thought were very nice. We noticed that in the past when she was with these friends, she often dictated what they should do, and it was obvious that they were getting turned off by her bossiness. We tried to talk with her about it, but she always says that we're wrong, that we never take her side, that these friends were mean to her for no reason. I must admit I got angry, and I told Ashley that she was the one who was wrong and that she never wants to look at what she is doing that could help the situation. After I said that, Ashley didn't want to talk about it anymore and felt I was blaming her."

"Ashley is having a hard time in school learning to read and at home completing her homework," Mrs. Satin said. "When we ask if she has done her work, she often tells us she did most of it and will finish the rest soon. Either she finishes it very late at night after she has watched television so that it is not done in a very careful way, or she doesn't finish it at all. Last night we told her that she had to start her work earlier, and she just sat there sulking. She complained that we always tell her what to do. We said that we tell her what to do because she doesn't do what she's supposed to do. She said that we should stop bugging her. There's no way we can talk with her. It's so frustrating."

Mr. Satin continued, "And she's having trouble reading but refuses to get help from a reading tutor, saying tutors don't help. Then she uses her learning problems as an excuse not to meet her household responsibilities, saying that she doesn't have time to clear the table or clean her room because she has so much work. We keep reminding her that she's not meeting her responsibilities, but our efforts just don't seem to matter."

Many parents can relate to the goings-on between the Satins and Ashley. In discussions with the parents, we flagged Ashley's difficulty accepting and appreciating the problems in her life and arriving at possible solutions. We interpreted her seeming dismissal of her problems and her contention that her parents were nagging her as both a consequence of her more impulsive temperament and a means of coping with situations that intimidated her. The approach for reinforcing problem-solving skills and a resilient mindset in children that we prescribed for the Satins is outlined later in this chapter.

Think about what you would do if you were Ashley's parents, to help her improve her problem-solving and decision-making skills. Some direction can be derived by studying the strategies used by Mr. and Mrs. Oakley with their daughter, Anna. The Oakleys shared these strategies at a parenting workshop.

Anna ran up against some of the same walls as Ashley. However, the ways in which she learned to surmount these barriers were significantly different from Ashley's behavior and are hallmarks of a resilient mindset. Anna was able to recognize and acknowledge that she had difficulty reading and getting organized to do her homework. Her parents suggested that she join them in a parent-teacher conference so that she could hear observations about her learning strengths and weaknesses and also participate in finding remedies where they were needed. Anna accepted.

"It was impressive to see Anna's involvement," Mrs. Oakley said. "Although there were a couple of times when she was a little defensive, she agreed that there were subjects that were causing her difficulty, and she told us what she thought would help. We talked about the problem of her waiting until late in the evening to do her homework, which added a lot of pressure on all of us. Anna said that she needed a break from work after school. We were able to establish a schedule in which she took a break when she first came home but then worked for an hour before dinner and finished her assignments immediately afterward."

Mr. Oakley noted, "The fact that Anna was involved in helping to solve this problem made her more motivated to follow through."

Mrs. Oakley added, "We used the same approach in getting her extra reading help. Anna did not want to miss any activities in class in order to go for extra help and didn't want the help after school or in the evening either. Her teacher said that some tutoring was available before school began. We were really surprised since Anna likes to sleep as late as possible, but she selected that option and most of the time has followed through on it.

"On a couple of occasions, she shut her alarm off and went back to sleep. She became angry with us for not waking her, but we had all agreed that it was her responsibility to get up on time since in the past when we did come in to wake her, she accused us of nagging her. We put the problem back on her shoulders and asked her to think of a solution. We told her we were there to help. She decided she needed a radio alarm clock with a snooze setting. She sets the alarm for the time she wants to wake up, but if she should go back to bed, she sets the snooze alarm for ten minutes later, which still gives her adequate time to be in school early enough for her tutoring session."

In our discussions with the Oakleys about Anna's peer relationships, they noted that at one time Anna's typical style was to dominate the conversation, which alienated her peers. They had an opportunity to sit down with Anna after she complained that she wasn't being invited to play at other children's homes nor were most of her peers accepting the invitation to play at her house. We asked the Oakleys what they said to Anna.

Mrs. Oakley responded, "It wasn't too difficult to get into a discussion with Anna, since she had mentioned her unhappiness about having few friends. We wanted her to be an active part of the conversation, so we asked her if she knew why kids were not inviting her to their homes.

"At first she said they were mean, but we asked her to think a little more about it. She told us again that she wasn't certain. We think she really didn't appreciate what she was doing to alienate her friends, so we said that we had noticed some things that might help explain what the problem was. We asked if it would be OK if we told her what we observed so that we could figure out a way to solve the problem."

Mr. and Mrs. Oakley were able to be empathic and to communicate in a manner that neutralized any possible defensiveness on Anna's part. From the perspective of problem solving, they deftly smoothed the way for Anna not only to define the nature of the problem but also to participate in its solution.

Another parent at the workshop wondered what would have happened if Anna had answered that she did *not* want her parents to share their observations about her problem. We proposed that they could have responded, "Maybe you can tell us why you don't want us to discuss what we have seen. We think it would be helpful if we did talk with you about it. If you don't want us to do it now, think about it. Maybe it'll be easier in a day or two."

We have typically found that giving children a little breathing room makes them more inclined to accept advice, a point that was reinforced as Mrs. Oakley continued.

"Anna was receptive to listening to us, which really helped. We selected a couple of examples in which she was almost dictatorial with her friends, telling them what to do. At first Anna said that she was just 'suggesting' things to them. We told her it might seem that way, but to us it came across as if she weren't giving them any choice. We basically told her that she didn't have to agree with what we said but that it would be helpful if she thought about it.

"She didn't become defensive," observed Mrs. Oakley. "Instead, a couple of days later she wanted to talk more about it, and before we knew it, we were discussing what she might do to change her style with her friends. Anna herself came up with one really good solution that seems so simple and has worked remarkably well: she asked her friends what they would like to do, and if they weren't certain, she mentioned a few possibilities but left it to them to choose. Once in a while she still slips into the dictatorial role, but usually she catches herself. It's been a pleasure to see the progress she has made."

The Oakleys' approach with Anna is a model for encouraging and reinforcing problem-solving and decision-making skills in a child, strengthening a sense of ownership, and nurturing a resilient mindset. The Satins, although well intentioned, frequently interacted with Ashley in a way that compromised opportunities for their daughter to develop these features of a resilient mindset.

What is it that the Oakleys did that was missing, in part, from the parenting repertoire of the Satins? We believe there are guiding principles that are part of a problem-solving approach. These can be used with our children from an early age, in almost any situation they encounter. As with the other components of a resilient mindset, subtle or not-so-subtle parenting practices intervene in the development of problem-solving skills in children. The following sections take you through these possible obstacles, as well as the principles you can follow to enhance your child's ability to handle challenges and problems.

Obstacles to Teaching Our Children How to Solve Problems and Make Decisions

Whether we realize it or not, all parents have certain assumptions about how to teach our children to handle problems. Sometimes these assumptions are roadblocks to nurturing our children's ability to make decisions and develop a sense of ownership for their lives. Here are the top three.

Obstacle One: Believing That Young Children Don't Have the Ability to Make Decisions, So We Must Do It for Them

Many parents do not fully appreciate the capacity of children to solve problems. This is especially true when our children are of preschool age or if they have "difficult" temperaments in which they act before they think. Robert's parents had nightly standoffs with their four-year-old before they realized the intense fears he was experiencing about going to bed. Once these fears were recognized, Robert arrived at a creative solution to his difficulties. The Ceranos likewise faced ongoing battles with their temperamentally difficult six-year-old daughter, Larissa. They attempted to provide Larissa with some choices; when these did not work, they resorted to spanking her and not involving her in the solution to the problem.

We are not advising that parents let children have the final say in making decisions. Certainly, parents must set guidelines, but they must also find opportunities, as the Ceranos eventually did, to offer choices that are within a child's cognitive and emotional capabilities.

If we do not perceive our children as capable of solving problems or making decisions, we will often delay teaching them these very important skills. Instead, we step in and tell them what to do. We must remember that problem-solving skills do not develop by osmosis when a youngster is thirteen years old. They must be continuously and carefully cultivated from an early age.

Obstacle Two: Expecting More than Our Children Can Deliver

This obstacle, in many ways the obverse of the first obstacle, echoes discussions in previous chapters of parents setting goals and expectations for their children that are too high. Larissa comes to mind once again. The Ceranos told her before entering a store that they would buy her one item of her choice as long as it was not too expensive. As Mr. Cerano lamented, "Larissa's idea of inexpensive just didn't match ours. Once again she ended up demanding and crying."

It is difficult to involve our children in the task of solving problems that require skills beyond their means. Mrs. Granatto, the mother of a child struggling with anxiety, attended one of our workshops in which we advocated giving children choices. We emphasized that doing so not only would reinforce a resilient mindset but also could curb power struggles. Mrs. Granatto called a couple of days later and said, "What you suggested didn't work."

We asked, "What didn't work?"

She responded, "I have one of those difficult children you discussed. She's six years old. Every morning is a real battle. She can't decide what to wear, and finally I get so angry that I just tell her what to wear, and soon we're screaming at each other. Talk about a negative script! After hearing you speak, I decided to give her a choice of what to wear and to do it the evening before so that it would be all set in the morning. I placed eight of her outfits on the bed and told her to select one to wear the next day. She stood there almost paralyzed and just began to say, 'I like this one, no this one, no this one.' It drove me crazy, and finally I resorted to my negative script and just told her what she would wear. So, you see, giving a choice didn't help at all."

Did you spot what's wrong with this picture? We empathized with Mrs. Granatto and applauded her attempts to help her daughter, but we also pointed out that providing too many choices for a temperamentally difficult child can be overwhelming, which can easily result in the child's becoming "paralyzed" with indecision.

She laughed and said, "I never thought of that. Would it be better if I just put out two outfits?"

"It's worth a try," we responded.

The next day, Mrs. Granatto called back with an update. "I put out two outfits: my daughter was still a little indecisive, so I came up with this plan. I felt, what did I have to lose? I was empathic (it was obvious this mother had heeded the advice we gave at our parenting workshop) and said to my daughter, 'I can see that it's not easy deciding what to wear tomorrow, since you seem to like both outfits. So, why don't we do this: decide what to wear tomorrow, and then you can wear the other outfit the next day.' To my amazement, it worked."

She said in high spirit, "Feel free to discuss my brilliant maneuver at your next parenting workshop." Then she added, "But I can't believe I didn't see that putting all those choices out for my daughter was just too much for her. Oh well, live and learn."

With much good humor, this anecdote goes to show you that if children are induced to make choices and solve problems that are beyond their capacity to do, they are less likely to feel secure about engaging in problem-solving tasks. As they feel less secure, we are more likely to step in and tell them what to do, compromising their sense of ownership.

Obstacle Three: Allowing Children to Make Decisions as Long as What They Decide Agrees with What We Feel Is Best

Most parents would maintain that they want their children to be "independent thinkers," to reflect on things, to be able to withstand peer pressure. Yet, often the unspoken message is "I want my children to be independent thinkers as long as their independent decisions are in accord with what I think is best." Though this dictum is most powerful during adolescence, it is actually present at all ages.

Mrs. Cerano once took her six-year-old daughter, Larissa, shopping for a dress and said, "Do you like the blue dress or the green dress better?" Larissa at first answered, "Both."

Mrs. Cerano specified, "Well, we can only buy one, so which one do you like?" Larissa finally said, "The green one."

"I can't believe what I actually said next," Mrs. Cerano groaned. "I said, 'The green one is nice, but I think you look better in blue.' Larissa rightfully yelled, 'You told me it was my choice.' I told her she was right, and we got the green dress, but I could see that she was upset."

While the selection of a green dress versus a blue dress may not seem like a major event, what occurred in the clothing store was a parent offering a choice that she herself had difficulty accepting. Often, the negotiations between a parent and child have far greater ramifications than the color of an article of clothing. As we provide children with opportunities to make choices and decisions, we must be certain that all of the choices offered are ones with which we feel reasonably comfortable. As logical as this point may seem, many parents are not comfortable with the possible choices they give their children. The results can be quite negative, including children's feeling deceived, losing trust in what their parents have to say, feeling robbed of the sense of ownership, and being drawn into power struggles.

Before moving on to the principles that foster the skills of problem solving and decision making, it may be helpful for you to reflect on how these three obstacles relate to your parenting practices. The more attuned you are to these possible negative scripts, the more likely you are to revise them.

Principles to Reinforce Problem-Solving and Decision-Making Skills

In presenting the guidelines for nurturing problem-solving abilities and a resilient mindset in our children, we acknowledge the contributions of our friend and colleague Dr. Myrna Shure, who was instrumental in developing the I Can Problem Solve (ICPS) program, which is discussed in her books *Raising a Thinking Child* and *Raising a Thinking Preteen*. Dr. Shure's work has highlighted that even preschool children can be taught skills to enhance their ability to learn how to solve problems. While we have added some of our own ideas to Dr. Shure's approach, the framework has been greatly influenced by her work.

Principle One: Serve as a Model of Problem Solving

Evidence abounds that our children are careful observers of our behaviors, including how we cope with various situations. For example, Chapter 8 profiled Rebecca, whose parents were concerned about her fear of making mistakes, which prompted her to back away from challenges. At one of our family meetings, Rebecca surprised her mother by noting that Mrs. Selig had turned down a request to speak at the local Rotary Club and querying how that differed from Rebecca's own behavior.

In accordance with the self-evaluations in previous chapters, think about how your children would answer the following two questions:

- "How do your parents solve problems and make decisions?"
- "How do they teach and involve you in decision making?"

There are some families in which effective problem solving appears to be a natural part of their repertoire, while the interactions of other families are characterized by arbitrary decisions with little, if any, input by the children.

A vivid example of the latter would be thirteen-year-old Trudy and her eleven-year-old brother, Wayne. Their parents, Mr. and Mrs. Betton, came to see us about Trudy, whom they described as "becoming increasingly rebellious, letting her schoolwork slip, being influenced by negative friends, and not doing any of her chores." Our work with the Betton family included one particular session that aired the parent's anger at their daughter for not thinking for herself and always being guided by the advice of her friends. The bone of contention that day was that Trudy wanted to spend a Saturday afternoon with her friends at the local mall and her parents said she could not.

In the session, Trudy said, "You never let me do what I want. All of my friends will be at the mall. We don't do anything wrong. It's just nice to be with your friends and walk around. I can't understand why you won't let me go."

Mr. Betton retorted, "You can't understand? There are a couple of reasons, but not that you would listen to them. You always have missing homework assignments that must be made up and chores that you haven't done. We don't think you should be going out to the mall when you haven't met your other responsibilities."

Trudy asked, "So, if I get my homework and chores done, I can go?"

"Actually, no," answered Mrs. Betton. "We don't think you should be hanging out at the mall, especially with some of your friends."

"Why not?" she persisted.

"We think they've been a bad influence on you. They suggest something, and you just follow along."

"What do you mean?" asked Trudy.

"Like the time you told us you were studying at Julie's house when a few of you actually went to the movies."

"I told you I made a mistake. Are you going to hold that over me for the rest of my life?"

"Not for the rest of your life," responded Mrs. Betton, "but you have to show us that you can be trusted and that you're not going to be influenced by the negative behavior of some of your friends. You have to be strong enough to make up your own mind."

Trudy was visibly upset when she said to her mother, "You say I should make up my own mind, think for myself, but whenever you and Dad disagree, he tells you you're wrong, and you just go along with him. You do the same with your friends; I've never seen you stick up for what you believe if the other person disagrees with you."

Mr. Betton barked, "Don't you talk to your mother like that!"

"I'm just telling you what I see," said Trudy.

Initially Mr. and Mrs. Betton were both very defensive about Trudy's remarks, but over the course of the next several weeks, it emerged that Trudy had hit the nail on the head: rather than attempting to resolve differences and deal with conflict, Mrs. Betton basically acquiesced. She and her husband did not serve as models for solving problems. Instead, what Trudy and Wayne constantly observed was Mr. Betton cutting off discussion, then telling his wife what should happen, and Mrs. Betton going along with it. In our sessions, we helped them to modify this family script.

We also recommended that the four of them set aside a weekly time to discuss different issues in the family and what each could do to help resolve conflicts. We helped them to create ground rules for these meetings, including that each of them could place items on the "family agenda" (a term that they used), that each would have a time to speak without being interrupted, that when dealing with a problem they would attempt to solve it together, and that if there were a disagreement, they would attempt to compromise as much as possible but that the parents would have the final say.

Trudy and Wayne were very motivated to participate in the family meetings. Mr. Betton, on the other hand, found it difficult to relinquish his role of telling his family what should be done, but with input and encouragement on our part, he learned that involving his wife and children in the discussion did not compromise his authority but rather led to a more unified, harmonious family. Mrs. Betton slowly developed an ability to deal with conflict not by fleeing from it but rather by offering her opinion. Trudy's oppositional behavior improved as she felt her parents paying closer attention to what she was saying.

Many months of family therapy were involved in changing the Bettons' script, but the outcome was a new script in which the parents served as models for solving problems and making decisions. Both Trudy and Wayne learned from what they observed in their parents and became more cooperative and receptive to seeking new ways to handle differences.

In light of the experience of the Bettons and the family pattern that had been established, think again about how your children would answer the questions posed at the beginning of this section: "How do your parents solve problems and make decisions?" and "How do they teach and involve you in decision making?"

Your thoughtful and informed answers will help you gauge to what extent you are helping to promote a resilient mindset in your children.

Principle Two: Provide Choices at an Early Age

If we want children to learn to solve problems and make decisions, we must build a solid foundation for these skills by providing them with simple choices. Most parents do so as part of their typical parenting practices. Many examples come to mind:

"Do you want pizza or lasagna for dinner?"
"Do you want to wear your yellow shirt or your blue shirt?"
"Do you want me to remind you ten minutes or fifteen minutes before
  bedtime to get ready for bed?" (This can be done with the help of a clock
  with hands that the child can see.)
"Do you want to play with this toy or that toy?"
"Do you want the night-light on or off when you go to bed?"

We often recommend that at the end of each such question, parents add the comment "It's your choice." We highlight the word *choice* to convey to children that we trust in their ability to make a decision. Such simple steps begin to establish and reinforce problem-solving skills in children.

Parents frequently ask how they should respond if children do not like *either* choice offered. With young children this rarely happens, but if it does parents can say, "Well, those are the only two choices. Think about them and let me know what will be best for you." In some situations, parents might ask the child to think of an alternative choice, and if the child's option is reasonable, the parent can agree to it. Remember that the choices that you offer must be ones with which you are comfortable.

Principle Three: Follow a Problem-Solving Sequence

The ability to solve problems and make decisions comprises a process with several interrelated components. The most important features of this sequence are highlighted here.

Articulate the problem and agree that it is a problem If a problem is not clearly defined, and if children do not agree with parents that it is a problem, then all of our exhortations to arrive at a solution will fall on deaf ears.

As parents, we must be careful not to misinterpret a problem. For example, Robert's parents saw his problem as his temper tantrums, but his problematic behavior turned out to be rooted in the terrible nightmares he was experiencing. Cindy's mother represented her daughter as having "a personal vendetta" against her, when in fact her daughter's behavior was based on a "difficult" temperament. Sarah's parents viewed her as a child who quits but failed to see that in many respects the problem resided in their unrealistic expectations of her. John's father perceived his son as an underachiever who would not get accepted to a good college, but a major determinant of John's difficulties was an undiagnosed learning disability.

The ways in which we understand our child's problems will play a large role in how we respond. If we experience a child as being willful, manipulative, out to get us, lazy, or a quitter, we are more likely to be angry and resort to a more authoritarian style. If we possess a better sense of the basis of the problem, if we recognize that some problems are predicated on a child's temperament or abilities, while other problems represent a child's attempts to deal with stress and pressure (e.g., children such as George, who set a fire because his parents harped on his weaknesses, or Sarah, who quit at skating because of the inflated expectations of her parents), our capacity for empathy and for engaging our children in effective problem-solving strategies will be enhanced.

As part of defining a problem, parent and child must agree that there is a problem. For instance, Gregory did not view his messy room as a problem. The problem for Gregory was his parents' nagging him about the room and a host of other transgressions. Larissa perceived the problem in the Cerano home as her parents' not buying her things she wanted, while her parents held that the problem was that she was insatiable and self-centered.

Ashley, whom we met at the beginning of this chapter, minimized or denied her difficulties with peers and school and tended to view the problem as residing in the way others treated her. In contrast, her parents, Mr. and Mrs. Satin, perceived the problem as Ashley's inability to accept responsibility for her behavior and her tendency to blame others. Our counseling with the Satins focused on how to bridge these different perspectives. We explained that we should first find areas of agreement on which to build.

"Probably the only thing we would agree on is that there is a problem with friends and schoolwork. That would be it," Mr. Satin said.

"Then, let's begin with that. What if you were to say to Ashley that you know that she feels that the two of you are on her back all the time, but you don't want to come across that way and you want to figure out what would help the situation."

Mrs. Satin responded, "Ashley would probably say that we *are* on her back all the time."

"That's OK," we said. "At least there would be some agreement. She might be more willing to listen to other things you had to say." We then suggested that they could even ask Ashley if she was feeling pressure about problems with friends and school. If she said no, they could say, "Maybe that's one of the reasons there's been so much tension between us. What we see as a problem, you don't. We would like to explain why we feel it's a problem. We want to do it because we really want to figure out how to be of help."

We added, "If she says that friendships and schoolwork have been a problem, you can ask her in what way they are problematic and can share your impressions. The important thing is to agree that there is a problem and to define what it is. Once you can do that, you can move to the next step."

Consider two or three possible solutions and the likely outcome of each Definition of and agreement about the problem lead naturally to the next step, coming up with possible solutions. You can engage children in this task by speculating about various courses. As much as possible, you should encourage your children to generate the solutions and should be cautious not to dismiss any suggestion unless it goes against a nonnegotiable rule. For instance, if you are discussing how late your ten-year-old child should be allowed to stay up on a school night and the child says 1:00 A.M., you have every right to say, "We know that you want to stay up that late, but if you did, you wouldn't be able to get up for school the next day, so we feel that either 9:30 or 9:45 would be the latest." This establishes parameters but still provides your child with some choice. When parents build in some leeway, children tend to be much more willing to compromise.

The Oakleys used this strategy with Anna regarding her tutoring. Anna agreed that she required extra help with reading. With the teacher's assistance, they reviewed with Anna the different possibilities of when the tutoring could take place. Anna chose to have the lessons before school and then had to ensure that she awoke on time. When she failed to do so on a couple of occasions, the Oakleys did not intervene, recognizing that Anna had to experience the consequences of not getting up. They were then able to encourage her to arrive at a solution, which she did: buying an alarm with a snooze.

Based on our suggestions, the Satins employed an approach with Ashley that was similar to that of the Oakleys. In changing their script, they engaged Ashley in a discussion by first acknowledging that they were probably coming across as nagging her. To their surprise, this tactic proved successful.

Mr. Satin recounted, "Ashley actually listened and acknowledged that friendships were a problem but quickly placed the blame on the other kids. We didn't get angry and tell her she always blamed others. Instead, we followed our plan and said to Ashley that certainly the other kids might be playing a role but that it might be helpful to think about what she could do differently. Ashley said she wasn't certain. We said that was OK; it was something to think about. We also asked Ashley if she would be open to hearing our thoughts if we could think of anything related to the problem. Ashley smiled and said, 'As long as you don't nag.' My wife said, 'If we do, you just let us know.'"

Picking up the story, Mrs. Satin reported, "The next day, Ashley came home from school very upset and told me that a girl had teased her and said that no one likes her. Ashley was close to tears. The positive side was that it gave me an entry into talking with her about it. I empathized with her sadness, but I also mentioned that sometimes I noticed ways she was acting toward other kids that could get them angry. She asked what I saw, and I said that sometimes she interrupted kids when they were speaking and told them what they should do. At first Ashley was defensive about what I said. She felt that she didn't interrupt and wasn't bossy. I simply said that it was something for her to think about. To help her to be less defensive, I told her that we have different views of what might be going on but that I wanted to share my view with her."

She went on, "I was surprised and pleased when Ashley said *maybe* she did interrupt at times and tell people what to do. Just as we discussed in here, I invited Ashley to think of a couple of solutions and what might happen with each. Her first thought was just not to say anything. I asked her what might happen if she did that. She laughed and said she wasn't sure if she could keep quiet. She also said that some of the other kids might think it was really weird if she said nothing. Her next solution was an interesting one: she said that when she was ready to talk, she would try to count to five, and while counting, she would ask herself if she should say anything. I thought this was an amazing step forward. The next day when she came home from school, she was excited. She said, 'Sometimes I forgot, but most of the time I remembered.' The knowledge that *she* had come up with a solution to the problem helped her greatly."

Mr. and Mrs. Satin used interventions with Ashley that facilitated the development of a resilient mindset: they were empathic, their communications permitted Ashley to listen to them rather than immediately become defensive, and they encouraged her to engage in problem-solving activities, for which she maintained a sense of ownership and accomplishment.

Develop a way to remind each other if someone forgets to follow through A refrain frequently heard from children and adolescents is that their parents are "nags." (Maybe it's part of the genetic code that when parents remind children to do something, it is immediately interpreted as an imposition and that the parents are nagging them.)

Even when families arrive at solutions to problems and everyone agrees to participate, there can be lapses. Family members may forget what they agreed on or may issue excuses for why they didn't follow through. One of the best remedies for forgetting is to establish a strategy to remind each other to follow through on the agreed-upon plan.

In our clinical work and parenting workshops, we suggest that once a family has decided on a plan to handle a problem, one of the parents should say, "This sounds great, but since we're human and we may forget what we agreed on, how can we remind each other so that we're not nagging each other?" Countless parents have attested that asking children how they would like to be reminded helps avoid the impression that parents are breathing down their backs since the children helped develop the plan.

We met with Mr. and Mrs. Sago and their son Kurt, a thirteen-year-old with attentional and learning problems as well as a seizure disorder. Kurt was taking multiple medications but frequently forgot his morning doses. Understandably, his parents would resort to reminding him.

Kurt would in turn respond, "You're always on my back. If you stopped being on my back, it would be easier for me to remember." However, when his parents demurred and didn't remind him, he would sometimes forget and then deny that he had forgotten.

In a family session, we empathized with Kurt, saying, "You really feel your parents are nagging you, huh?"

"Yeah."

We asked, "Do you have any questions about whether you need to take medication?" We often ask this kind of question to make certain that there is agreement about the subject at hand. If Kurt were to answer that he felt that the medication did not help and he did not have to take it, then we could say, "We're glad you told us that. We understand why you might not want to take something that you feel isn't helpful. However, maybe we should review why your doctor and parents think it is important to take." In this instance, Kurt agreed that he needed the medication.

Once Kurt acknowledged that the medication was necessary, we asked, "Do you need your parents to remind you to take it?"

"No."

We then said, "We're glad to hear that, Kurt." He seemed pleased, and we waited for a few moments before adding, "Kurt, if you're like most of us, you sometimes can forget to do something you're supposed to do."

"I won't forget."

"We think you probably won't, but it's always good to have a backup plan so that in case you should forget, your parents won't be yelling at you."

We loved Kurt's response: "Well, I don't like them to *talk* to me to remind me."

We wondered aloud if there were any other way they could remind him.

Kurt thought for a moment and answered, half-kidding, half-not, "Let them hold up a sign."

His parents looked stunned yet amused. We said evenly, "That sounds like a great idea." Turning to the Sagos, we asked what they thought.

Fortunately, they didn't answer that it sounds crazy. Instead, they said, "That's fine."

We then entered into a twenty-minute discussion of what the sign should say and at what time the Sagos could hold it up. Interesting topics can arise in family therapy. The family agreed that the sign should read "Please remember to take your meds" and that the Sagos should wait until 7:25 A.M. before holding it up.

The plan was successful, most likely, because *Kurt* had suggested how best to be reminded. As a sidelight, several weeks after Kurt engineered this solution, a major parenting magazine published an article about the use of signs to remind your children to do things. We made a copy for Kurt. When we gave it to him, we said jokingly, "The only thing we were upset about was that they didn't quote you in the article."

Kurt retorted, "Don't worry, they don't know about me yet, but they will someday."

What to do if it doesn't work Similar to the importance of ensuring follow-through is to plan for possible obstacles to the success of a strategy. Some people may object, "Why bring up possible obstacles? Can't that be interpreted as a self-fulfilling prophecy for failure?" The benefit is that when the potential trouble spots are defined, families are better prepared to avoid them, or deal with them if necessary, or switch to a backup intervention.

We learned the value of foreseeing possible roadblocks to success from experiences in our work with families. We discovered that what appeared to be brilliant strategies in our offices were not as brilliant in actual practice. Moreover, we found that when parents and children attempted strategies that they helped to design and these strategies didn't deliver, the family often felt more defeated and less disposed to attempt other interventions. However, considering possible roadblocks in advance and knowing that if one approach did not work, there were others that might, provided families with a sense of hope and perseverance. An important by-product is the reinforcement of the principle that mistakes are experiences from which to learn rather than defeats.

Learning to Steer Life's Ship

Whenever possible, use the typical everyday problems and challenges that arise in your children's lives as opportunities to hone problem-solving and decision-making skills. When children can articulate problems, reflect on and engage in possible solutions, and consider other options if the initial solutions don't pan out, they demonstrate a resilient mindset. These skills foster a sense of ownership for and control of their own lives. They are not overwhelmed by everyday problems, since they believe that they have the skills to manage and learn from these problems. They develop the mindset that whatever challenges may await them, they have the inner resources to meet them. In other words, they believe that as they learn to steer their life's ship, they will become captains of their own fate.

As parents, we must never underestimate the importance of nurturing these feelings and beliefs in our children. We must be available to provide input, support, and limits when necessary, but we must also know how to increasingly delegate decision making and ownership to our children.

11

Disciplining in Ways That Promote Self-Discipline and Self-Worth

Perhaps the most frequently asked questions at our workshops and in our clinical practice pertain to discipline. The plethora of books that have been written (and sold) about the topic gives testimony to its importance to parents. Rarely a day goes by that we do not hear from a parent, teacher, or other child care specialist about the best approach to disciplining children. Invite a panel of child care professionals to express their views about discipline and it would not be surprising to hear a wide spectrum of opinions. In reaction to transgressions against society by our youth, politicians and law enforcement professionals also often enter the debate.

With some amusement and confusion, parents have shared with us the varying advice they have received from mental health professionals. For example, one mother with a temperamentally difficult four-year-old son "devoured" all the books she could locate about discipline. She also attended many parenting workshops, including one we offered at which she bemoaned, "I feel as if I'm going crazy when it comes to how to handle my son. One expert told me to use time-out and lock my son's door if he tried to get out. Another called that approach abusive. I read that spanking was OK as long as the parent didn't lose control. Then I was told that spanking could damage your child's psyche and that children didn't have a test to determine when a parent was out of control or not. Someone else said to reason with children and tell them why they can't do something, but someone else said many children saw reasoning as a sign of weakness. You mentioned that you should be empathic, but if you're too empathic, won't your children take advantage of you? Now do you see why I feel as if I'm going crazy? And guess what, it seems as if nothing I do works with my son anyway."

Parents in the room smiled and nodded in agreement. Many were eager to share some of their own tribulations with discipline. One father singled it out as the main source of stress in his marital relationship: "My wife says that I don't support her when she sets limits for our two sons, but I feel the limits she sets are too harsh. When we try to talk about what limits we should set, we never seem to agree."

His wife, who was seated next to him, noted, "My husband's view of discipline is that if kids grow up in a loving home, they will just learn the rules and parents don't really have to set limits. I say that's how you raise spoiled children."

Her husband interrupted, "I don't think kids learn when parents yell and scream at them."

She countered, "I only yell and scream when they get wild or disrespectful, and I don't think they would be wild or disrespectful if you were more forceful with them and more supportive of me."

After a few moments of this couple's bickering back and forth, we asked if we were observing what typically occurs at home. Although they were arguing, it was obvious that they cared a great deal about each other and about their role as parents. They also had a healthy sense of humor. In response to our question about how typical this discussion was, the husband said with a smile, "This is rather typical, except that if we were at home, we would probably either be yelling at this point or have left the room in frustration with no solution to the problem. But in front of everyone here, we're on our best behavior." His wife smiled in agreement.

The audience laughed, but as several parents declared, the philosophy and practice of discipline do not typically elicit humor in the home but rather tension and confusion.

This chapter mines the topic of discipline from the perspective of resilience. If our parenting activities are directed toward the goal of nurturing resilient mindsets in our children, then our understanding of the function of discipline and the most effective forms of applying it will also be guided and enhanced by this goal.

Discipline and the Resilient Mindset

One of the most important parenting roles is to serve as disciplinarians. The ways in which we enact this role can either diminish a child's self-esteem, dignity, hope, and resilience or strengthen these qualities.

The word *discipline* is rooted in the word *disciple* and best understood as a teaching process. As a form of education and as a correlative to the concept of disciple, discipline should not be associated with so-called teaching practices that intimidate, humiliate, or embarrass children.

If discipline is placed in the context of an educational process, what is it that we are attempting to teach? Discipline has two key functions. Most parents at our workshops readily identify the first: to make certain that adults provide a consistent, safe, and secure environment in which children not only learn that reasonable rules, limits, and consequences exist in the household but also that they exist for a reason. The second function of discipline, which is equally important but not as readily identified by parents, is to nurture self-discipline or self-control in children. Dr. Daniel Goleman has classified self-discipline as one of the pillars of emotional intelligence, a predictor of satisfying interpersonal relationships and success in life.

Self-discipline implies that a child has internalized rules so that even if a parent is not present, the child will act in a thoughtful, reflective manner. Self-discipline may be understood as a significant component of a sense of ownership and responsibility for one's behavior. If we subscribe to this view, then parents must develop disciplinary practices that reinforce self-control within a safe and secure environment rather than generating feelings of resentment and anger in children.

The disciplinary practices we recommend are closely related to features of a resilient mindset. Being an effective disciplinarian presupposes empathy, the use of communication skills, the ability to modify negative scripts in ourselves and in our children, and an appreciation of each child's unique temperament. The process should strengthen a responsible and compassionate attitude in our children as well as advance their decision-making and problem-solving skills. Discipline should teach children to reflect on their actions and foresee the likely consequences for their behavior. It is difficult to ever develop a resilient mindset without these skills.

Being a disciplinarian is often filled with untold uncertainties and anxieties. You've been privy to many instances in this book of well-meaning parents imposing rules and consequences on their children that brought about resentment and anger rather than learning. Mr. and Mrs. Fischer thought that they could modify Brendan's poor grades by using youth group leadership as a carrot. As we learned, this form of discipline did not lead Brendan to be more responsible in his schoolwork but rather increased the level of tension and anger in their home. Cindy's mother, viewing her daughter as having "a personal vendetta" against her, often responded to Cindy's behavior by yelling and spanking, which further soured their relationship. Mrs. Cerano resorted to spanking Larissa when attempts to reason with her temperamentally insatiable daughter did not change Larissa's behavior (nor did the spanking). In all of these families as well as others, parents groped for more reliable forms of teaching their children since their regular practices did not lead to positive change. If anything, their discipline eroded self-esteem and resilience.

Mr. and Mrs. Morris consulted with us about their seven-year-old son, Charlie. They described him as "provocative" and "rebellious" and very different from his nine-year-old sister, Marnie. As they reviewed Charlie's developmental history, it was obvious that Charlie possessed a difficult temperament characterized by seeming to never be satisfied, an inability to be flexible and compromise, and a perception of others as being unfair and not acting as he desired.

"All we had to say to Marnie is not to do something, and she would stop," explained Mrs. Morris. "On the few occasions in which she continued to do something we didn't like, we sent her to her room, and she came out after a few minutes and told us how sorry she was. We could sit down and explain things to her even when she was just four or five. But with Charlie it's an entirely different matter. He never listens; he is always yelling, although he tells us that we yell at him all the time; and it seems as if he looks for opportunities to provoke us. Everything we've tried seems to be of little use, except when we've gotten so frustrated that we've spanked him. But even that doesn't last for long."

Mr. Morris echoed, "If someone had told me before Charlie was born that I would ever spank my child, I would have said that person was crazy. But the only thing Charlie seems to listen to is a good spanking on his rear end. Like my wife said, though, it works for a short time, and soon Charlie is acting up again."

We empathized with their frustration and asked them for a few examples of what it was that upset them about Charlie and what things they had done that weren't working.

Mrs. Morris sputtered, "I don't know where to begin, since almost everything Charlie does frustrates us. When we tell him it's time to go to bed, he will get into a long argument that he shouldn't have to go to bed because he's not tired. When we ask him to clean his room, he either throws everything under his bed or tells us that it's clean, even though all his stuff is on the floor. If we give him a choice of two kinds of cereal to eat in the morning, he will tell us that we don't have a third cereal, which that morning he claims is his 'most favorite' cereal."

"And we don't like his lying," intoned Mr. Morris. "He'll tell us he didn't do something, such as sneak cookies into his room, when we know he did. He'll tell us he washed his hands or brushed his teeth, but he didn't. Once, right in front of us, he hit his sister, who was just sitting there, and he said that she tried to hit him first. I was so angry that I told him he was always lying and to go to his room. I couldn't believe his answer: he yelled back at me, 'You can't make me!' He's only seven. I went over and told him I could and gave him a spanking and brought him to his room."

After hearing a sampling of Charlie's negative behaviors, we asked the Morrises if they could tell us about some of their son's strengths and what he enjoyed doing.

In a somewhat joking frame, Mr. Morris quipped, "He is skilled at aggravating us and producing tension in the household." Then he acknowledged, "He is very good at playing computer games. Also, when he has our undivided attention, he enjoys playing games like chess and checkers with us and is actually quite good at those too."

Mrs. Morris interrupted to clarify, "But if you should beat him in a game, he can quickly resort to his Dr. Jekyll and Mr. Hyde personality and accuse us of cheating."

Given their frustration, it was not easy for Mr. and Mrs. Morris to think about Charlie's islands of competence. Beyond spanking Charlie, we asked what other forms of discipline they had attempted.

Mrs. Morris smiled weakly and said, "I think everything. I think we have read every book on discipline there is, but we think Charlie has read them as well and keeps one step ahead of us. I hate to say this, but sometimes I feel that nothing we do will work, that he is *incorrigible*."

Upon saying that, Mrs. Morris teared up and confided, "I'm so angry at Charlie and so upset with myself. I feel like such a failure."

The Morrises reviewed many of the disciplinary techniques they had attempted: they had sent him to his room, taken away television or the computer for several evenings, refused to take him out for ice cream, screamed, yelled, and spanked him.

Based on this brief excerpt from our meeting with the Morrises, what questions would you ask yourself about Charlie and the ways in which they disciplined their son? What might they do differently to motivate Charlie to respond to them positively rather than challenge their authority? Later we will return to the Morrises and see how they changed their approach so that discipline in their household increasingly became an intervention for reinforcing a resilient mindset in Charlie.

In keeping with the established format, this chapter first describes obstacles to effective discipline and then outlines principles that parents can follow to promote self-discipline and resilience in their children.

Obstacles to Using Discipline to Develop a Resilient Mindset

The assumptions that each of us holds about child rearing influence the particular ways in which we understand and interact with our children. Some assumptions prompt us to behave in ways that nurture resilience in our children, while others impede this process. For example, the last chapter highlighted the importance of parents' believing that from an early age children can be involved in discovering solutions to problems rather than perceiving children as always having to be told what to do. To become a more effective disciplinarian, it is important to understand the assumptions and obstacles that serve as roadblocks to reaching this goal. Several of these obstacles were also addressed in earlier chapters, especially in the discussion of empathy and negative scripts in Chapters 2 and 4.

Obstacle One: Practicing What We Have Been Taught, or "If It Was Good Enough for Me, It's Good Enough for My Kids"

Many parents repeat the same forms of discipline that they experienced as children. Such a pattern would be fine if the parents grew up in homes in which the disciplinary practices of their parents nurtured a resilient mindset. However, if this is not the case, if discipline did not promote self-discipline and problem-solving skills, then parents may be mirroring ineffective forms of discipline without realizing it. Many parents at some point have lamented, "I swore I would never say or do that to my children, since I didn't like it when my parents did it to me." However, as discussed in Chapter 4, it is not always easy to rewrite our own scripts from childhood, to free ourselves from the excess baggage that we're hauling.

For example, John, the seventh-grade student introduced in the first chapter, had a father who fell into disciplining his son based on his own childhood experiences rather than on what John needed. John was a gifted athlete but not a gifted student. He suffered undiagnosed problems with learning and attention. Mr. Kahn adhered to the view that John's problems would be solved with harsher, more punitive discipline measures, prompting the increasing use of corporal punishment, the same kind of parenting that he had experienced from his father. It was only in the context of parent counseling that Mr. Kahn could talk about the "beatings" he had received from his father and the resentment they triggered, enabling him to give up the myth that these beatings made him a better person.

Obstacle Two: Discipline That Is Crisis Oriented and Punitive

Many of the questions and comments we receive about discipline fall under "crisis intervention" or "punishment." The following is a representative sample:

"What should I do when my older son hits my younger son?"

"Is it OK to spank my six-year-old daughter when she is rude? That's the only way she seems to listen."

"My five-year-old son ran into a busy street after we warned him not to. We took television away for a week. Was that a good thing to do?"

"My sixteen-year-old daughter challenges all of my authority. Now the moment she does, I tell her that she can't use the car on weekends. Do you think that's effective? She's lost the use of the car for the next five weeks and says it doesn't bother her and that I'm a mean mother."

"I screamed and yelled at my fifteen-year-old son when I discovered pot in his room. He's grounded for the next two months. Is there anything else I could have done?"

While these are all valid and important concerns, when discipline takes on the air of urgency, we typically become reactive rather than proactive, punitive rather than educational. We are less likely to ask such questions as:

"Is there anything I can do to help prevent problems from emerging in the first place?"

"Are my children learning from my disciplinary practices, or are these practices eliciting resentment and anger?"

The parents of four-year-old Robert, who first appeared in Chapter 2, initially resorted to crisis-oriented, reactive, and harsh discipline. To tame Robert's resistance to bedtime, they eventually spanked him. To them, his behavior was oppositional and manipulative. They failed to ask what might be prompting his difficulty going to sleep and what might they do differently to overcome his resistance. When we discovered that Robert's problem was nightmares and engaged him in the proactive process of considering possible solutions, which included his suggestion of having a photo of his parents by his bedside, his tantrums stopped.

Similarly, Mr. and Mrs. Cerano spanked Larissa, their six-year-old daughter, in response to her demandingness and insatiability. Even when they tried to prepare her to enter a supermarket or department store and not ask them to buy her things, she persisted to do so. The Ceranos understandably became increasingly frustrated and punitive. Without realizing, they also became increasingly reactive, even as they sought ways to handle and minimize Larissa's demands. However, with the input of counseling, their approach to discipline shifted to teaching and being proactive rather than punishing and being reactive. They adopted more realistic goals, such as going to a convenience store rather than a large supermarket, being more specific about choices that Larissa could have, and being clearer about the consequences that would follow if her behavior was not appropriate. Their new approach, although not without hitches, eventually resulted in noticeable improvement in Larissa's behavior.

Ask yourself, "Do I rely primarily on punishment and punitive measures to teach my child? Are my actions typically spur-of-the-moment responses to my child's behavior?" If your answer is yes to either of these questions, then changes are indicated in how you discipline.

It is helpful to remember that punishment is one form of discipline. Often it is the least effective form since it teaches children what not to do rather than what to do. A reactive, crisis approach typically weakens the teaching process, especially since we are often angry and upset when we use it.

Obstacle Three: Discipline That Is Harsh and Belittling as Exemplified by Spanking and by Verbal Assaults

Most parents are likely to lose their temper with their children at times. Obviously, we should strive to avoid doing so. Unfortunately, for some parents, discipline is characterized by harshness, whether physical or verbal. The reasons for this behavior are complex and are rooted in such factors as their own histories, their frustration tolerance, their level of anger, and their mistaken belief that children learn best when fearful and intimidated. For example, when Billy spilled milk, he was told he was clumsy; Carl's parents yelled at him for not getting ready for school and not sitting at the dinner table for the entire meal; Danny's father sternly scolded him for misbehavior; Larissa's parents constantly yelled and spanked her in response to her demandingness and insatiability; Michael's father lobbed demeaning comments when his son quit at building a radio.

When discipline is riddled with anger and physical and verbal punishment, children are more likely to remember the punishment than the reasons they are being punished. With the pollution of this form of discipline, there is little opportunity for a resilient mindset to develop since children are unlikely to experience unconditional love, to intuit how to solve problems and make decisions, and to learn from mistakes. What they do learn is that if someone bigger than you doesn't like what you do, that person can hit you rather than figure out how to resolve the difficulty.

We are often asked about our position on corporal punishment. Some parents have told us that the only way they can get their children to listen to them is to spank them. Mr. and Mrs. Cranston, for instance, came to see us about their ten-year-old son, Frank, after hearing one of our presentations. They were concerned by Frank's "belligerence, his anger, especially when he lost at a game or couldn't figure out his homework, and his refusal to help out at home."

At the workshop the Cranstons had attended, we discouraged the use of spanking. Not only does it impair development of a resilient mindset, but also, according to research studies, the more spanking that children received at home, the more aggressive they were toward their peers.

During our parent counseling session, the discussion quickly turned to the topic of discipline. Mr. Cranston opened with, "I should let you know that I disagree with what you said about discipline when I heard you speak. I don't think there's anything wrong with hitting your children if they do something wrong. When I spank Frank, he stops what he's doing and listens to me. Sometimes, a good smack is the only thing that children understand."

At one point we asked Mr. Cranston how often he found himself hitting his son. He answered, "I would say I hit him three or four times a week, and when I do, he listens. He has to learn that he can't mouth off and that when we ask him to do something, he has to do it."

We asked him to explain why, if the spanking was *effective*, he had to resort to its use so often.

Mr. Cranston responded, "I think it's effective. Imagine what he would be like if I didn't use it."

Mrs. Cranston then said to her husband, "I'm not sure if it's working. I think it just makes Frank angrier and angrier. You should see the look he gives you when you come near him. He seems scared and angry."

"Well, then he should learn the right way to behave, and I wouldn't have to hit him. I'd rather he be scared and angry than act with such a lack of respect."

It was apparent that discipline had taken the form of a very negative script in the Cranston household and that Mr. Cranston was rather fixed in his views about discipline. We also knew that if we were to help change Mr. Cranston's views, we needed to be empathic and begin to present alternatives. Thus, we made a point to "join" Mr. Cranston in an area of agreement.

We said, "We agree with you that it's important for children to learn respect and cooperation and how to get along with people. We think where we have a difference of opinion with you is in the best way of reaching those goals." By communicating agreement with Mr. Cranston's goals, we reinforced what he was attempting to accomplish as a parent, so that he might be more receptive to alternative views of how best to accomplish these goals.

We discussed why spanking often gives parents a false impression of its effectiveness. "When you spank children, they typically will stop their behavior but only temporarily. What many parents don't realize is that once they leave the room, children will often resume the behavior that the parents wanted them to stop. Many parents who believe that spanking works will then assume that the child needs *more* spanking if its effects don't last. Unfortunately, increased spanking typically causes more anger."

Mr. Cranston then said something that we hear from many parents, "But *my* father hit me, and I turned out OK."

We answered, "Every child is different. Maybe some kids learn from the spanking, but there can be side effects, such as resentment. That's one reason we feel spanking should not be used. Other kids seem to learn very little from spanking. If you've been spanking Frank for years and he's still doing many of the things you want him to stop, then you have to ask yourself, Is Frank a slow learner, or is the way I'm teaching him not the best way?"

This comment caused Mr. Cranston to pause and reflect, "I never really thought about it in that way."

We said, "You also mentioned that you were spanked. Sometimes it's helpful to think about what effect it had on you and on your relationship with your parents, and whether that's what you want with your son."

"I didn't like it when my parents spanked me," he answered, "especially when they used a belt on my rear end, but I learned how to behave."

"How did you feel when they hit you?" we asked.

He hedged, "I was very angry, but I knew it was for my own good."

As soon as her husband finished, Mrs. Cranston said to him calmly, "But you've told me how angry you were with your parents and how you'd then find ways to do the things they didn't want you to do. Also, even today when you and your parents get together, some kind of argument always seems to break out immediately."

He listened before replying, "I know. But I think they were just trying to teach me."

Sensing that Mr. Cranston trusted us and the direction in which we were moving, we then phrased a rather pointed series of questions. "We know that what we are going to ask you might not be easy to answer, but it can be helpful to think about. If we asked Frank to describe you, what words would you *hope* he used, and what words would he *actually* use. Also, would you want him to describe you with the same words that you would use to describe *your* father and mother?"

As occurs with most parents, these questions stirred up many thoughts and feelings. Mr. Cranston told us, "You asked questions like that in your workshop, and I had never really thought of them before. However, I have thought about what you asked. I think Frank would say that I'm always on his back, that I have little patience with what he does, that I'm too harsh, and that I never say anything nice to him. I think I do say positive things, but I'm not sure he hears them. Maybe he's too angry with me. Why do I think that's how he would describe me? I'm not certain, but I think that's how I would have described my own father at Frank's age."

Mr. Cranston then added, "And you know your comments about negative scripts and how if something isn't working you have to find another approach? I think you're right. I'm the one who has to find the other approach first."

We told him that we were very impressed by his honesty and directness. Mrs. Cranston took her husband's hand and said, "I know how much Frank means to my husband. That's why we came to see you, so that we could all have a better relationship with each other. We also know that our arguments with Frank are affecting his sister, and we just want to have a less angry home."

During the next few weeks, they engaged Frank in the problem-solving tasks described in the previous chapter. They reviewed what they considered a few nonnegotiable rules, inviting him to think of ways he would comply. They realized that they had been imposing more and more rules on their son and that as they did, he was feeling as if they were "placing him in a cage." Thus, they decided to let certain things go, such as whether he made his bed in the morning, and instead devote their energy to important matters.

They also recognized that, given their frustration and anger, they had developed a "praise deficit" and rarely complimented or encouraged Frank. Mr. Cranston especially found opportunities to express positive feelings to his son, which Frank at first had difficulty accepting, since it was so different from what he had experienced to date in his relationship with his father. However, as Mr. Cranston held to a more positive approach, Frank's behavior improved.

Obstacle Four: Discipline That Is Arbitrary and Inconsistent

Although most parents appreciate that discipline will be more effective when it is governed by clear and reasonable expectations, and when consequences follow consistently, achieving this kind of practice is often a challenge. Many flies in the ointment can prevent parents from adhering to fair and consistent disciplinary behaviors, including the mood of a parent on a particular day or the persistent nagging of a child. No parent can be consistent all of the time. There may even be occasions when it makes more sense for a parent to modify a rule because of certain circumstances.

As an example of the latter, a couple at one of our workshops said that they were fairly strict about the time in the evening when their six-year-old son and eight-year-old daughter should go to bed. Since both parents worked, they felt that it was important to have a routine in which they spent time with their children but also had some time for themselves. However, after the children heard about a shooting in a school, they both became more clingy. For several days, the parents spent extra time talking with them about how upsetting the shooting was and reassuring them that although shootings *had* taken place in schools, this rarely happened. The parents also were more tolerant when either of the children called for them from bed and asked for a glass of water, recognizing that the real agenda was the child's need to be soothed. During this time of anxiety, the children went to bed a little later than usual. In this situation, the extenuating circumstances justified a temporary modification of the rules.

However, in many homes there is little rhyme or reason to changes in rules, limits, and consequences. A parent may have had a difficult day at work and punish a child for a behavior that the day before was acceptable. Or one day a parent may respond to a child's transgressions by taking away a privilege such as television, and a week later a similar transgression may be met with a spanking. Mr. and Mrs. Morris became so frustrated with their son, Charlie, that the only consistency in their disciplinary practices was their inconsistency, fueled by feelings of confusion and helplessness. While many youngsters, especially those with difficult temperaments, may manifest inconsistent behaviors, for discipline to be meaningful parents must follow a consistent course of action.

Consistency does not imply a lack of flexibility, but rather that when changes are made, they are based on a careful consideration of the situation. For example, when Mr. and Mrs. Fischer told Brendan that they had reconsidered their position and would allow him to become head of his youth group even if he did not reach a B average, they did so after they realized that their original expectations and consequences were counterproductive.

Obstacle Five: Disciplinary Styles of Parents That Are Miles Apart

It is not unusual for a husband and wife, based on their own backgrounds and experiences, to have different views and styles regarding disciplining children. An example at the beginning of this chapter included a couple at one of our workshops who exhibited this divergence of opinion. The wife complained that her husband did not support her when she disciplined their sons, and he felt that he could not support her because she yelled and was harsh. She countered that her husband's philosophy was that if kids grow up in a loving home, they will just learn the rules and parents don't really have to set limits; she was convinced that this approach would produce spoiled children. Divergent views about discipline typically cause noticeable tension between parents and do not help children to learn clear-cut rules and consequences.

Parents don't have to be clones of each other and agree about every parenting decision and practice. However, in far too many homes, differences in discipline styles are so constant and significant that they greatly influence children's development of self-discipline and problem-solving skills. Many parents even argue about discipline in front of their children. Children can become experts at splitting parents in order to get their way, not because they are "bad" children but because children are often dominated by the wish to get what they want. It is not unusual to see children running from one parent to the other as they seek to persuade one parent to go along with something even if the other disagrees.

Adding to the problem of parents disagreeing in front of children is that the presence of an audience (i.e., the children) often reduces the possibility of compromise since compromise may be interpreted as "giving in" or "losing face" (think of the news "blackouts" that are often imposed during sensitive negotiations between warring parties). It is much wiser for parents to discuss their differences by themselves and arrive at a mutually acceptable position before talking with their children about it.

This is true even when parents are separated or divorced, a situation that often heightens the possibility of children's splitting parents since in actuality they are already split. In situations in which a child catches a parent off guard by questioning an existing limit or consequence in the absence of the other parent, the parent who is "on the spot" could say, "You are raising a very important point but one that I wouldn't feel comfortable making a decision about without first discussing it with your mother (father)."

In the best scenario, different beliefs about discipline should be seen as opportunities to consider various viewpoints. Ongoing, intense arguments between parents about discipline will not help children develop the characteristics of a resilient mindset.

Obstacle Six: "I Want My Child to Love Me."

Some parents have difficulty setting realistic expectations, limits, and consequences because they fear that their children will be angry with them and not love them. It is amazing how children frequently pick up on this fear and use it to their advantage by dropping such lines as, "I don't love you" or "If you loved me, you wouldn't ground me" or "If you loved me, you would let me get that bike." We must remember that even though most children feel safer when parents set realistic guidelines and consequences, they are not going to respond to limits by saying to their parents, "I know that when you set limits, it's because you love me. I am so fortunate to live in this household."

Being a "good" parent requires that we learn to tolerate our children's being temporarily angry with us when we set limits, especially if we know that we have established these limits in a fair and reasonable way. Some parents are burdened by such strong feelings of doubt and guilt that they become almost paralyzed when they have to set guidelines and follow through with consequences.

Mr. and Mrs. Brown came to see us about their six-year-old son, Drew. They cast Drew as a child whose "life is dominated by tantrums and who won't take no for an answer." They quickly contrasted him with his younger brother, who "at three would listen to what we asked."

Mr. Brown noted, "Drew is such an immature kid. He wants us to do everything for him: cut his food, put on his shoes, put his toys away. If we don't do it, he whines."

We inquired what they did when Drew asked for help.

"We tell him he can do it and he should just make the effort. But then he begins to whine, and before you know it, we're doing it for him."

"What would happen if you told Drew that you knew he wanted you to do it for him but you felt it was important for him to do it by himself?" we asked.

Mr. Brown responded, "We've tried, but to be honest, he just outlasts us."

In our first meeting with Drew, we witnessed firsthand his "helpless" style. During the session, he asked to use the bathroom. When he exited the bathroom, he could hardly walk since both his pants and underpants were still down around his ankles. The scene had a surreal, almost humorous quality.

We asked, "Drew, do you realize that you forgot to pull up your pants and underwear?"

He answered, "I can't."

Therapy began at that moment when we said, "You may feel you can't, but we think it's something you can learn." We then encouraged Drew to pull up his pants, and although hesitant at first, he did so.

When we discussed Drew's behavior with his parents, they responded that if *they* had asked him to pull his pants up, he would have whined and cried until they finally did it for him. "We know we shouldn't, but sometimes it's easier just to do things for him and give in."

During the next few sessions with Mr. and Mrs. Brown, we discussed the ramifications of not having realistic expectations for children or holding children accountable. We noted that appropriate limits and consequences are the foundation for a resilient mindset. To handle Drew's temper tantrums, our advice was that they should tell him that he could continue to scream and shout but it would not get him what he wanted. We also suggested that if he had his tantrum in a store or restaurant, they pick him up calmly and take him home.

Mr. and Mrs. Brown began to be more consistent, but then an incident occurred that Mr. Brown was embarrassed to recount. They were in a department store, and Drew spotted a small guitar, which he said he wanted. Mr. Brown said that it was not something he could have, and Drew began to scream that he wanted it. Rather than follow the course of action we had agreed on, Mr. Brown acquiesced and bought Drew the guitar.

We asked, "What do you think Drew learned from that interaction?"

Mrs. Brown quickly supplied, "That his whining and crying will get him what he wants. I told my husband not to do it, but he did."

Mr. Brown responded, "I didn't have the heart to disappoint him. My job requires me to travel a lot, and I had just returned home a few hours earlier. Drew doesn't like it when I travel. I just didn't have the heart to say no to him. I was afraid he would even be more upset with me."

A key issue in our work with this family was Mr. Brown's mistaken belief that setting limits and disciplining Drew would compromise a positive relationship with his son. This belief was fed by his feelings of guilt related to his frequent business trips. Mr. Brown believed that Drew wouldn't love him if he disciplined him. Drew was perceptive enough to recognize his father's ambivalence about setting limits. Drew, like many other children, took advantage of his father's waffling.

In our meetings, we helped Mr. Brown recognize that while Drew might get upset with the imposition of limits and consequences, the alternative was to raise a child with little sense of accountability. As we do with other parents, we distinguished between harsh and arbitrary punishment that generates anger and resentment on the part of children toward their parents and realistic and fair consequences that teach children self-discipline and self-control.

Obstacle Seven: Punishing Children for Unrealistic Expectations

You've seen a parade of examples of parents setting the bar too high, holding expectations that their children could not meet. When the children failed to meet these expectations, the parental response was to punish them. Carl's parents would yell at him when he had difficulty remaining seated at the dinner table; likewise, Cindy's mother and the Ceranos would scream at their temperamentally difficult daughters; John's father became more punitive in response to his son's seeming irresponsibility, a reaction traceable to beatings he had received from his own father as well as his belief that to back off from his demands would equate to giving in.

To punish children for actions over which they have little, if any, control is unfair. To teach our children self-control, we must be realistic in our expectations. In our workshops, we often ask parents how they would feel in the workplace if they were asked to do things that were beyond their ability, and then when they could not accomplish the task, they were punished for their failure. Parents readily respond that they would be very angry in such a situation and that if they had difficulty with a particular task, they should first be taught how to do it.

Of course, our expectations for our children should be raised as their skills improve, but the raising of the bar must be done in a reasonable fashion. If our children demonstrate difficulty with the height of the bar, then we may have to lower it for at least a short time until they have succeeded at that level. Obviously, if our children feel that they cannot meet the expectations that we have set, but we continue to push and punish instead of teach them, the outcome is likely to include anger, doubts about their ability, fear of failure, and low self-esteem—all characteristics that will work against their becoming resilient.

Principles of Effective Discipline to Nurture a Resilient Mindset

As we have seen, many obstacles exist day in and day out to our becoming effective disciplinarians. The good news is that we have a number of principles to guide us in using discipline to reinforce a resilient mindset.

Principle One: A Major Goal of Discipline Is to Promote Self-Discipline and Self-Control

An end product of discipline is for our children to develop self-discipline and self-control, characteristics that are essential for success in all aspects of our lives. To accomplish this goal, we must use interventions that help children understand the importance of limits, guidelines, and consequences, and, when indicated, enlist their input in the disciplinary process. With our input and support, our children will comprehend the rationale for limits and consequences. As they are asked to rely on their own problem-solving skills to deal with issues of discipline, they will begin to feel a sense of ownership for rules, to perceive these rules as reasonable and not arbitrary, and eventually to adhere to these rules.

The process of effective discipline reflects many of the principles outlined in the previous chapter for effective problem solving and decision making. It is important to discuss with your children discipline problems that exist and involve them in strategies for solving these problems. As seen in the last chapter, even preschool children can be engaged in examining problems and arriving at solutions. Obviously, if a situation concerns risks to safety or security (e.g., playing with matches, riding a bike on a busy street, climbing on the roof), parents must step in immediately. However, once the immediate danger is defused, parents can then sit down with their children to recap the situation and explore ways of remedying the problem in the future.

The previous chapter introduced Ashley, the eleven-year-old daughter of Mr. and Mrs. Satin. Ashley was seen as impulsive, bossy with other children, and struggling to finish her schoolwork. Her parents also noted that she refused to work with a tutor but instead leveraged her learning difficulties as an excuse not to meet household responsibilities. Their discipline approach was not working: Ashley experienced it as an attempt to impose rules and conditions on her. It was only after the Satins acknowledged that they probably came across as nagging, and included Ashley in a discussion of the problems she was experiencing, that she became less defensive. This change permitted Ashley to consider alternatives for solving her problems, and once she was an active participant in this process, her feeling of ownership increased. In this way, she was developing self-discipline, or a sense of accountability and responsibility for rules, rather than experiencing her parents as dictating rules and consequences for her.

Another instance of developing self-discipline involved Len and his younger brother, Barry. They often quarreled about what television show to watch and who would occupy the front seat of the car. Their parents realized that when they yelled at their sons, it had little effect, especially when they placed most of the responsibility for fighting on Len since he was the older of the two. However, when the parents shifted their approach and told Len and Barry that they should try to come up with solutions to these problems, the boys were able to do so. If they had difficulty arriving at solutions, their parents could assist them but still delegate much of the responsibility to their sons.

Earlier in this chapter, we told how Mr. and Mrs. Morris were encountering problems and frustrations with their seven-year-old son, Charlie, to the point that they were reduced to spanking him. Our work with the Morrises stressed the importance of involving Charlie in developing rules and consequences. We suggested that they sit down with Charlie during a calm moment and select two or three of the most important areas of concern and explain to Charlie why these were problems. They could then ask their son if he also saw these areas as problematic. If he said no, they could review why they thought these particular areas were causing difficulties and then enlist him in a dialogue of how best to solve these conflicts. We explained that the discussion should cover (a) why the problem was a problem, (b) possible solutions, (c) ways of reminding each family member of the new rules, and (d) consequences should a rule be forgotten.

Mr. and Mrs. Morris professed that they had already attempted this approach, with little gain. As an example, even when they gave Charlie a choice of two kinds of cereals, he would say he didn't like either. We told the Morrises that we felt that they had attempted *some* of what we were suggesting but that we thought Charlie had to be more actively involved since he quickly perceived his parents as trying to control him even when they offered choices. Involving Charlie in a discussion of rules and consequences should not exacerbate his demandingness and opposition but actually could discourage these behaviors.

Mr. and Mrs. Morris talked with Charlie about a few areas, including his hitting his sister, his battles with them about bedtime, and his messy room. They had also wondered about addressing his habit of lying, but as we spoke, they came to the conclusion that this was a form of protection for him and that if he began to feel more in control, the lying would decrease. They also decided that if any lying occurred, instead of telling him he was "always lying," they would first calmly validate his perception by acknowledging that they knew he saw things the way he was describing, but they saw things differently and that it was important to examine these differences. We all believed that this approach would help to minimize Charlie's feeling of being interrogated and render him more open to hearing what they had to say.

When Mr. and Mrs. Morris talked with Charlie about their not wanting to yell at or spank him, he quickly said, "Then you shouldn't. I don't deserve it. You're not fair. You never yell at Marnie or hit her."

Responding that his sister behaved appropriately and that's why they didn't have to yell at her would have triggered Charlie's anger and defensiveness and intensified his feeling that they loved Marnie more than him. Instead they kept the focus on Charlie and said, "Let's look at what we can all do differently to be more cooperative."

During the next few weeks, they invited Charlie to join in problem-solving discussions as a form of developing self-discipline. For example, one solution for Charlie's getting to bed on time was that if he went into his room on time, he could stay up an extra fifteen minutes each evening to read. But if he stayed up beyond the designated time with the light on, the consequence was that he could not stay up an extra fifteen minutes the next night. Also, he could select one night a week to stay up an extra half hour to watch television; if he stayed up beyond that time, he lost the privilege the next week. Mr. and Mrs. Morris were initially convinced that Charlie would soon ask for these extra half hours on all of the other evenings of the week, but to their surprise and delight he did not. The fact that he was involved in setting the rules helped him to feel a greater sense of responsibility for honoring them.

Firm rules were also established for hitting and applied to all family members. Charlie, in a somewhat provocative way, had said, "If I hit Marnie and get punished, then why shouldn't you be punished when you hit me?"

Once again, Mr. and Mrs. Morris did not respond impulsively by declaring, "We're your parents, and when we hit you, it's because you deserve it; it's the only way you seem to listen." Instead, knowing how quick Charlie was to perceive their treatment of him as "unfair," they affirmed that hitting was not the way to teach any of them how to behave. All four members of the family agreed on consequences should any hitting take place. They also discussed the best ways to remember not to hit or scream and made a "reminder list" that Charlie recommended be posted in the kitchen and on the doors of all of their rooms.

We worked with the Morris family for a couple of years. It was slow going to develop more effective disciplinary practices that led to the emergence of self-control. Charlie, as could be expected, often resorted to old patterns when frustrated. However, a structure was now in place that provided guideposts to handle these old patterns. Since Charlie had helped to create this structure, it was easier to apply limits and consequences without his feeling that his parents were imposing arbitrary rules.

Principle Two: Prevention, Prevention, Prevention

The saying "An ounce of prevention is worth a pound of cure" has much validity. It is vital for parents to become proactive rather than reactive in their interactions with their children, and especially in regard to discipline.

As you observe your children's problematic behaviors, try to understand what prompts these behaviors. Then you can ask, "Are there ways of modifying the situation in order to deter my child from behaving in this way?"

Remember that Robert's tantrums ceased when his parents permitted him to have a night-light and a photo of them by his bed; Charlie felt more in control when he could select one night a week to stay up an extra half hour; Carl, the boy with hyperactivity, was permitted to get up from the dinner table when he could no longer remain seated and developed the ability to sit through a meal without being disruptive; Laurie was able to get to school on time when given the responsibility of working in the nursery school before classes. In all of these instances, parents implemented strategies to lower the probability of their child's acting up, thereby minimizing the need for punishment.

The process of prevention can be greatly enhanced when parents establish a regular time each week or every other week to meet as a family and discuss the positive things occurring in the household as well as behaviors that require modification (including parents' behaviors). A problem-solving, proactive approach to discipline can more easily be accomplished if a time is set aside to sift through family issues. If such a time is not carved out, the more likely scenario is that parents will be catching their children on the run or during moments of crisis. These are not conducive moments to tackling disciplinary matters.

Mr. and Mrs. Morris arranged time each week to discuss family issues with Charlie and Marnie. They presented the meeting as an opportunity for their children to share their concerns. Charlie was enthusiastic about the meetings since he had an "agenda of complaints" to submit. While the Morrises allowed

Charlie to air these complaints, they also used the forum to discuss and resolve some of the friction between them. For example, they told him that they realized he was not happy with the choice of cereals they had, and together with their son they arrived at a solution: Charlie would accompany them to the supermarket and select two brands of cereal. Also, they told him that if he did not put his dirty clothes in the hamper but instead threw them on the floor or under his bed, he would not have clean clothes to wear. With Charlie's input, they moved a small hamper into his room.

The Morrises took the position that the more choices they could provide Charlie about "non-life-threatening" situations, the fewer conflicts they would have and the more cooperative he might be about truly important matters. This approach helped ease the tension in the household and led to positive changes in Charlie's behavior.

Principle Three: Work as a Parental Team

In the previous section, the fifth obstacle cautioned that problems occur when parents are figuratively miles apart in their understanding of the role of discipline. If parents' differing views are constantly aired in front of the children, and if they lead to inconsistent expectations and goals, children have difficulty developing self-discipline and are likely to take advantage of their parents' divergence.

We strongly recommend to parents that they set aside a time for themselves (similar to the family time we advocate) to examine the expectations they have for their children as well as the discipline they use. While parents cannot and should not become clones of each other, they should strive to arrive at common goals and disciplinary practices, which most likely will involve negotiation and compromise. We recommend this even when parents are divorced. The beneficiaries of a more unified approach will be the children. We always remind parents that if a particular intervention is not effective, then others can be attempted. It will be less difficult to do so when they are on the same page.

Mr. Brown was prone to acquiesce to his son Drew's crying and whining, given his feelings of guilt for not being as available as he would like because of his travel schedule. For instance, he bought Drew the guitar in response to one of his tantrums. Mrs. Brown was more comfortable in setting limits and not responding to Drew's outbursts. Consequently, Drew quickly learned that if his mother said he could not have something he wanted, he could go to his father, who was more likely to agree. In Drew's eyes Mrs. Brown had become the withholding, "mean" parent, while Mr. Brown was the sugar daddy.

The situation that existed in the Brown household is found in many other homes and leads to a great deal of stress and tension. In our work with the Browns, we encouraged them to consider what behaviors they would like to teach Drew in their disciplinary activities. We asked them to reflect on whether what they were currently doing was helping Drew to learn these behaviors, which included being more responsible, more flexible, more reasonable, and less demanding when he could not get what he wanted.

Mrs. Brown said, "We want to be able to say no to Drew and not have him stage a two-hour tantrum."

The Browns audited their different styles. Mr. Brown admittedly was prone to just "give in" to Drew's demands, but he realized that this was counterproductive since it essentially taught Drew that tantrums could lead to gratification of one's desires.

For her part, perhaps to counterbalance her husband's style and as a reflection of her frustration, Mrs. Brown had "become a real yeller and even said some mean things to Drew."

Their honest self-appraisal resulted in Mr. Brown's being able to set limits more readily when Drew was demanding and even tolerating his son's voicing such comments as "You're so mean" or "I don't like you."

Mrs. Brown became calmer in her interactions with Drew. If he should utter, "You're yelling at me," rather than becoming defensive, she simply changed the script. She lowered the volume of her voice and said, "Thanks for telling me. It would be hard for you to listen to me if I was yelling." This script was so different from what Drew expected that the wind was taken out of his sail and he was more receptive to hearing what his mother had to say.

In addition, the Browns agreed that if situations arose in which Drew might try to split them, either of them would say to him, "This is very important and something that I want to discuss with your mother (father)."

At one point, Drew said to his father, "Can't you think for yourself? You always have to ask Mom."

Mr. Brown simply answered, "There are some decisions that Mom or I would feel comfortable making without consulting each other, but there are other decisions that we feel we should discuss with each other since that discussion will help us to be better parents."

Using the Browns as a frame of reference, think about how you and your spouse handle differences of opinion regarding discipline. Do you negotiate and compromise beforehand to present a united position to your children, or are your children wedged in the middle of parental battles?

Principle Four: Be Consistent, Not Rigid

Our workshops and clinical practice bring many examples of parents whose disciplinary styles vary from one moment to the next. Similar to Principle Three, working together as a team, parents have to be consistent over time. The behavior of our children sometimes makes consistency a herculean labor. Some children believe that they can outlast their parents and that eventually their parents will succumb to their whining, crying, or tantrums. We certainly witnessed this with Drew. Psychology teaches the concept of "intermittent reinforcement," which, translated to the topic at hand, means that if you remain firm on twenty-five occasions but acquiesce to a child's inappropriate demands on the twenty-sixth, the child will continue to act inappropriately in the knowledge that at some point, parents will give in.

As stated earlier, at times inconsistency is caused by our mood or level of fatigue. If guidelines and consequences have been established for acceptable behavior, it is important that we adhere to them, unless extenuating circumstances require that we modify our expectations.

Consistency is not synonymous with rigidity or inflexibility. A consistent approach to discipline invites thoughtful modification of rules and consequences, such as when a child reaches adolescence and is permitted to stay out later on the weekend. When modifications are necessary, they should be discussed with your children so that they understand the reasons for the changes and can offer input.

Principle Five: Serve as a Calm, Rational Model

If discipline is conceptualized as a teaching process, then parents must think about how effective they are as teachers and how they model what they teach. For example, parents who simultaneously hit their child and say, "That will teach you not to hit your sister again" are engaging in the very behavior they profess to punish.

Reprising several of the earlier exercises in the use of empathy, how would your children answer the following questions, and how would you *wish* them to respond?

- "When you do something that is not right, what do your parents do?"
- "When your parents correct something that you have done, are they usually calm, or do they yell a great deal?"
- "How do your parents solve problems between each other?"
- "Do your parents ever spank you? If so, what does that teach you?"
- "Do your parents compliment you when you have done things well?"

We have interviewed many adults who grew up in homes in which discipline was harsh and arbitrary. Invariably, they recount a similar theme: "I don't even remember what my parents were punishing me for; all I remember is how angry I was and how mean they were." Children will observe what we *do* more than what we say. If, in attempting to discipline and teach our children, we are angry, punitive, and unreasonable, then we are teaching our children to be the same. If we act in an arbitrary manner, failing to use a problem-solving approach, our children are more likely to be arbitrary in their thinking and behavior.

Children also notice how parents react to and treat each other. What they notice will influence how much they listen to their parents and how they respond to discipline. Chapter 2 showed Simon's parents punishing him for teasing his sister Lucy. In one of our family sessions, Simon's father criticized his wife's ability to set limits and told her that she lacked courage. His wife burst into tears and said, "All you do is put me down in front of the kids. You never say anything positive. You're such a critical person."

This prompted Simon to say to his father, "And you tell me to speak in a nice way to Lucy, but look how you talk to Mom." Children are incredibly perceptive in observing their parents' behavior.

Similarly, when we met with Mr. and Mrs. Palmer and their sons, Roy and Duane, the Palmers complained about the boys' lack of responsibility. Duane trumped them by reciting that his parents didn't always meet their responsibilities, that their bedroom was not very neat, and that Mr. Palmer at times did not keep his promises to do things with them, often coming home late from work. It is hypocritical to discipline our children for behavior in which we ourselves engage.

Think again about how your children would describe your disciplining. Ideally, they would use words such as *calm, reasonable, in control,* and *loving*.

Principle Six: Select Your Battles Carefully

How important is it for your child to remember to put the toothpaste cap back on the tube? Is there a book about discipline that does not suggest that we should select our battles carefully? If parents were the disciplinary gestapo, we could spend almost every waking hour of our lives finding something that our children did wrong. In some homes there are ten times more negative comments than positive comments. Children growing up in such homes will tune out their parents as they become increasingly annoyed and frustrated by the constant put-downs and negativity.

Here's another helpful exercise: During the course of a week, make a list of the behaviors exhibited by your children that lead to punishment. Then ask yourself, "In the course of my child's life, how important is the behavior in question, and is it worth the battle?" This question is especially relevant for children with difficult temperaments who tend to be more inflexible, rigid, and angry, typically perceiving the world as unfair and unjust. As psychologist Dr. Ross Greene has noted in his book *The Explosive Child*, parents must learn to devote most of their attention and energy to behaviors that carry risks of safety and security, while not wasting effort on less important actions. Dwelling on less important behaviors will only lead to increased stress and tension in parent-child relationships and weaken our attempts to change the behaviors that are relevant in a child's current and future life.

Fifteen-year-old Gregory was punished for having a messy room, but as his parents admonished him about his room, they brought up a rap sheet of other transgressions. Gregory eventually became angry and tuned out what they had to say.

Parents often ask us what behaviors merit discipline. Obviously, behaviors concerning safety deserve immediate attention. Other behaviors take on importance because of the expectations and values in a particular home but may not be relevant in another household. Whatever the guiding values, first and foremost, your disciplinary practices should have as a goal teaching children to be more responsible, more effective problem solvers, and more resilient. If we punish our children for countless behaviors, if we are constantly on their backs telling them what to do, and if we do not take the time to understand their points of view, then the significant goal of using discipline to support a resilient mindset will be greatly compromised or not realized at all.

Principle Seven: Rely When Possible on Natural and Logical Consequences Rather than on Arbitrary and Punitive Measures

Children must learn that there are consequences to their behavior and that they are neither harsh nor arbitrary but are based on discussions that parents have had with them. Natural and logical consequences can be very effective controls, especially when the situation does not threaten the child's safety or the safety of others.

Natural consequences are those that result from a child's actions; parents don't have to enforce them because they follow naturally from the child's behavior. For example, at one of our workshops, a parent described a situation in which her nine-year-old daughter went out to play on a chilly day. This mother found herself getting into an argument with her daughter about wearing gloves. Finally, she told herself that this really was not a matter of safety, that if her daughter's hands got cold, her daughter would either place them in her jacket or come into the house at some point to get gloves. About thirty minutes after going outside, the girl came in and got her gloves, telling her mother that the temperature had dropped a lot in the past half hour, a face-saving statement that was accepted by her mother.

Another illustration of a natural consequence comes from a father who had bought his son a new baseball glove and some oil to rub into the glove to soften the leather. He told his son that softening the glove would make it easier to catch the ball. His son neglected to do so, and in a game the son dropped two throws, in part because the glove was still rather stiff. Immediately after the game, his son went home and applied the oil.

While *logical* consequences sometimes overlap with natural consequences, logical consequences typically involve some action taken on the part of parents in response to a child's behavior. For instance, a mother told us her eleven-year-old son was late getting ready for school each morning, and then when he missed the school bus, she or her husband had to drive him. She said that she believed her son was capable of being ready and that she realized that when they drove him to school, they were actually reinforcing his lateness. So, they told their son that if he was not ready when the bus came, he would have a choice: either walk to school (a safe, one-mile walk) or stay home. They felt comfortable with this second choice since they knew that he wanted to be in school; obviously, the same choice would not be wise if the child did not want to go to school. They also discussed with him how he might ensure that he would be ready on time.

All of these discussions notwithstanding, he was late for the school bus. His parents did not drive him, and he ended up walking to school, where a notation was made by his teacher that he was tardy. It was the last time he was late for the bus.

Another logical consequence followed after a father at one of our workshops had to repeatedly remind his nine-year-old son to put his bicycle in the garage at the end of the day. He told his son that if it rained, the bike could be damaged, or if it were left outside overnight, someone could even take it. He finally got tired of reminding his son and told him it would be his responsibility to remember. His son left the bike out, and during a rainstorm it was damaged.

The damage to the bike could be seen as a natural consequence of the son's behavior. Then, when the son cried and asked his father to have the bike repaired, the father's response represented a logical consequence. He did not say, "I told you so." Instead, when his son said that the bike was "ruined," the father responded that they could take it to the bike store to see if it could be repaired but that it would be the boy's responsibility to pay for the repairs. If the bike were beyond fixing, the son would be responsible for purchasing a new bike out of his savings.

In essence, consequences should fit the "crime." As much as possible, our children should be aware of the rules and consequences in advance. For instance, if a seventeen-year-old plans to go out on a Saturday night and has a midnight curfew, it should be made very clear to this adolescent what the consequences are if the curfew is broken. In one household, breaking curfew meant that the boy would be grounded the following Saturday night. The boy came in at 12:30 A.M. and explained that he was late because he had to drive several friends home from a party.

His father calmly said, "Next time you have friends to drive home, you have to start earlier so that you can be home by midnight. But this was your choice. You know the consequence we agreed on: next week you cannot go out on Saturday night."

The boy argued that he was just trying to help his friends. The father remained calm and said, "I'm glad you wanted to help your friends by driving them home, but you'll have to figure out a way of doing so in the future without breaking your curfew."

This father added at our workshop, "I was almost ready to give in, but I realized that my son had not met his responsibility and for me to excuse his being late would communicate that I did not take our agreement seriously. Of course, if some extenuating circumstance had come up such as the car having mechanical problems, I would have been more tolerant, but in this case what happened was within my son's control. By the way, I think the approach worked, since it was the last time he broke his curfew."

These examples drive home the ways in which discipline can reinforce a resilient mindset. They involve (a) articulating with your children the behaviors in question that require modification, (b) searching for possible solutions to problematic behaviors, and (c) highlighting for your children that they have choices in what solutions to use but that each choice leads to different consequences. This process reinforces a feeling of accountability and ownership as well as a sense of control over one's life.

Before ending the topic of natural and logical consequences, it is relevant to briefly address the question of the effectiveness of a disciplinary tactic used a great deal: time-out. Typically time-out involves removing children from a certain setting when they misbehave to another setting, such as a chair or their room. The rationale is that separation from desirable activities as well as from others as a consequence of misbehavior will help the child learn to change whatever behavior led to the time-out. Time-out was initially perceived as an alternative to spanking and other humiliating consequences. However, while time-out may be less aversive than hitting or humiliating a child, it must also be used with care and thoughtfulness. With some children, time-out may backfire.

When time-out is used, the message to the child should be "You need time to calm down." Child development specialists have found that it is best to add, "You can let me know when you feel calm," since this statement places control and responsibility back in the hands of the child. Some child care professionals have observed that time-out is not very effective for children over the age of seven, especially children who may be temperamentally stubborn. These children may say to their parents, "You can't make me sit in that chair or send me to my room." At this point the consequence becomes the lightning rod for further confrontation. We typically recommend not to use time-out with an oppositional child (or a hyperactive child who is asked to sit still in a chair) but instead to take away a privilege, since that is something over which a parent has control. Thus, a parent could say, "If you continue to scream and shout, it will still not get you what you want and it will also lead to not watching television tonight. It's your choice."

If children view time-out as an opportunity to calm down and think of alternatives to their misbehavior, it can be an effective consequence. However, if it results in greater frustration and confrontation, other strategies are warranted.

Several parents have told us that they have found the situation to improve when *they* take a time-out rather than asking the child to do so. One mother told us, "When I find that I'm ready to scream at my daughter, I simply tell her that when I'm getting that angry at her, I need time to cool off before I say or do something that I'll regret. I then go to my room for a couple of minutes and return much calmer. I find that it works for me, and I think it helps to model for my daughter a better way of handling anger."

Principle Eight: Know Your Children's Capabilities, and Do Not Punish Them for Unrealistic Expectations

When parents establish guidelines for behavior, they must consider if the behaviors in question are (a) important and (b) within the control of their child. As we have seen, some behaviors are of little significance in the course of a child's upbringing. Other behaviors may be important, but if they involve the bar being set too high, parents must modify their expectations. Otherwise, the atmosphere of the household will be characterized by nagging, stress, and tension, and the educational value of discipline will be lost.

Of course, children must be held accountable, but for accountability to be developed, it must go hand in glove with realistic and attainable expectations. If an expectation requires modification so that it can be achieved, then we must do so. With each success, the bar can be placed at a higher level.

Principle Nine: Remember That Positive Feedback and Encouragement Are Often the Most Powerful Forms of Discipline

It is telling that most of the questions we are asked about discipline pertain to punishment. We are less often asked about what we consider to be the most influential component of discipline, especially in terms of developing a resilient mindset, which is positive feedback and encouragement. The emphasis on positive feedback and encouragement is in concert with other tenets of this book, including the need for parents to identify and reinforce their children's islands of competence and the importance of overcoming a "praise deficit" and helping each child to feel special and appreciated.

Chapter 5 offered numerous examples of parents serving as "charismatic adults," adults from whom children gathered strength. In the daily hassles of parenting, many well-meaning parents neglect to notice or acknowledge when their children are behaving well or have been helpful. Instead, we lock in to telling our children how they must change. Ms. Malone, for example, saw Marty, her eleven-year-old son, whom we met in Chapter 9, as irresponsible in not cleaning up or doing his chores. Yet, when we asked if he assisted in *any* way, she mentioned that he helped to do the shopping and even some of the cooking. Once she recognized the many positive things that her son did, her "praise deficit" was replaced by positive comments. This reinforced Marty's cooperative behavior. Similarly, when Mr. and Mrs. Lemrow identified nine-year-old Amelia's islands of competence, her behavior improved. Amelia had developmental problems but found great joy in assisting others. Thus, when she began to help at a nursing home and received positive feedback, her sense of pride and accomplishment improved, she became more responsible, and her resilient mindset was nurtured.

Recall that we recommended to Mr. and Mrs. Morris that they put more emphasis on Charlie's islands of competence, which they identified as playing computer games, chess, and checkers. However, that presented a problem because when he lost, he accused them of cheating. So, we suggested that they allow Charlie to "teach" them how to play computer games and the best moves to make in chess or checkers. At first they were hesitant, given their history with their son.

Mr. Morris ventured, "I think he will act like a little dictator and even tell us how dumb we are."

We said that since he often acted rude anyway, we wondered if there was anything to lose by saying to him that they were impressed with his game skills and would love to learn more. They said they were willing to try.

The following week, Mr. Morris told us, "I was impressed with Charlie's ability to show us how to play computer games. He even accepted our compliments when we told him how proud we were of his ability. He seemed less angry and even cleaned up his room a little. We know that it's going to take time for him and us to change, but I guess we hadn't realized how negative we had become. All my wife and I had been discussing for the past couple of years were different ways of punishing Charlie, even spanking him. It was helpful to think about how we might compliment him, especially since he often feels we love Marnie more and she gets all of our positive attention. In many ways, that did happen in our home since Marnie is such an easy kid."

We advise parents to "catch your children doing things right and let them know." Well-timed positive feedback and expressions of encouragement and love are more valuable to children's self-esteem than stars or stickers. When children feel loved and appreciated, when they receive encouragement and support, they are less likely to engage in negative behaviors. Isn't this true for all of us? Some children, especially those with a difficult, insatiable temperament, may require more positive feedback than others, but as many parents have reported, devoting that extra time is the best form of discipline they have attempted.

Teach Your Children Well

How well we handle the role of disciplinarian will determine the extent to which our children develop resilient mindsets. Discipline is a teaching process: we hope our children learn self-discipline and self-control rather than let anger or resentment fester. To accomplish this task, we must involve our children in the disciplinary process by helping them to understand the importance of limits, rules, and consequences. We must help them to see that they can learn to make appropriate choices and decisions, and that they can gain increasing control of their behavior.

12

The Alliance Between Parents and Schools

Previous chapters dealt almost exclusively with the function of parents in nurturing a resilient mindset in children. This chapter surveys the noteworthy influence of schools in reinforcing resilience as well as the importance of developing productive, respectful parent-teacher relationships.

Schools and Resilience

With the exception of parents, over the course of a year teachers typically spend more time in a child's life than any other adult. In some instances teachers actually spend more time in a child's waking life than parents. In fact, when educators describe the numerous added responsibilities they face in their jobs, they often include feeling that they have been cast in the role of surrogate parents. Thus, while parents are the most influential adults in a child's life, it is important to appreciate the impact that teachers and the school environment have on a child's emotional development and resilience.

When Dr. Julius Segal wrote of the "charismatic adult" from whom children and adolescents "gather strength," he observed that in a "surprising number of cases that person turns out to be a teacher." Given the thousands of interactions that children have with parents and teachers, it is imperative that these significant adults in a child's life collaborate in the quest to develop a resilient mindset in children. All of the guideposts described for parents raising resilient youngsters are applicable for educators in the school environment. This chapter first articulates principles that parents and teachers can follow to solidify their relationship and then describes interventions that teachers can implement in the school setting to reinforce resilience in all students.

Principles for Effective Parent-Teacher Relationships

Principle One: Parents and Teachers Are Partners

This guiding principle is housed in the four subsequent principles. Parents and teachers must strive to form a respectful, working partnership, one that will enhance the process of educating and developing resilient mindsets in children. Studies of excellent schools, those in which children feel safe and learn successfully, highlight the essential ingredient that this partnership represents. As in any partnership, tensions may arise at times, given differing expectations and goals for children. In a collaborative atmosphere in which the parties involved demonstrate genuine respect for each other, these tensions can be managed and lead to positive outcomes.

We visited one elementary school in which for the past four years teachers had agreed on a policy that involved calling each of the parents and students in their class a day or two before the school year began to welcome them. They adopted this practice after realizing that heretofore, the first time they called parents typically was when a child was experiencing problems. When the first contact concerned problems, a negative or defensive tone was set with parents.

We asked these teachers what they said to students and parents when they called to welcome them. Several teachers laughed. One noted, "Students are often so stunned by the call that they quickly say hello and good-bye, but we have found that just calling to say hello is a good start to our relationship with them. When we speak with parents, we tell them that one of the most important things in their child's education is for us to work together. We encourage them to contact us if they have any questions or concerns and tell them that we will do the same. We want them to feel that they have an open invitation to visit the school. We always encourage them to be active participants in their children's education."

We wondered how much time was invested in making these phone calls. Almost all of the teachers responded that since these conversations tended to be relatively brief, the total activity consumed about one hour. When we asked what they learned from this practice, one teacher answered, "I learned that I should have been calling parents right before school began when I first started teaching twenty-five years ago. I now have a much better relationship with parents. This translates into better attendance, better-behaved students, and better learning."

Another teacher said, "I must admit that when we first discussed doing this, I had reservations." She continued with a smile, "I was even concerned that parents might begin to tell me how to teach and would spend hours observing me during the year. However, I found the opposite happened. When parents feel that we want their input and participation, they are more supportive, not intrusive. When they have concerns about how and what we are teaching, they discuss the subject in a respectful way. That's not to say there haven't been some parents who have exhausted our patience and challenged what we do, but by and large, our relationships with parents have improved over the past four years, and the children have benefited."

For the partnership to be successful, parents must be active and respectful in their interactions with their children's teachers. We know parents who have written notes to teachers at the beginning of the school year informing them that they would like to be of whatever help they can and that they would welcome having the teachers contact them with any questions that may arise.

An effective parent-teacher partnership does not suggest that differences of opinion will not arise. They often will. However, when mutual respect exists, these differences can be aired in a climate characterized by trust and a problem-solving attitude so that there is greater opportunity for eventual agreement. This kind of climate is one in which children are the beneficiaries and resilient mindsets are nurtured.

Principle Two: Maintain Regular Contact Throughout the School Year

The recommended contact prior to and at the beginning of the school year must be maintained throughout the year. Most schools send newsletters to parents about class or school activities as a general way of keeping parents informed of what is transpiring in their child's class or within the entire school.

Teachers often communicate more specifically to parents about their individual child's progress through quarterly notes or report cards. With all of the responsibilities that fall on the shoulders of educators, they can't spend blocks of time outside of school composing progress reports, but well-designed forms can capture a child's progress in a concise, helpful format. These forms should call out not only children's difficulties but also their islands of competence, with recommendations of how to address their vulnerabilities and utilize their strengths so that the child feels more comfortable and successful in school.

Bradley, a nine-year-old with learning and attentional problems, had difficulty getting to school on time and completing all of his homework. While his teacher permitted modifications in his homework and ensured that before he left school at the end of the day, he had his homework assignments written in his assignment book, the problem of his tardiness persisted, even when his parents, Mr. and Mrs. Dawson, woke him up early. On a progress update Bradley's teacher commented on how much he enjoyed taking care of the flowers that adorned the school lobby during recess, an observation supported by his parents, who noted that Bradley had several plants in his room at home and that he never neglected watering them.

Mr. Dawson said proudly, "My son may have problems learning some things, but he has a green thumb."

His wife smiled and said, "He gets that from his father."

The Dawsons appreciated the teacher's spotlighting an activity in which Bradley (and his father) showed proficiency. Bradley's parents and teacher worked in concert to devise the strategy that Bradley come to school a little early each morning and, with the help of the custodian, examine the plants, water them when necessary, and make sure that any decaying leaves were removed. Having this activity motivated Bradley to arrive at school on time, and it originated in his teacher's belief that a progress report as well as yearly goals should include descriptions of a student's strengths as well as his or her weaknesses, all of which could then be discussed with parents.

Ongoing communication between home and school takes on greater urgency when a youngster is facing learning or social difficulties in the school environment. In such cases more frequent communication is typically necessary. While this may appear to be extra work, the greater frequency of contact can actually save time since it serves as a preventive measure.

In sum, if written or oral communications between teachers and parents are to have maximum effectiveness, they should include a student's strengths and possible ways of capitalizing on these strengths, a student's weaknesses and possible interventions to remediate them, the goals and expectations of the class, and what parents and teachers can do to support each other in implementing any recommendations.

Principle Three: Practice Empathy, Empathy, Empathy

This point is closely related to Principle One, viewing parent-teacher relationships as a partnership. Just as it is much easier to be empathic with our children when they behave in ways that we like them to behave than when we are annoyed or disappointed with them, so parents and educators are more likely to be empathic with each other when their views are similar. Not surprisingly, this is more apt to occur when the child enjoys and is doing well in school. There is a greater probability of tension between parents and teachers when long-standing academic or behavioral problems occur in school.

Yet, it is precisely when the child is having ongoing setbacks that parents and teachers must expend increasing time and energy to ensure that they are each attempting to understand and validate the perspective of the other. Reaching understanding and validation does not imply that they agree with each other, only that they acknowledge that differences of opinion may exist. In the interest of the child, they work to resolve these differences to the greatest extent possible in order to develop the most effective school program. When empathy is lacking, parent-teacher relationships will become tenuous, and children will be the ones most affected.

In our clinical practices, we have witnessed the detrimental impact of a lack of empathy between parents and teachers. In one example, parents of a nine-year-old girl who was anxious about school and experiencing headaches and stomachaches each morning began a parent-teacher conference by saying to their daughter's teacher, "Last year our daughter loved school, was not nervous, and did not have headaches or stomachaches each morning. What have you been doing to her? What are you doing in your class?"

As could be expected, the teacher became defensive, and within a few seconds there was a noticeable tension in the room. Although the teacher's style might have been contributing to this child's anxiety (the teacher's demeanor tended to be less warm and supportive than that of the teacher from the previous year), the failure of these parents to be empathic mediated against the possibility of their developing a working relationship with the teacher. In the absence of such a relationship, the child's problems were not successfully addressed.

You may wonder why these parents started the meeting in this way since their comment was obviously judgmental and likely to trigger defensiveness. It is not unusual for our own anxieties and anger to become roadblocks to empathy and the successful resolution of problems. In this case if these parents had raised the following two questions for themselves prior to the school conference, their approach might have been different:

> In the school meeting, what do we hope to accomplish with the teacher? How can we say things so that our daughter's teacher will be most responsive to listening to our message and working closely with us?

These parents knew that their daughter, who tended to be somewhat shy and insecure, would adjust more comfortably to school with a teacher who spent a few extra moments each day offering support and encouragement. They felt that this teacher, compared with last year's, did not go out of her way to provide this support. While they knew that their goal was for the teacher to be more encouraging, the way in which they attempted to present this goal elicited anger, resentment, and defensiveness. When such feelings fill the room, empathy is eclipsed, as are effective solutions.

Another example is Dennis's teacher. Dennis was a six-year-old client of ours who exhibited hyperactivity and impulsivity. At the initial parent-teacher conference, which we attended, Dennis's teacher began the meeting much to our consternation by saying, "I've been teaching thirteen years, and your child is the worst child I have ever taught." Needless to say, we were all taken aback, and the parents, Mr. and Mrs. Vintor, became visibly upset and defensive. The meeting was characterized by accusations and mistrust rather than problem solving. After the teacher's opening sally, a more positive tone could not be established.

Subsequent to the parent-teacher conference, we spoke briefly to the teacher, endeavoring to be empathic in the hope of developing a better relationship for the future. We talked about her opening remark.

"I was just trying to be honest," she said. "Too often when a student has a problem, we downplay it for the parents. Our not being truthful comes back to haunt us years later when the student continues to have problems. Parents wonder why we weren't honest initially about the severity of the problem. I wanted to emphasize to the Vintors that their son had significant problems."

Applying the two questions presented earlier to this situation, "In the school meeting, what do I hope to accomplish with the parents?" and "Am I saying things in a way that will make the parents most responsive to hearing my message and working with me?," it appears that the teacher knew what her goals were: to inform the parents of the severity of their son's problems.

However, she neglected to reflect on the question of whether she was communicating this information in a manner that would encourage Mr. and Mrs. Vintor to listen to what she had to say and enter into a positive, respectful relationship in which they could assess the problems and brainstorm possible solutions.

Principle Four: Parent-Teacher Collaboration Should Be Guided by the Goal of Developing a Resilient Mindset in Our Children

All of the interactions that parents have with their children should have as a goal the nurturing of a resilient mindset. The same goal applies as parents and teachers collaborate about a specific child. We have been asked, "If teachers spend a lot of time and attention on so-called social and emotional issues in a classroom, including reinforcing resilience, wouldn't that take away valuable time from teaching academic subjects?"

It is unfortunate that in the minds of many, a dichotomy has been established that suggests that fostering self-worth and resilience is separate from teaching a child basic academic skills and content. This dichotomy has, at times, been unintentionally fueled by individuals who hold that a child's emotional well-being is an important ingredient of the school environment. While these advocates make the excellent case that when children feel confident about themselves they are more motivated to learn, the ways in which they attempt to reinforce children's self-esteem actually work against development of a positive self-image.

We know of educators who have given children false praise or minimized or denied the problems that children were encountering. In some instances they rushed in so that a child would not experience making a mistake (rather than helping youngsters discover that they could learn from mistakes). In one school, children were given buttons to wear that said "I'm capable and lovable" as remedies to low self-esteem. Children are much more sophisticated than many adults realize in recognizing these various forms of false positive feedback. If anything, they learn to resent these less-than-honest attempts to make them feel more competent.

Children's self-esteem and resilience *will* be heightened when they truly experience accomplishments in school and at home, when they truly begin to learn and succeed. A focus on a student's social-emotional life does not take time away from academic achievement; it enhances the learning process. Success breeds self-worth, a sense of ownership, and confidence—feelings that help children recover from mistakes, that foster problem-solving skills, and that motivate them to continue to learn and achieve. We must help children to experience realistic success as the foundation for the development of a resilient mindset.

Principle Five: Parents and Teachers Must Be Proactive

In light of the importance of school success in a child's development, it is imperative that parents and teachers appreciate the components of a resilient mindset as they collaborate to establish strategies for academic achievement. As much as possible, this partnership must be guided by a proactive, rather than reactive, approach.

To help make this collaboration proactive as well as smooth and productive, teachers and parents should prepare in advance for their contacts, whether the contacts take place on the phone or, ideally, in face-to-face meetings. Preparations should typically include the following responsibilities:

1. Teachers should be ready to clearly define for parents a child's strengths and weaknesses. This information should be gathered early in the year, first through meetings with parents and then through ongoing observations of the child. In articulating a child's strengths and weaknesses, teachers should begin to develop a plan that includes proposed interventions to deal with the child's difficulties, how the effectiveness of the interventions will be evaluated, and possible backup strategies should the initial interventions prove unsuccessful. Interventions should also include the ways in which a child's strengths will be utilized in any school program.

2. For their part, parents should be prepared with their observations from the home environment. These could include comments that their child has made about school, how long it typically takes the child to complete homework, the amount of assistance they give the child, and observations about specific work the child is doing. For example, at our workshops it is not unusual for parents to comment that in school their children do not demonstrate any behavior problems, but the moment the children arrive home, they scream and yell. This does not necessarily mean that the school setting is more supportive than the home environment. Some children expend all of their

time and energy to hold it together in school, only to "fall apart" when they arrive home. Obviously, it is imperative for all parties involved to know what is occurring so that plans can be established to ease the pressure in school (e.g., some extra help or some modification in the requirements in a particular subject) while building in safety valves at home (e.g., giving the child a half hour to relax at home before commencing homework).

3. At all meetings, teachers should initially review the child's strengths and then the areas of difficulties, both in a jargon-free manner. Teachers and other school personnel should make sure that parents understand the concepts being discussed. To facilitate this understanding, they could tell the parents at the beginning of the meeting that if any terms used are not clear, parents should inform them, and they will be glad to explain.

One father and mother who consulted with us mentioned that at their last school conference, concepts such as *sensory integration, auditory processing,* and *spatial relations* were tossed around, but they weren't certain what these terms meant or what their implication was for their child's school program. The father added, "We asked the teacher and school psychologist a couple of times to explain these terms, but we still had difficulty understanding, and by the third time we felt foolish asking." School officials must create a climate at meetings such that no parent feels foolish asking questions.

Along these lines, as teachers discuss a child's strengths and weaknesses, they should continually seek feedback from parents to ensure that their descriptions are clear and should restate any points that are not. These descriptions should be followed by consideration of proposed strategies, which may include a wide variety of interventions in the academic arena as well as pertain to social and emotional issues.

4. As strategies are considered and those most likely to succeed are agreed on, teachers and parents should ask: (a) Are these strategies guided in great part by the goal of developing a resilient mindset?, (b) How will the effectiveness of the interventions at school and home be assessed?, and (c) What are the backup interventions should the initial ones prove unsuccessful? The particular criteria to assess effectiveness may be applied to a wide spectrum of behaviors, such as improving or learning a specific academic skill (e.g., long division or decoding of new words), staying on task for a certain amount of time, not blurting out answers in class, getting to school on time, not cutting classes, or not teasing one's classmates. For instance, to assess improvement in a particular academic skill, a specific educational test may be used, while

to assess tardiness, the teacher may simply maintain a daily record of whether the child gets to school on time. Number counts may be used to evaluate whether a child has decreased blurting out answers or cutting classes.

Not to lose sight of a child's strengths, interventions and criteria should also be established that identify and build on a child's islands of competence. As an illustration, fifteen-year-old Laurie was able to arrive at school on time when her love of children was used to enlist her to help in the nursery school next to her high school each morning before classes.

5. As these assessment criteria are established, parents and teachers should decide how much time is necessary to evaluate the effectiveness of the designated interventions. It is also imperative that during their collaboration, parents and teachers establish a system for communicating their observations and questions. Variables include:

- Who is the designated person in the school for parents to contact? This is especially important if the child has several teachers and the counselor and principal are also involved. Parents should not be puzzled about which staff member to call if questions arise.
- Is it easier and preferable for the teachers to call parents, and what is the best time to reach the parent? For example, it is difficult for some parents to receive personal phone calls at work.
- If parents are separated or divorced, should both be contacted? This answer will be determined in great part by the custody arrangements.
- How will more formal feedback be provided about the child's progress, particularly in the specified problem areas?
- When will the next formal meeting occur? It is typically easier to schedule the next appointment when all of the parties involved are seated in the same room.

6. We are often asked if children should attend parent-teacher conferences. In many states the law *requires* that adolescents be invited to these conferences. However, even in the absence of legal requirements, we believe that children should be active participants in their education. This includes attendance at school conferences. A key component of a resilient mindset is a sense of ownership and responsibility for what transpires in one's life.

There are some parameters to consider when inviting children and adolescents to attend school conferences. For one, the purpose of a school conference should be explained to children. We tell youngsters that what we hope to accomplish at a school meeting is for parents, teachers, and student to review the current school program and assess whether it is best meeting the needs of the student. If it is not, the input of all of these parties is necessary to improve the program.

If after the purpose and goals of the meeting are explained, youngsters say they do not wish to attend, they should not be forced to do so, but they should be asked what their reluctance is based on. One ten-year-old boy we know said, "I don't want to be sitting there while everyone says how dumb I am and how I don't try to do my work." We clarified for this boy that the purpose of the meeting was not for everyone to say how dumb he was but to evaluate what changes would help the school program best meet his needs and what he might do to be more successful. We emphasized that a school conference was not a forum for put-downs, that it was to solve problems.

Even with these parameters and guidelines, some youngsters may not wish to attend even for part of the meeting. In such instances it is helpful to discuss in advance with children what they would like to have addressed at the meeting, including what they enjoy about school, what they believe their strengths are, what they perceive as difficulties, and what they think would help them to be more successful. Children as young as five or six years can offer insights into their school program. If children are not at the conference, a parent as well as a teacher or school counselor should talk with them afterward about what transpired and encourage their ongoing input.

Children need not attend the entire meeting. This is especially true for younger children, who may have an attention span of five or ten minutes. However, whether children attend for just a few minutes or for most of the meeting, they should be prepared for what will occur, especially if it is the first school meeting in which they have participated. There should be no surprises that cause the child or anyone else at the meeting to feel ill at ease.

Children should also be seen as active participants in the conference. When problems are presented, parents and teachers should make certain that children understand the nature of the difficulties and should seek their thoughts about addressing the problem. For example, nine-year-old Melissa, introduced in Chapter 8, arrived at two possible solutions to her test anxiety. When the first option of sitting in the front of the room proved unsuccessful, she moved to the second plan, taking tests outside of the room so that she would not become anxious watching her peers, assuming that they knew all of the answers and were completing their tests faster and better than she. Similarly, Anna, from Chapter 10, chose from among several possible times to be tutored. Having backup plans such as these communicates to children that if one solution does not work, we can learn from this seeming failure rather than feel defeated by a lack of immediate success.

Never underestimate the importance of involving children in the process of reviewing their own education and offering suggestions and insights. This sense of involvement and ownership is what we must strive to nurture in our children.

Interventions in School

If the interactions of parents and educators adhere to the principles and practices we suggested in the preceding section, then the interventions implemented in school can follow the same guidelines advocated for parents in the home environment.

Guideline One: Practice Empathy

Chapter 2 emphasized that if parents are to nurture a resilient mindset in their children, they must become increasingly empathic, and the same holds true for teachers in their interactions with students. Our workshops for educators stress the importance of reflecting on how their students perceive school and their teachers. Similar to the exercises we use with parents to promote a more empathic stance with their children, we ask teachers the following questions:

Think of one of your childhood teachers you liked: What did you like about that teacher? What words would you use to describe that teacher? Now think of a teacher you did not like: What didn't you like about that teacher? What words would you use to describe that teacher?

We then note, "Just as you have words to describe your teachers when you were a student, your students have words to describe you. What words would you *hope* they would use to describe you? What words would they *actually* use?"

Obviously, these questions are posed to encourage educators to recognize what may seem obvious: that as they say and do things in class, students form opinions of them. This recognition is important since children's opinions of their teachers affect how motivated, respectful, and disciplined they are in class and how safe, secure, and comfortable they feel.

For example, Dennis, whose teacher characterized him as the worst child she had ever taught, was well aware of how much his teacher disliked him. In one of our therapy sessions, he said, "The teacher just thinks I'm a bad boy. I can't do anything right." Given his age and impulsive style, it was difficult for Dennis to appreciate the role his behavior played in his teacher's perception of him. If the teacher had not been as angry or frustrated, she might have assumed a more empathic position and asked, "I wonder how Dennis feels in class?" or "I wonder how Dennis would describe me?" or "I wonder if Dennis thinks I say or do anything positive toward him?" We believe that a display of greater empathy on the teacher's part would also have contributed to a more productive relationship with the parents and increased the possibility of their targeting several of Dennis's strengths as a team and incorporating them in his school program.

In this case the parents instead requested and received permission to have their son transferred to another teacher. His new teacher was able to "look beyond" his immediate behavior. At the first meeting with the parents and us, she asked what we saw as Dennis's strengths. We noted that, similar to most other children, he liked to help others and that perhaps his hyperactivity could be used in a positive manner. The teacher responded immediately, suggesting that Dennis come to school a few minutes early each morning to make certain the chairs and tables in the room were all in order. She added that she would tell Dennis that to do so would be very helpful to her. Given his need for activity, she also said that she would ask him to take a message to the office each morning and afternoon. In addition to these strategies, she discussed with Dennis his proclivity for calling out answers. Together they worked out a special signal to curb that behavior.

All of these interventions helped to foster a resilient mindset, by playing to Dennis's strengths, by changing the negative script that had existed in the previous classroom, by appreciating his inborn temperament and developing more realistic expectations for his behavior, by teaching him responsibility through the act of contributing, and by involving him in the decision-making process so that his sense of ownership and commitment increased.

When we consult to schools, we often use exercises to promote empathy in a meeting attended by the entire staff. We have found that the presence of all staff typically leads to a productive discussion in which a group energy is harnessed that facilitates changes in staff attitudes. These changes promote a more positive school climate.

Guideline Two: Change Negative Scripts if Students Are to Change Theirs

If a child is having difficulty adjusting to and succeeding in school but teachers and school administrators continue to follow the same practices and adhere to the same expectations, one can predict that the results will also continue to be the same. Remember that if children are to change their behaviors, it is incumbent on the adults to change their own. Negative scripts—predictable, ineffective ways of communicating and behaving—must be modified if a more positive outcome is to be achieved.

A consultation we held with a team of high school teachers concerned a freshman whom they referred to as a "roamer," that is, a student who had difficulty finding his way to homeroom. As the label they gave him implies, he was prone to roam the halls. Rewards and punishments appeared to have little effect on his behavior. Since we had worked with this group of teachers for months and they knew about our approach to changing negative scripts, we felt comfortable saying, "Perhaps one of the reasons that typical consequences had limited impact is that this boy has a 'need' to roam."

One of them said, "A need to roam?"

We elaborated, "We think this is a very active adolescent. He requires physical activity not only when he first arrives in school but also at other points during the school day."

We added to the mood of changing the script by saying, "And his need to roam may actually be his island of competence. By stopping him, we may deprive him of displaying his strength."

Another teacher said with a smile, "Don't you think you're stretching things a little?"

We answered, "Perhaps. But why don't we think about how we can use his need to roam constructively so that he doesn't bother you, he contributes to the school, and you know where he is even while he is roaming."

As we have discovered with other educators who are "given permission" to consider the unexpected, this group of teachers became increasingly relaxed as they pondered ways to display the student's "need to roam." He was appointed the "attendance monitor," a position that involved walking down the hall each morning with a clipboard supplied by the principal. The principal told the boy that it would be of great help to the school if while teachers were taking student attendance, he took "teacher attendance" to verify that there was a teacher in each classroom. This intervention, although rather different from most, helped to acclimate this adolescent to the school environment each morning, making it easier for him to adjust to the requirements of the school day.

The educators in this school, rather than continuing to see this student as a resistant or oppositional adolescent who should first change his behavior, had the courage to ask what they could do differently and then proceeded to change their script. As we'd hoped, having the opportunity to be the attendance monitor at the beginning of the day helped this boy to become more calm and focused. A humorous footnote to the story is that with the principal's permission, this young man "recruited" another "active" freshman as an "assistant attendance monitor" to help him in his rounds.

If an educational plan that has been attempted for a relatively long time is not productive in school, then teachers and parents, often in collaboration with students, must change the plan.

Guideline Three: Help All Students Feel Welcome and Appreciated

Students will learn best from teachers when they believe that teachers care about them and take a personal interest. With this in mind, we asked more than 300 students between the ages of five and eighteen what they thought teachers could do every morning to help them feel welcome in school. Regardless of the age of the student, the two most common responses we heard were: "Say hello to me while using my name" and "Smile."

Need we point out that this is not the same as greeting a student in the morning with comments such as "Jimmy, are we in for another miserable day today?" or "Susie, did you finally remember to bring in your homework?"

A smile serves as a wonderful connection between people, so there is little wonder that students mentioned it so frequently as a sign that teachers care about them. It also follows that students are very aware when a smile is absent. We experienced this firsthand while working with Roland, a seventh-grade middle school student with learning and attentional problems.

Shortly after we began to see Roland, we mentioned that we were going to his school to meet his teachers. We frequently ask children to describe their teachers before a school meeting so that we have a sense of the ways in which they perceive them and can assist in changing negative scripts. Although Roland did not want to attend even part of the school conference, he had a fascinating agenda, which, given his impulsivity, was delivered in rapid-fire form with little room for questions.

"I love five of my six teachers, and I know they love me. One teacher hates me, and I don't like her either. So, when you go to school would you do me a favor? Would you tell one of your funniest stories?"

We asked why.

Roland answered, "The five teachers who love me and I love them will all smile and laugh. The teacher who hates me won't even smile."

We asked Roland, "Why won't she smile?"

He answered, "She can't. I think she has paralysis of the mouth."

It took all of our restraint not to break out laughing, since Roland was very serious.

Honoring Roland's request (and also because we were admittedly interested in observing what would happen), at the school meeting we told one of our favorite "war stories" that typically elicited laughter. It was as if Roland had scripted the response: Five teachers smiled and laughed and shared their own stories. One teacher sat there with what appeared to be a perpetual frown on her face. Several times we were tempted to ask, "Excuse me, but do you suffer from paralysis of the mouth?"

Our next session with Roland following the school conference was memorable. He immediately asked, "So, was I right about the smile?"

"Yes, you were."

Making a joke of it, he chirped, "Can you help her?" In keeping with his tone, we responded, "We're not sure; paralysis of the mouth is tough to cure since we're not plastic surgeons."

While there was a playful atmosphere during this session, what was obvious is that a warm smile—or the lack thereof—can have a far-reaching impact on children (and adults as well).

Guideline Four: Develop Realistic Expectations for Each Child, and Make Accommodations when Indicated

Chapter 6 made the case that children are born with different temperaments, learning and attentional styles, activity levels, and islands of competence. Parents have to start with each child's unique makeup in order to develop realistic expectations and goals for their children. Examples in this book highlight the fact that too often the expectations that parents have for their children are not in keeping with what the children are capable of doing; when bars are set too high, frustration and failure are likely to follow.

If teachers are to nurture resilient mindsets, it is imperative that children experience success in the school setting. For certain youngsters this will require that educators offer well-designed accommodations both in the way children are taught and in the kinds of work they are expected to produce. We are not suggesting that teachers have a different educational plan for each student in the classroom; a large "middle ground" will address the learning needs of the majority of students. What we are recommending are modifications that do not require an inordinate amount of time and that are based on the input of teachers, parents, and students. To set these accommodations in motion requires that we demystify for students what it means to learn differently from others and why certain modifications in their program will help them to succeed.

For example, some youngsters with learning or attentional problems benefit from the following accommodations:

- Taking tests without a time limit.
- Having a maximum time established in which to complete a homework assignment. Thus, if most students can finish eight math problems in thirty minutes, then thirty minutes may be set as the maximum time to spend on math problems. If a child can do only three problems in that period and the parents write a note confirming that the child worked for thirty minutes on the assignment and in that time completed three problems, it is often better to accept the three completed problems than to insist that all eight be finished since working any longer than thirty minutes is likely to be frustrating and ineffective for the child.
- Being provided with a printout of homework assignments or, if the homework is listed on the blackboard, having a class "buddy" check to see that the child recorded the assignment correctly. This is particularly important for students who have difficulty copying things from the board.
- Being permitted to use a computer to write papers. Some students have trouble writing their thoughts on a piece of paper. While most teachers allow students to use a computer, there are still a number of educators who believe, in the absence of supporting research, that students should use a pen or pencil. We believe that if available technology can facilitate learning, we should apply that technology.
- For students who are more active, such as the "roamer," building physical activity into the classroom routine.

Obviously, many other accommodations are possible. Any accommodation used should be designed and implemented based on the strengths and vulnerabilities of the particular student. Also, teachers who openly discuss with their students at the beginning of the school year that they all learn differently and that the most equitable approach is to make modifications, help to foster an atmosphere of understanding and compassion and refute the notion that accommodations are "unfair." Demystifying for students the nature of their learning problems has the added benefit of offering a sense of control and involving them more actively in decisions that influence their education. Carefully planned accommodations also increase the likelihood of success, as well as a sense of ownership in the success. These characteristics are all part of a resilient mindset.

Guideline Five: Discuss the Role of Mistakes in the Learning Process

As set forth in Chapter 8, children with a resilient mindset perceive mistakes as experiences from which to learn rather than defeats. They do not constantly attribute mistakes to things that they cannot change such as low intelligence. Instead, they believe that while some learning is difficult, with the input and support of adults, they will be able to learn. They also are realistic, recognizing that even with the support of adults, they may not be able to score 100 percent, but they can still learn a great deal of the material.

Unfortunately, school is an environment that often exposes what children do not know. When children have difficulty reading in front of the class, when they become anxious if called on to answer a question, when they fail a test, or when they fumble with gross motor skills in physical education, their vulnerabilities are readily apparent to their peers. Since self-worth and resilience are linked to a child's response to mistakes and failure, educators must find ways to convey the message that mistakes are part of the learning process. They must help students appreciate that mistakes are not the problem; the problem is the fear of making mistakes and feeling humiliated.

The fear of making mistakes in the classroom is often like the elephant that no one talks about but everyone knows is present: it is a hidden presence that casts a large shadow over what transpires in class. Thus, similar to the previous guideline, everyone gains when teachers openly discuss with students the fear of making mistakes, and the best time to do so is at the beginning of the school year, before any work has been assigned.

Teachers can do this by asking the class, "Who feels you are going to make a mistake or not understand something in class this year?" Before any student can respond, we recommend that teachers quickly raise their own hands. They can then involve the class in a problem-solving activity by asking what the teacher as well as the students can do to minimize the fear of being called on, of making a mistake, and of feeling foolish. Teachers who use this activity maintain that openly acknowledging the fear of failure renders it less potent.

One elementary school teacher told her class on the first day of school that throughout the year they would celebrate mistakes. She humorously explained that if her students did not make mistakes, she might lose her job, since it would mean that they already knew everything she had to teach them. She placed a glass jar on her desk and next to it a box of stones and told them, "Whenever you or I make a mistake, someone will come up and drop a stone into the jar. As soon as the jar is filled, I will bring in the popcorn for our celebration." Apparently the jar was small enough and the stones large enough that the party always took place within the first week. Students who typically would not raise their hands for fear of making a mistake now volunteered to answer; after all, if their answer was incorrect, they would be helping the class move one step closer to the celebration.

The upshot of this teacher's approach was to transform the fear of mistakes into a fun, positive force. Through the ritual of celebration she accentuated the belief that mistakes are a natural part of the learning process and not something to be feared. As the school year progressed, the achievement scores in her class were very good, and she had few, if any, discipline problems. This is not surprising, since many discipline problems are rooted in the fear of looking foolish—that is, some students would rather act up, be aggressive, or play the class clown than look dumb. This particular teacher was gifted in recognizing that one of the main tasks in developing a resilient mindset in students is to banish the fear of failure and humiliation.

Guideline Six: Develop Responsibility and Compassion

Schools are fertile ground for teaching children to be responsible and compassionate. As we reported in Chapter 9, many adults retain positive memories of being asked by a teacher to contribute in some manner to the school environment. When we consult with teachers about students in their classes, we ask them to describe the islands of competence of each child and then to consider ways in which the child can use these strengths to help others and to facilitate learning.

As examples, when fifteen-year-old Laurie and seven-year-old Ryan were offered "jobs" before school, each was motivated to get to school on time. Laurie was asked to come in early to assist in the nursery school (she also wrote an article about her experience for the school newspaper), while Ryan became the "Assistant Custodian." The adolescent "roamer" who was appointed the "attendance monitor" is another illustration of teaching responsibility by asking a student to help out.

That brings us to William, an aggressive nine-year-old with learning problems. William typically hid behind the bushes instead of entering the school when he got off the bus. During our first session he was very direct in explaining this behavior: "I like the bushes better than school." Rather than debate the relative merits of bushes versus schools, we asked William what he enjoyed doing. His face lit up as he told us that he enjoyed taking care of his dog. This prompted us to call the school principal and ask if the school would benefit from the presence of a "pet monitor." When the principal expressed bafflement at what a "pet monitor" was, we provided a quickly conceived job description.

The next day, the principal—an educator with the courage to change an obviously negative script—met with William and said that he needed his help as a "pet monitor." He even handed him a "Pet Monitor Union" card. When William asked what the position entailed, the principal said that to begin with, William would be expected to come to school ten minutes before class began each day to take care of a rabbit that the school had recently purchased. Within a short time, William began to take care of other animals as well. His teacher told him how impressed she was with his knowledge of animals and encouraged him to write a manual about animal care. William's initial response was that he had difficulty writing. His teacher said that she would help him. When the manual was finished, it was bound and became part of the school library, and by the end of the year, William had "lectured" in every classroom in the building about taking care of pets. He never headed for the bushes again as his confidence and resilient mindset grew.

Having children tutor other students, or involving students in cooperative learning activities in which all members of the group offer their expertise to the completion of a task, can also teach children that they have something to offer their world. The potential benefits of adopting these practices are supported by research in British schools undertaken by psychiatrist Michael Rutter and his colleagues, who noted:

> *Ample opportunities for children to take responsibility and to participate in the running of their school lives appear conducive to good attainments, attendance, and behavior. . . . There is some indication that holding positions of responsibility at school may help students' commitment to education.* (Rutter 1980, 216)

Our position is that every student should engage in at least one task that contributes to the school environment. As these examples indicate, even one responsibility can reinforce self-esteem, compassion, and resilience.

Guideline Seven: Teach Students How to Solve Problems and Make Decisions

School presents numerous opportunities for children to learn how to solve problems. Many academic tasks lend themselves to problem-solving activities. In addition to arithmetic functions, these include discussing how a character in a book might have handled a situation differently, weighing different options that historical figures might have taken when confronted with challenges, and planning a scientific experiment.

At a school we visited, teachers put into practice the principle that involving students in making decisions reinforces their feelings of ownership and motivation. These educators found that when they changed their homework routine from simply dictating a number of problems to do each night to saying, "Here are eight homework problems. Look at them and then do the five that you think will be most helpful for you to learn," the amount of homework completed increased noticeably, and the quality of the work improved. As one teacher summarized, "By being offered a choice like this, students felt it was *their* homework, not ours."

Problem solving and decision making need not be confined to academic tasks in school, either. We know of teachers who have engaged their classes in a discussion of ways to handle social issues such as scapegoating or bullying. In one class, the teacher's use of rewards and punishments to discourage put-downs was having little impact. However, when she launched a discussion about the possible reasons that scapegoating was a problem, rather than just telling her students that it was not appropriate behavior, and then enlisted their assistance in how to control it, the class was motivated to arrive at a solution. They decided that each student would create an "anti-scapegoating" poster and that these posters would be placed at the top of the wall around the room. The students explained that rather than "nag" them the teacher could simply point "up," and wherever she pointed, she would be pointing at a poster, which would remind them not to put other students "down." Since the solution arose from the students, it was not surprising that their intervention proved successful.

Guideline Eight: Use Discipline to Promote Self-Discipline

Disciplinary practices in school should be guided by the goals of creating safe and secure environments and of developing self-discipline and self-control in students. To help accomplish these goals, teachers should also discuss the topic of rules and consequences with students at the beginning of the school year. Teachers can define "nonnegotiable" rules that concern safety and security but then can pose the following questions:

What rules do you think we need in this class for students to feel safe and comfortable and to learn best?
What's the best way to remember rules so that it doesn't come across that I'm nagging you or you're nagging me?
What should the consequences be if you or I forget a rule?

Teachers have affirmed that when students recommend how they should be reminded of rules, the sense that they are being nagged is minimized. One example is the handy "anti-scapegoating" posters described in the last section.

As for consequences, teachers have reported that rather than trying to get away without being held responsible, students often proffered consequences that were more harsh than what teachers thought were reasonable. One teacher said, "My biggest job was to help students be less punitive."

Addressing these kinds of questions promotes decision-making skills in students as well as fostering self-discipline and a feeling of ownership and responsibility. It is also important to remember that positive feedback and encouragement are powerful forms of discipline. Teachers should ensure that they overcome "praise deficits" when relating to their students. A smile, a note, or a phone call may go a long way to help students feel that they are appreciated.

Much research supports the premise that when students feel that there is at least one person at school who knows them, believes in them, and is an advocate for them, they are more likely to succeed in the school environment and less likely to become alienated or to drop out.

Dusting Off the Welcome Mat

In our clinical practice and consultation to schools, we have experienced first-hand the significant benefits that accrue when parents and teachers work as partners toward the goal of nurturing components of a resilient mindset. As a Massachusetts Department of Education report concluded:

> *Since both the parent and the school are concerned about the child, their con-*
> *tinued cooperation and communication are vital in helping children develop*
> *the cognitive and affective skills necessary to achieve academic success.*
> *Research has shown that this cooperative effort succeeds when the school envi-*
> *ronment is welcoming to parents and encouraging of their participation and*
> *input.* (Massachusetts Department of Education 1989, 9)

We would add to this statement by emphasizing the importance not only of teachers finding ways of welcoming and being supportive of parents but also of parents finding ways of doing the same for teachers. When parents and teachers are working in concert in an atmosphere of mutual respect and when their interactions with children are guided by similar principles for nurturing a resilient mindset, the energy, productivity, and excitement of this partnership will yield lifelong benefits for the children in their care.

13

Hope and Courage

The second author met Ed last spring on an airline flight from Salt Lake City to Cincinnati. The first author met Lisa several years ago when she was referred to him for therapy. The stories of Ed and Lisa begin this final chapter because they powerfully exemplify the themes of this book.

Ed's Story

Ed was one of those men whom people immediately notice—at a party, in a store, or walking into a room. He was well over six feet tall, with chiseled good looks, an infectious smile, and a firm handshake. Most people would probably take him for an athlete. His looks and bearing suggested the quarterback throwing the winning touchdown or the point guard making the final basket.

The flight attendant smiled and greeted Ed as he boarded the airplane. As it turned out, his seat was next to mine.

"Good morning," he said with a smile.

"Good morning. How are you?"

"Just great."

As the aircraft taxied out to the runway, Ed and I struck up a conversation. Soon I learned that at a young age, he had risen through his company to the position of national sales manager. He was flying east for a convention. When he inquired about my work, I explained that I was a psychologist and worked with children and families experiencing a variety of medical and developmental problems. Although Ed was single and had no children, he expressed interest in what I did to help children in need. As we talked, he became more animated and began telling me about his life.

"When I was thirteen," he said, "you would have bet all your money that I wouldn't have amounted to anything. I was skipping school, I was drinking, and I had been arrested for joyriding."

"Sounds as if you were having a difficult time."

"I sure was," Ed replied. "My dad was in the army. We moved five times before I turned twelve. Just when I would make friends, we would move. I was not a very good student, but I could always play ball."

Ed's comments suggested that perhaps sports was the island of competence he had developed to help him cope with the adversities he faced. I took the opportunity to explain the concept of resilience and the work that my colleague and I were undertaking. He listened carefully and then resumed.

"We finally settled down in the Midwest. My dad had trouble finding consistent work, and we lived mostly on his pension from the army. He had always liked his alcohol, but he began drinking heavily. When Dad drank, all of his frustrations and anger came out through his fists. He didn't just hit *us*; he hit most objects in the house as well. I don't know why my mom stayed with him. I guess she felt she just couldn't make it on her own; they were married very young.

"Eventually Dad's routine was to get up, hang around the house, get drunk, and wait for us to get home to pick fights. I stopped coming home. I also stopped going to school. So, what you just said about resilience and having an island of competence is very interesting. I think I understand now not just how but why I was able to turn my life around."

I asked what had made the difference in his life. The answer didn't surprise me.

"It certainly wasn't my parents. My mom tried to protect us and keep the family together, but the worse my father got, the more trouble my younger brother and I got into. It was then that I met my high school football coach."

I said, "I knew you looked like an athlete."

"People tell me that all the time," Ed replied.

Then I asked, "How did your coach help?"

"He watched me play a pickup game of touch football in gym as a ninth-grader. It's funny because I usually skipped gym class, but for some reason I went that day. He asked me if I was interested in joining the football team, which at the time I certainly was not. But he told me something that I remember to this day: he told me that he had never seen anyone throw the ball with as much pure talent as I did. I thought maybe he was pulling my leg, but he seemed serious."

"Was that a transitional moment for you?" I asked, explaining that a transitional moment is an occurrence that seemed to take a person's life in a different direction.

"It sure was. I thought about what he said and his offer. I decided I had nothing to lose, and the next day I went to see him. He told me he thought I could be an exceptional quarterback. He asked if I would work with him three days a week after school. I agreed. The following summer, I attended football tryouts and became the starting sophomore-team quarterback. In my senior year, I was named to the All State team as quarterback."

"How did things change at home?"

"They really didn't. My dad continued drinking and finally drank himself to death three years ago. But my coach not only taught me but also believed in me. I spent more and more time at his house and less and less time at mine."

"Sounds as if he was a father figure for you."

"He sure was. He took a chance with me. He knew I had been in trouble and wasn't attending school. I went on to receive a four-year college scholarship and had offers to play in the pros, but I injured my shoulder in my senior year and knew that full-time athletics wasn't in the cards."

Suddenly Ed stopped talking and stared straight ahead. It was obvious that he was thinking about something. I just waited.

After a few moments, he said, "Now I finally understand why my brother has had so much trouble in his life." He said that his younger brother of two years never did turn his life around. He never finished high school, had been in and out of jail a number of times, and was a substance abuser.

"My brother never found something he was good at, someone who believed in him, or the opportunity to develop what you call his island of competence. But I did. Not only that, I found an adult who supported and believed in me. My coach offered me the hope that my life could be better and provided the encouragement to make it happen."

Sessions with Lisa

One of the first sessions I had with ten-year-old Lisa and her mother, Mrs. Newman, dramatically and poignantly captured the themes of hope, courage, and resilience that underlie this book. Lisa was burdened by learning disabilities, poor peer relationships, and a growth hormone deficiency. Because of this last problem, she appeared several years younger than her actual age and received growth hormone shots five times a week (eventually they were administered daily).

In the session, to assess what Lisa perceived to be her islands of competence, I asked her what she thought she did well.

Lisa responded, "Nothing."

I asked her again and received the same answer. By the third time, Lisa, becoming exasperated, replied, "Dr. Brooks, do you know what it feels like every day in school to be chosen last when the other kids choose up teams? I don't even know why the other team cheers when they beat my team. Look who they've beaten."

Her words laid bare the pain of feeling that she had few, if any, strengths and was a virtual outcast among her peers. Both Lisa and her mother looked sad. As I searched for a response that would be helpful, Lisa began to smile. Then the smile broadened, and with obvious delight she said, "I never really thought about your question before. I just thought about something I do better than anyone in the whole school."

Now, this was intriguing. In just a few seconds, Lisa made the leap from saying she felt worthless to voicing the belief that there was something she did better than anyone else in her school.

I implored, "What do you think you do better than anyone else in the school?"

With sparkling eyes, she answered, "I take shots better than anyone in the school."

Mrs. Newman's face filled with joy. She looked at Lisa and then at me and said from the heart, "Dr. Brooks, you will find as you work with my daughter that she is one of the most courageous children you will ever meet. She has gone through so much but has not lost hope."

Lisa warmly clutched her mother's arm, and it was obvious that for Lisa, her mother truly was the "charismatic adult" from whom she gathered strength.

Mrs. Newman's use of the word *courageous* had a profound impact on me. I realized more than I ever had before the *courage* that many children display day in and day out as they encounter challenges in school, in sporting events, or even at birthday parties.

I worked with and kept in touch with Lisa for several years. At the beginning of our final therapy session, Lisa gushed, "Guess what? I'm off my growth hormone shots. Do you know how tall I got?"

"No, how tall?"

"Four feet, eleven inches. My goal was five feet."

I was ready to say, "Well that's only one inch." However, before I could utter a word, Lisa consoled, "Don't worry, it's only an inch."

Lisa and I began to reminisce about our initial sessions together and the problems that brought her to therapy. We next discussed her impressive progress from a sad child who had difficulty in school, with peers, and with self-worth to a teenager who had good friends, excellent grades, and renewed confidence (she even joined the drama club so that she could perform in plays). Lisa had acquired the characteristics of a resilient mindset *in spades*: she knew how to solve problems, had assumed ownership for her successes, accepted what she could not change while focusing on what was within her control to influence, was not derailed by mistakes, felt loved and appreciated, found ways to help others, and showed a zest and satisfaction for life.

As we talked about the changes that had taken place since we first met, Lisa said something that any adult would love to hear from a child since it vividly highlights the positive impact adults can have on children. While the comment was directed at me, it certainly included her parents:

"We really showed them, Dr. Brooks. We really showed them. Thank you."

What Do Children Need?

Ed is one of the fortunate individuals who found—or, to be more accurate, was found by—what he needed to help him divert his life from stress and seeming tragedy to happiness and success. Lisa had supportive parents who looked beyond her frustrations, pessimism, and tears and saw a courageous child with many untapped strengths. What both Ed and Lisa shared was the presence of adults who would not give up on them, who served as reservoirs from which they could draw strength.

Children require hope and the courage to follow their goals. These qualities help them develop the inner strength and resilience necessary to succeed despite the adversities that may and often do come their way. To develop a resilient mindset, children need more than just support and care. They require daily affirmation and encouragement, parents' active involvement in their lives, opportunities to participate in the community, and a supportive neighborhood. Children require boundaries, values, realistic expectations, and caring schools. While there is no precise formula, there are common themes, issues, and opportunities that all parents must provide to their children.

For too long we have been influenced by a culturally driven, deficit-thinking model. Consequently, as our children have experienced increasing problems, our efforts have been directed toward how to "fix" these problems. This orientation has proved counterproductive. It is time to give heed to what is right about our children, to strengthening and building on their assets and abilities rather than on fixing their problems and liabilities. It is time that our children begin to turn to the adults in their lives as supports and resources rather than shun them as judges and critics.

The increasing body of research on resilience and success in our kids suggests that there are powerful factors that contribute to a positive outcome. Many of these are manifested in the quality of parent-child relationships. Resilient children, those who are happy and successful, learn to manage their emotions, thoughts, and behavior in part through the common denominator of living, working with, and being educated by available and caring adults. No doubt other resilient or protective processes promote competence, but they also come into play primarily through the agency of parents and teachers. Poverty, domestic violence, disasters, and the stress of everyday life can be and are mediated through the protective environments that parents and teachers provide.

Increasingly, scientific research demonstrates the importance of parent-child relationships to the development of competence and resilience. This is true not just for children facing extraordinary challenges but for all children. A combination of warm yet structured child-rearing practices forges the trail to success in many areas of children's lives and the development of a resilient mindset. When adversity is present and effective adults are unavailable, risk for serious life problems is high. There can be no doubt: The development of a resilient mindset requires the involvement of caring adults in a child's life. These adults possess the mindset and skills necessary to nurture resilience in their children.

Why has it taken us so long as a society to recognize the importance of resilience as a central concept in parenting? Perhaps, as just noted, there has been too much emphasis on fixing rather than strengthening. Or possibly we have assumed that only some children are at risk.

In 1990 the American Medical Association cited evidence that for the first time in history, young people were less healthy and less prepared to take their places in society than were their parents. Half of all children aged ten to seventeen were at high or moderate risk of undermining their chances for a healthy lifestyle owing to substance abuse, unsafe sex, teenage pregnancy, school failure, delinquency, crime, or violence. In a 1999 report on children at risk, the Casey Foundation stated that more than nine million American children confronted numerous adverse family conditions, robbing them of their ability to become productive, functional members of society (Casey Foundation 1999). The report estimated that one in seven children in America faced at least four risk factors affecting their chance for success. Among them were growing up in a single-parent household or with parents who lacked a high school education, did not have a full-time job, or were uninvolved with their children. Children growing up with these risk factors were reported to fail more often than other children. According to the same study, four-year-olds coming from families with multiple risk factors were twice as likely to have difficulty concentrating, three times as likely to experience communication problems, and nearly five times as likely to be in poor health as other children.

The message here is not that factors such as growing up in a single-parent home preordain children for a life of hardship and failure or that these children cannot be provided with experiences for developing a resilient mindset. Rather, these studies indicate that parents in such homes typically require additional support to engage in activities with their children that nurture resilience.

Although the data from these studies may lead some people to conclude that things are falling apart for our youth, the scene can be viewed from another perspective. One possibility is that as a society, we are moving too slowly to make the changes necessary to prepare our youth to become resilient, successful members of a future society. Then again, it may be not that we are particularly slow in modifying our approach but rather that the world is changing so rapidly that parents, educators, and the community at large have had difficulty keeping up. This latter explanation likely is closest to the truth.

In fact, many statistics argue that risk factors alone cannot provide a satisfactory explanation for the troubles among our youth. For example, in this demographic study the rates of poverty, violent crime, teen pregnancy, and even traffic deaths related to alcohol are less today than in recent years. Yet, children are obviously struggling with a world moving at breakneck speed and fueled by complex technological development.

The solution, therefore, lies not just in reducing these risk factors but also in changing our mindset to adapt to the rapid changes in our society. We must shift our view and place our emphasis and energy on what it takes to raise resilient children. To do so, we must promote assets rather than reduce deficits. We must place the development of a resilient mindset first and foremost in our parenting goals. We must avoid becoming parents with the characteristics of the Red Queen or Rumpelstiltskin.

The Red Queen and Rumpelstiltskin Parents

In Lewis Carroll's classic *Alice in Wonderland*, Alice along her journey comes upon the Red Queen. The Queen admonishes Alice to run faster. Yet, the faster Alice runs, the more apparent it becomes that she is not getting anywhere. When Alice complains, the Queen points out that this is how fast you have to run just to keep up; getting ahead is an entirely different matter. As parents, we must be on guard not to become Red Queens.

Our personal, professional, and family lives are filled with increasing responsibilities, draining available time for ourselves and, more important, our children. In response, many parents act like Rumpelstiltskin. In the fairy tale, Rumpelstiltskin asks for more and more from the miller's daughter to spin her straw into gold. Each time, the miller's daughter provides what is asked, and each time, Rumpelstiltskin requests more.

The pressure of everyday life prompts many parents to ask or, for that matter, demand more and more from their children. We must be vigilant not to become present-day Red Queens or Rumpelstiltskins, imprisoned by a negative script dominated by unrealistic expectations and a loss of empathy. If we become trapped in such a script, our actions will convey the message to our children that what they have done at school, on the playground, or at home is never good enough and that we are disappointed in them. Like Rumpelstiltskin, we are likely to respond angrily when our expectations are not met; our children in turn will experience fear and frustration. In this sad scenario our parenting efforts will run counter to the very goals we seek. Rather than preparing our children to be happy and successful, we may unintentionally strip away their resilience in our often desperate efforts to help and motivate them.

Unfortunately, there is a little Rumpelstiltskin in all of us. The more stressed and harried we become, the more like Rumpelstiltskin our parenting becomes. We must summon the courage to block the intrusion of the Red Queen or Rumpelstiltskin into our parenting practices and instead be guided by a mindset that fosters acceptance, realistic expectations, hope, and resilience in our children. Preparing children to be happy, productive, and successful in their adult lives is our goal.

Our Legacy to the Next Generation

Despite well-founded worries for our children and their future, there is reason to be optimistic about counteracting the negative influences in their lives. The goal of raising resilient children is of paramount importance to ensure future success for each individual and for the collective culture we have created. Resilience conveys a sense of optimism, ownership, and personal control. In 1994, as part of the National Movement for Children, William Raspberry wrote about adults helping children attain their life possibilities:

> *I wish I understood by what chemistry these individual and local efforts could be transformed into a movement with a power to reach beyond the particulars of time and place and make our children . . . know they are valued and loved and counted on.* (Raspberry 1994, A25)

The new millennium offers unlimited possibilities and unimagined advances. But the future lies not in technology but in our children, children instilled by their parents, teachers, and other adults with the resilient qualities necessary to help them shape a future with satisfaction and confidence. We can all serve as the charismatic adults in children's lives—believing in them and providing them with opportunities that reinforce their islands of competence and feelings of self-worth. This is not only a wonderful gift to our children but also an essential ingredient for the future. It is part of our legacy to the next generation.

Appendix

Guideposts and Principles for Raising Resilient Children

Chapter 1 The Dreams and Wishes of Parents

Ten Guideposts

1. Teach and convey empathy.
2. Listen, learn, and influence in order to communicate effectively.
3. To change your words of parenting, rewrite your negative scripts.
4. Find ways to love your children that help them feel special and appreciated.
5. Accept your children for who they are, and help them set realistic expectations and goals.
6. Nurture islands of competence; every child must experience success.
7. Mistakes are teachable moments.
8. Help your child develop responsibility, compassion, and a social conscience.
9. Teach and emphasize the importance of solving problems and making choices and decisions.
10. Discipline in ways that promote self-discipline and self-worth.

Chapter 2 Teaching and Conveying Empathy

Obstacles to Empathy

1. We often practice what we have lived, or History has a nasty way of repeating itself.
2. It is difficult to be empathic when you are angry.
3. "My child's goal in life is to make me angry."
4. Believing that empathy interferes with parenting.

Guidelines to Becoming an Empathic Parent

1. Begin with empathy.
2. Let experience be your guide.
3. Put empathy into action.

Chapter 3 Communicating Effectively: To Listen, to Learn, to Influence

Obstacles to Climbing the Stairway to Successful Communication

1. We practice what we have lived.
2. Anger clouds effective communication.
3. We sometimes believe that our children's goal is to wear us down.

Ten Steps for Effective Communication: To Listen, to Learn, to Influence

1. Begin at birth.
2. Be proactive.
3. Become an active listener.
4. Make sure you say, "I heard you."
5. Do unto others . . .
6. Use nonjudgmental and nonaccusatory communication.
7. Communicate clearly and briefly.
8. Serve as a model of honesty and dignity.
9. Accept repetition.
10. Make humor an integral part of your communication.

Chapter 4 Changing the Words of Parenting: Rewriting Negative Scripts

How Negative Scripts Come to Be Written and the Obstacles That Perpetuate Unhappy Reruns

1. One size fits all; all children are basically the same.
2. Changing my words will spoil my child.
3. It was good enough for me, or I turned out OK.
4. Our children should be more appreciative of our hard work and parental effort.
5. A goal is realistic—if I say so.
6. Carrying around excess baggage from the past.

Five Principles to Writing Positive Scripts

1. Accept your responsibility to change.
2. Know the problem—know the goal.
3. Know what you have done so far and why it hasn't worked.
4. Seek and ye shall find—every problem has a positive solution.
5. If at first you don't succeed, try again.

Chapter 5 Loving Our Children in Ways That Help Them Feel Special and Appreciated

Obstacles

1. The process of love is difficult if you haven't been on the receiving end.
2. Confusing love and a lack of discipline.

*Six Steps to Helping Your Children Feel Loved, Special,
and Appreciated*

1. Let your memories of childhood be your guide.
2. Create traditions and special times.
3. Don't miss significant occasions.
4. Be demonstrative with your love.
5. Build up; don't chip away at your children.
6. Accept your children for who they are, not what you want them to be.

Chapter 6   Accepting Our Children for Who They Are: The Foundation for Setting Realistic Goals and Expectations

Temperament

1. The easy child.
2. The slow-to-warm-up child.
3. The difficult child.

*Four Steps to Developing an Accepting Mindset with
Your Children*

1. Become educated.
2. Measure your mindset.
3. Make necessary adjustments.
4. Begin the process of collaboration.

Chapter 7 Experiencing Success: Nurturing Islands of Competence

Obstacles to Nurturing Islands of Competence

1. The inability to experience the joy of success.
2. Reinforcing low self-esteem.
3. Misattributing success.
4. Setting the bar too high.
5. Parents alone defining a successful experience.

Principles for Experiencing Acceptance and Success

1. Openly enjoy and celebrate your children's accomplishments.
2. Emphasize your children's input in creating success.
3. Identify and reinforce your child's islands of competence by engaging in environmental engineering.
4. Give strengths time to develop.
5. Accept the unique strengths and successes of each child.

Chapter 8 Learning from Mistakes

Obstacles to a Positive Outlook About Mistakes

1. The power of temperament and biological factors.
2. The negative comments of parents.
3. Parents setting the bar too high.
4. Dealing with the fear of making mistakes in ways that worsen the situation.

Guiding Principles to Help Children with Mistakes

1. Serve as a model for dealing with mistakes and setbacks.
2. Set and evaluate realistic expectations.
3. In different ways, emphasize that mistakes are not only accepted but also expected.

4. Loving our children should not be contingent on whether or not they make mistakes.

Chapter 9 Developing Responsibility, Compassion, and a Social Conscience

The Myths of Irresponsibility

1. Equating chores with responsibilities.
2. Taking a narrow view.
3. A mismatch of expectations and abilities.

Guiding Principles to Help Children Develop Responsibility, Compassion, and a Social Conscience

1. Serve as a model of responsibility.
2. Provide opportunities for children to feel they are helping others.
3. Develop traditions to become a charitable family.
4. We can't get away from "chores," so distribute them fairly.
5. Take a helicopter view of your child's life.

Chapter 10 Teaching Our Children to Make Decisions and Solve Problems

Obstacles to Teaching Our Children How to Solve Problems and Make Decisions

1. Believing that young children don't have the ability to make decisions, so we must do it for them.
2. Expecting more than our children can deliver.
3. Allowing children to make decisions as long as what they decide agrees with what we feel is best.

Principles to Reinforce Problem-Solving and Decision-Making Skills

1. Serve as a model of problem solving.
2. Provide choices at an early age.
3. Follow a problem-solving sequence:
   - Articulate the problem and agree that it is a problem.
   - Consider two or three possible solutions and the likely outcome of each.
   - Develop a way to remind each other if someone forgets to follow through.
   - What to do if it doesn't work.

Chapter 11 Disciplining in Ways That Promote Self-Discipline and Self-Worth

Obstacles to Using Discipline to Develop a Resilient Mindset

1. Practicing what we have been taught, or "If it was good enough for me, it's good enough for my kids."
2. Discipline that is crisis oriented and punitive.
3. Discipline that is harsh and belittling as exemplified by spanking and verbal assaults.
4. Discipline that is arbitrary and inconsistent.
5. Disciplinary styles of parents that are miles apart.
6. "I want my child to love me."
7. Punishing children for unrealistic expectations.

Principles of Effective Discipline to Nurture a Resilient Mindset

1. A major goal of discipline is to promote self-discipline and self-control.
2. Prevention, prevention, prevention.
3. Work as a parental team.
4. Be consistent, not rigid.
5. Serve as a calm, rational model.

6. Select your battles carefully.
7. Rely when possible on natural and logical consequences rather than on arbitrary and punitive measures.
8. Know your children's capabilities, and do not punish them for unrealistic expectations.
9. Remember that positive feedback and encouragement are often the most powerful forms of discipline.

Chapter 12 The Alliance Between Parents and Schools

Principles for Effective Parent-Teacher Relationships

1. Parents and teachers are partners.
2. Maintain regular contact throughout the school year.
3. Practice empathy, empathy, empathy.
4. Parent-teacher collaboration should be guided by the goal of developing a resilient mindset in our children.
5. Parents and teachers must be proactive.

Interventions in School

1. Practice empathy.
2. Change negative scripts if students are to change theirs.
3. Help all students feel welcome and appreciated.
4. Develop realistic expectations for each child, and make accommodations when indicated.
5. Discuss the role of mistakes in the learning process.
6. Develop responsibility and compassion.
7. Teach students how to solve problems and make decisions.
8. Use discipline to promote self-discipline.

Recommended Reading

Barkley, R. A. 1995. *Taking Charge of ADHD: The Complete, Authoritative Guide for Parents.* New York: Guilford Press.

Brazelton, T. B. 1994. *Touchpoints: Your Child's Emotional and Behavioral Development.* Cambridge, MA: Perseus Publishing.

Brazelton, T. B., and S. I. Greenspan. 2000. *The Irreducible Needs of Children: What Every Child Must Have to Grow, Learn and Flourish.* Cambridge, MA: Perseus Publishing.

Brooks, R. 1991. *The Self-Esteem Teacher.* Loveland, OH: Treehaus Communications.

Chess, S., and A. Thomas. 1996. *Know Your Child.* New York: Basic Books.

Clark, L. 1998. *SOS Help for Emotions: Managing Anxiety, Anger and Depression.* Bowling Green, KY: Parents Press.

Dendy, C. Z. 1995. *Teenagers with Attention Deficit.* Bethesda, MD: Woodbine House.

Goldstein, S., and N. Mather. 1998. *Overcoming Underachieving: An Action Guide to Helping Your Child Succeed in School.* New York: Wiley.

Greene, R. W. 1998. *The Explosive Child: A New Approach for Understanding and Parenting Easily Frustrated, Chronically Inflexible Children.* New York: HarperCollins.

Greenspan, S., and N. B. Lewis. 1999. *Building Healthy Minds: The Six Experiences That Create Intelligence and Emotional Growth in Babies and Young Children.* Cambridge, MA: Perseus Publishing.

Hallowell, E. 1997. *When You Worry About the Child You Love: Emotional and Learning Problems in Children.* New York: Pantheon Books.

Heininger, J. E., and Weiss, S. K. 2001. *From Chaos to Calm: Effective Parenting of Challenging Children with ADHD and Other Behavioral Problems.* New York: Perigee Books.

Higgins, G. O. 1994. *Resilient Adults: Overcoming a Cruel Past.* San Francisco: Jossey-Bass.

Ingersoll, B. D. 1998. *Daredevils and Daydreamers: New Perspectives on Attention-Deficit/Hyperactivity Disorder.* New York: Doubleday.

Ingersoll, B. D., and S. Goldstein. 1993. *Attention Deficit Disorder and Learning Disabilities: Realities, Myths and Controversial Treatments.* New York: Doubleday.

Ingersoll, B. D., and S. Goldstein. 2001. *Lonely, Sad, and Angry: How to Help Your Unhappy Child.* Plantation, FL: Specialty Press.

Jones, C. 1994. *ADD: Strategies for School Age Children.* San Antonio, TX: Communication Skill Builders—A Division of Psychological Corporation.

Jones, C. B. 1991. *Sourcebook on Attention Disorders: A Management Guide for Early Childhood Professionals and Parents.* San Antonio, TX: Communication Skill Builders—A Division of Psychological Corporation.

Katz, M. 1997. *On Playing a Poor Hand Well: Insights from the Lives of Those Who Have Overcome Childhood Risks and Adversities.* New York: Norton.

Kindlon, D. J., and M. Thompson. 2000. *Raising Cain: Protecting the Emotional Life of Boys.* New York: Ballantine Books.

Kurcinka, M. S. 1991. *Raising Your Spirited Child.* New York: HarperCollins.

Kutner, L. 1992. *Parent and Child: Getting Through to Each Other.* New York: William Morrow.

Levine, M. D. 1992. *All Kinds of Minds.* New York: Educators Publishing Services.

Levine, M. D. 1994. *Educational Care: A System for Understanding and Helping Children with Learning Problems at Home and in School.* Cambridge, MA: Educators Publishing Service.

Levine, M. D. 1996. *Keeping a Head in School.* New York: Educators Publishing Services.

Manassis, K. 1996. *Keys to Parenting Your Anxious Child.* Hauppauge, NY: Barrons Educating Services.

Phelan, T. W. 1998. *1-2-3 Magic: Effective Discipline for Children 2–12* (2nd ed.). Glen Ellyn, IL: Child Management Press.

Phelan, T. W. 1998. *Surviving Your Adolescents: How to Manage and Let Go of Your 13–18 Year Olds.* Glen Ellyn, IL: Child Management Press.

Pollack, W. 1999. *Real Boys: Rescuing Our Sons from the Myths of Boyhood.* New York: Owl Books.

Pollack, W. S. 2000. *Real Boys' Voices.* New York: Random House.

Samalin, N. 1998. *Loving Your Child Is Not Enough: Positive Discipline That Works.* New York: Penguin.

Shure, M. 1996. *Raising a Thinking Child.* New York: Pocket Books.

Shure, M. 2000. *Raising a Thinking Preteen.* New York: Henry Holt.

Silver, L. B. 1998. *The Misunderstood Child: Understanding and Coping with Your Child's Learning Disabilities.* New York: Crown Publishing.

Taffel, R. 2000. *Getting Through to Difficult Kids and Parents: Uncommon Sense for Child Professionals.* New York: Guilford Press.

Thompson, M. 2000. *Speaking of Boys.* New York: Ballantine Books.

Werner, E., and S. Smith. 1992. *Overcoming the Odds: High Risk Children from Birth to Adulthood.* Ithaca, NY: Cornell University Press.

Zentall, S., and S. Goldstein. 1999. *Seven Steps to Homework Success: A Family Guide for Solving Common Homework Problems.* Plantation, FL: Specialty Press.

References

California State Department of Education. 1990. "Toward a State of Esteem: The Final Report of the Task Force to Promote Self-Esteem in Personal and Social Responsibility." The California Self-Esteem Report, 31. Sacramento, California.

Casey Foundation. 1999. "At Greatest Risk: Identifying America's Most Vulnerable Children." *Kids Count Data Book*. Baltimore: Casey Foundation.

Collins, W. A., Maccoby, E. E., et al. 2000. "Contemporary Research on Parenting: The Case for Nature and Nurture." *American Psychologist* (February): 228.

Covey, S. 1989. *Seven Habits of Highly Successful People*. New York: Simon and Schuster, Inc.

Donahue, D. 1998. "Struggling to Raise Good Kids in Toxic Times: Is Innocence Evaporating in an Open Door Society?" *USA Today*, October 1, 1d.

Frank, A. 1993. *Anne Frank: The Diary of a Young Girl*. New York: Bantam Books.

Massachusetts Department of Education, Bureau of Student Development and Health. 1989. "Educating the Whole Student: The School's Role in the Physical, Intellectual, Social and Emotional Development of Children." Massachusetts Department of Education Report, 9. Boston.

Raspberry, W. 1994. "A Crusade for America's Children: They Need to Know They're Valued, Loved, and Counted On." *The Washington Post*, February 18, A25.

Rutter, M. 1980. "School Influences on Children's Behavior and Development." *Pediatrics* 65: 216.

Stargell, W. 1983. "Yes I Am Ready." *Parade*, April 3, 11.

Weltner, L. 1997. "Ever So Humble: Kids Need to Give as Well as Get." *Boston Globe*, December 11, E2.

Index